Controversial Issues in Special Education

Garry Hornby, Mary Atkinson
and Jean Howard

David Fulton Publishers

London

David Fulton Publishers Ltd
Ormond House, 26–27 Boswell Street, London WC1N 3JD

First published in Great Britain by David Fulton Publishers 1997

Note: The right of Garry Hornby, Mary Atkinson and Jean Howard to be identified as the authors of this work has been asserted by them in accordance with the Copyright, Designs and Patents Act 1988.

British Library Cataloguing in Publication Data
A catalogue record for this book is available from the British Library

ISBN 1–85346–462–7

Typeset by Textype Typesetters, Cambridge
Printed in Great Britain by BPC Books and Journals, Exeter

Contents

1 Introduction

Practitioners must offer both appropriate treatment and protection from inappropriate care. They need the skills to know the difference.

(Jacobson, Mulick and Schwartz, 1995: 762)

This quotation highlights the rationale of this book, which is to provide practitioners in the field of special education with the information they need to decide whether controversial diagnoses and treatments in this field are valid. Being able to discriminate valid from invalid treatments enables professionals to select and use effective interventions in their work and to provide guidance to parents so that they can make informed choices about treatment programmes suitable for their children.

This is particularly important in special education because of the nature of the field. Its focus is the education of children who are considered to differ from the norm in some significant way, to the extent that they have special educational needs (SEN). With most of them this is due to difficulties in learning. The slow progress of many children with SEN often leads to practitioners and parents becoming frustrated. Linked with this are the difficulties of accepting limitations in the potential of such children. Both of these factors tend to lead those concerned with children with SEN to seek alternative treatments in the hope of accelerating progress. Therefore, practitioners and parents in the field of special education are particularly vulnerable to dubious diagnoses, over-optimistic prognoses and 'fad' treatments. This is especially true with regard to children with low-incidence disabilities such as autism, hearing impairment, physical disability and severe learning difficulty.

The impact of controversial diagnoses and treatments is not benign. Their attraction is that they create (false) hope of a cure among parents who are desperate to help their children and relieve their own feelings of loss. These parents are especially vulnerable for two reasons. Firstly, since the majority of them have no knowledge of the field of special education they rarely understand the issues involved in deciding on appropriate treatment for children with disabilities. Secondly, the intense feelings and adjustment process initiated by a diagnosis of disability are such that, for many parents, the ability to make a rational decision about their child's treatment is reduced.

Further, by creating false hopes of a cure, 'fad' treatments delay acceptance of a child's disability by the parents, thereby prolonging denial and delaying the application of appropriate treatments (Vernon and Alles,1994). In this way, they take up valuable time and deflect financial and human resources away from conventional methods and therefore hold back the progress of children with SEN. They also create conflict between practitioners using conventional methods and parents who choose 'fad' treatments, which can make it difficult for parents to re-establish collaboration with these practitioners when alternative treatments fail.

Examples of controversial issues

Oralism or signing in deaf education

Special education has a long history of controversial issues. The longest running controversy has been raging for over two hundred years. This is the controversy concerning the best method of educating severely and profoundly deaf children. This conflict, over the use of oral methods or signing in deaf education, began in the second half of the eighteenth century, and is still very much alive today (Lynas,1994). Oral methods involve auditory training to help children make optimal use of residual hearing and the teaching of lip-reading or speech-reading to enable children to make optimum use of visual information in understanding what is being said to them. Signing involves the teaching of organised sign systems – such as British Sign Language, Signed English, Sign Supported English and Makaton as well as finger-spelling – to teach children to communicate manually without the need to use speech.

Signing was the preferred method for teaching deaf children from the first efforts at deaf education until the middle of the nineteenth century. From then until the middle of the twentieth century the oral approach has dominated deaf education. However, in the 1960s concern began to develop about the standards being achieved in schools for the deaf using oral methods of teaching. This was reinforced by the results of a survey of all deaf school leavers in England and Wales which was undertaken in the 1970s (Conrad, 1979). This revealed that the average reading age of deaf school leavers was below 9 years and that almost three-quarters of them had unintelligible speech. The results of this survey supported a pendulum swing back towards signing during the 1970s and 1980s. During this time a new philosophy and methodology called Total Communication (TC) became the predominant approach (Schlesinger,1986). TC combines listening, lip-reading, signing and finger-spelling in simultaneous communication to represent English for the receiver.

In the past two decades research evidence has been building in support of the greater effectiveness of signing, over oral methods, in facilitating the acquisition of a first language (Mason and Ewoldt, 1996). For example, there is now considerable evidence that deaf children who are exposed to sign language in the early years of life learn language in a similar way and at a similar or even faster rate than hearing children acquiring speech (Caselli, 1983; Lewis, 1987). It is notable how deaf children with parents who are also deaf and who are exposed to signs from birth onwards tend to outperform other deaf children in learning their first language (Brasel and Quigley, 1977).

Also, in the past two decades there has been considerable growth in the influence of the disability rights movement which has emphasised that people with disabilities should be viewed as different, not deficient (Oliver, 1996). In line with this philosophy the adult deaf community has asserted the rights of deaf children to learn a sign language as their first language to acquire a social identity and gain entry to deaf culture.

These two factors, recognition of the value of signing in first language acquisition and the influence of the deaf community, have promoted a new approach to deaf education which has emerged in the 1990s. The approach is termed bilingualism and involves teaching deaf children their native sign language as their first language and then teaching them English as a second language (Mashie,1995). This approach is supported by linguistic analyses which have shown that sign languages such as British Sign Language and American Sign Language are distinct languages in their own right with the same capacity as any verbal language for the expression of concepts and ideas (Sacks, 1989).

Bilingualism requires a total commitment to exposing deaf children to an environment in which signing is competently used by parents, teachers and other members of the community, as illustrated by the following quotation:

> If hearing parents are taught sign language and have social contacts with deaf people, and if young deaf children can spend time with each other and deaf adults, then sign language can develop as a mother tongue for the deaf and as a second language for their hearing parents.
>
> (Ahlgren, 1994: 60)

However, as Lynas (1994) has pointed out, past experience has taught us that many parents of deaf children will be unable or unwilling to devote the time necessary to become fluent in a sign language. Also, there is currently a shortage of teachers of the deaf and teacher trainers who are sufficiently fluent in sign language. Therefore, it will be difficult if not impossible to provide all deaf children with a rich language learning environment based on their native sign languages.

Lynas (1994) also claims that services for hearing impaired children and their families and the technology associated with oral methods of education have improved drastically in the past two decades. Deaf children are now able to be diagnosed in the first few days of life and technologically advanced hearing aids may be fitted earlier and better maintained. In addition, techniques for making earmoulds and the widespread availability of radio hearing aids in schools have had a significant impact. These factors, she claims, have enabled severely and profoundly deaf children to make better use of their residual hearing in the 1980s and 1990s than was possible before this time.

She cites the results of three recent large-scale studies of the outcomes of orally based education programmes for deaf children which suggest that most deaf children who are orally educated are now achieving success in developing literacy skills and intelligible speech as opposed to the minority achieving success which was the case at the time of the Conrad (1979) study. However, she suggests that evidence for the effectiveness of total communication in achieving these outcomes has not been forthcoming.

In contrast, Hyde and Power's (1992) recent study suggests that no single method of communication is suitable for all deaf students. They consider that signing is generally needed for profoundly deaf children but that some severely deaf children can benefit from the oral approach. So the controversy continues, with bilingualism at present holding sway.

Cochlea implants for deaf children

As if there was not enough controversy in the field of deaf education a recent innovation threatens to return the focus to oral methods of teaching. This is the increasing use of cochlea implants with children who are prelingually deaf, that is those who are congenitally deaf or who become deaf before they have developed speech. Cochlea implantation involves surgically inserting an electronic device into the inner ear to increase the perception of sound. Cochlea implants have been pioneered with individuals who have become deaf as adults after developing speech and language normally as children. The implants have generally been found to be successful with this group and it is now widely accepted that the cochlea implant is a viable rehabilitative device for these postlingually deafened individuals (Rose *et al.*, 1996).

In recent years the use of cochlea implants has been extended to prelingually deaf children, which is a much more controversial procedure. It is now estimated that around two thousand implants have been performed on such children in North America and Europe (Rose *et al.*, 1996). One programme, based in Nottingham, reported that, by 1995, 80 children had received implants from the team (Twomey and Dyar, 1995). Follow-up data on these children have prompted the authors, who work on the Nottingham Paediatric Cochlea Implant Programme, to conclude that:

> The research literature and clinical outcomes predict a bright future for the families of very young profoundly deaf children who elect to have a cochlea implant for their child. The majority of those implanted before the age of 5 years and

without additional problems can be expected to use spoken language as their everyday means of communication.

(Twomey and Dyar, 1995: 13)

However, the results of independent studies of the success of cochlea implants with prelingually deaf children tell a very different story. Longitudinal research conducted by Geers and Moog (1992) in the USA indicated that auditory gains for implanted children was limited and that even after 2 or 3 years of implant use most of the children relied primarily on lip-reading or signing. Further, in a recent follow-up study of 151 implanted children in the USA, 71 or almost half of them were no longer wearing their cochlea implants. Many of the remaining 80 children still wearing the device were doing so only intermittently or because they were part of a research programme and were primarily dependent on signing and speech reading (Rose *et al.*, 1996).

The selection criteria, established in the USA, for considering children for implantation includes their participation in orally oriented education programmes, the absence of other disabilities and a profound level of hearing loss. However, Twomey and Dyar (1995) talk of implanting severely and profoundly deaf children and in the USA a study by Allen *et al.* (1993) found that some children with severe losses and some with severe learning difficulties had been implanted.

Several studies have reported increased perception of sound in implanted children (e.g. Twomey and Dyar, 1995) but there is no evidence that this increase has been substantial enough to bring about meaningful changes in children's communication abilities (Vernon and Alles, 1994). That is, there is no evidence of significantly improved speech or educational achievement for implanted children.

Given the findings of the studies conducted to date it is difficult to disagree with the position statement of the National Association of the Deaf (NAD, 1990) in the USA which suggested that prelingually deaf children are being used as guinea pigs for a procedure which has been a demonstrated failure for the majority of prelingually deafened patients on whom it has been tried.

The only reasonable conclusion which can be reached at present is that the use of cochlea implants with prelingually deaf children cannot be justified and should not be undertaken.

Doman–Delacato programme for brain-injured children

Possibly the best known controversy about an intervention outside the field of deaf education has been that surrounding the Doman–Delacato programme for brain-injured children (Delacato, 1966; Doman, 1974). This programme was originated by Glen Doman and Carl Delacato who established the Institute for the Achievement of Human Potential in Philadelphia in the 1960s. The Institute and its offshoots in various parts of the world continue to enrol children in the programme to this day despite the controversy about its use.

The programme is claimed to be effective for children with a wide range of disabilities resulting from neurological impairment (or brain damage). Clients include children with cerebral palsy and those with mental handicap of unknown or known causation, such as children with Down's syndrome.

A key component of the programme is 'patterning' which involves passive manipulation of the limbs and body for a number of hours each day to produce normal motor function. The rationale for this is that it will imprint a normal pattern of movements into a different part of the child's brain to that which has been damaged and thereby bring about normal motor functioning. Patterning requires the child to lie on a table while a team of adults manipulate legs, arms and head to simulate normal patterns of movement. The programme requires patterning to be carried out several times a day and on each day of the week for a period of several months or years. It therefore requires intensive involvement of the parents and the organisation of a team of volunteers who will help the family on a regular basis over a long period of time.

Another component is 'gagging' in which the child breathes into a plastic bag until he or she is gasping for breath. This is done in the belief that it will ensure maximum use of the lungs and thereby maximum circulation of oxygen to the brain. It is often, understandably, distressing for the child. The programme also involves the teaching of reading through the use of a series of flashcards. These are used regardless of the developmental or mental age of the child. In fact, Doman has extended this approach to reading to nondisabled children in a commercially available programme aimed at teaching babies as young as 1 year of age to read.

Doman and his colleagues published data in the 1960s which appeared to demonstrate the effectiveness of their programme with brain-injured children. However, it has been reported that parents of children involved in the programme are instructed not to allow their children to participate in any independent studies designed to evaluate its effectiveness (Bridgman, 1977). Probably because of this, the professional literature concerning its effectiveness is sparse, despite the length of time for which the programme has been operating.

The earliest report which could be located (Kershner,1967) investigated the impact of an intervention based on Doman–Delacato techniques on children with severe learning difficulties aged 8–18 years. The experimental group of 13 children received 74 daily sessions of five and a half hours duration based on Doman–Delacato techniques. The control group of 16 children participated in alternative activities which enabled them to receive an equivalent amount of praise and attention. The results of pre- and post-test assessments indicated that the experimental group improved significantly more than the control group on creeping and crawling and IQ but not on perceptual-motor proficiency. Kershner concluded that the Doman–Delacato techniques had a facilitating effect on both the physical and intellectual development of the children in the experimental group.

In another early study Fredericks (1969) compared the effects of Doman–Delacato techniques with behaviour modification procedures. The subjects were 72 children with Down's syndrome aged 7–12 years. Subjects were randomly assigned to either of the two treatment programmes which were run concurrently for 9 weeks. They were pre- and post-tested with a motor development scale and the Doman–Delacato profile. The results indicated that there were no significant differences between the two treatments, although children receiving behaviour modification demonstrated greater improvements in co-ordination than those in the Doman–Delacato group.

In a later report Bochner (1977) described a Melbourne based offshoot of the Doman–Delacato programme. She concluded that there was, at that time, no evidence to support claims about the effectiveness of the programme, while there was growing concern about the negative effects of the methods used, particularly on parents. A New Zealand study (Bridgman, 1977) compared a group of children on the Doman–Delacato programme with a matched group following a typical programme within a special school for children with severe learning difficulties. No significant differences between the groups were found after 6 months or 1 year on the respective programmes. A British study (MacKay *et al.*, 1986) followed up 36 children who had undergone the Doman–Delacato treatment programme and found that they had not made significant progress.

The most comprehensive analysis of the rationale and effectiveness of the Doman–Delacato programme to date is the book by Cummins (1988) dedicated to this topic. Cummins draws on data from neuro-anatomy and neurophysiology to demonstrate that there is no sound scientific basis for the techniques, such as patterning, used in the programme. He concludes that any improvements observed in children on the programme can be attributed to the increased activity level and attention paid to them. He notes that many professional bodies have denounced the approach as overly-expensive, ineffective, raising false hopes and destructive to family life. An example of this is the statement from the American Academy of Pediatrics (1983) which cites a lack of research support for the programme and concludes that its demands may overburden families without achieving progress beyond that which could be accounted for by expected growth and development.

In more recent articles Cummins (1987, 1992) has extended his critique of the Doman-Delacato approach. It is now clear that the only results supporting the effectiveness of the programme come from a handful of early, poorly controlled studies. Therefore, the conclusion must be that this treatment programme is not only ineffective with brain-injured children but also potentially damaging to the functioning of their families. Yet, as noted earlier, it continues to be available in various parts of the world.

Gentle Teaching

A more recent example of a controversial treatment is Gentle Teaching (GT). This approach was developed in the 1980s by McGee and his colleagues (McGee, 1985; McGee *et al.*, 1987). GT is a philosophy of treatment which involves non-aversive techniques for reducing challenging behaviours of children and adults with severe or profound learning difficulties. Its aims are to teach bonding and independence through gentleness, respect and solidarity. The techniques employed in GT include: interrupt–ignore–redirect–reward; environmental control; stimulus control; task analysis; prompting; shaping; fading; co-participation; identification of antecedents; reduced verbal instruction and physical demands; choice-making; dialogue; and errorless learning (McGee, 1992). These techniques are to be used flexibly within a humanistic framework in which the caregiver is expected to change as part of a two-way process.

McGee *et al.* (1987) have claimed that GT has been successful with over 600 clients. For example, grouped data are presented from 73 individuals treated for self-injurious behaviour in the state of Nebraska, where the approach was developed. Before treatment 63 of these were reported to exhibit a high intensity of self-injury. Following a maximum of 11 weeks of GT, 30 individuals exhibited a low intensity of self-injury and 43 did not injure themselves at all.

However, several writers have expressed doubts about the validity of such accounts reported by proponents of GT (Bailey, 1992; Jones and McCaughey, 1992; Mudford, 1995). It has been suggested that the findings reported by McGee and colleagues have been mainly from informal observations, personal descriptions, or videos of client behaviour before and after treatment with GT. Further, that research conducted by proponents has generally not included baseline or control conditions and has been subject to other methodological deficiencies.

Jones and McCaughey (1992), in their critical review of GT, included five studies conducted by researchers other than McGee and colleagues. They report that, in four out of five of these GT was found to be ineffective and in the fifth the results were mixed. Mudford (1995), in his review of data on GT, concluded that independent studies have included nine clients who received GT. Of these nine, two exhibited clinically significant reductions in problem behaviours, five showed no clinically significant changes in levels of problem behaviours, and two exhibited increased levels of self-injury following GT. In contrast, the seven unsuccessful cases were all effectively treated using behaviour analytic techniques such as differential reinforcement and visual screening.

Therefore, it is clear that there is, at present, insufficient independent data supporting the effectiveness of GT to justify its use as an alternative to more established and validated behavioural methods (see Singh, 1997). Other criticisms levelled at GT are that it is based on vague concepts such as 'bonding' (Bailey, 1992), consists primarily of existing behavioural procedures dressed up and re-marketed (Glynn, 1985) and that it is potentially highly aversive to clients whose self-injury is an attempt to escape contact from others (Emerson, 1990).

However, GT does highlight some important perspectives which are perhaps paid insufficient attention in behaviour analytic treatments. For example, it emphasises the importance of wider ecological variables in the analysis of inappropriate behaviour. GT also emphasises the importance of the personal characteristics and behaviour of the caregiver in the treatment process. In addition, GT highlights the contribution of non-contingent reinforcement in the elimination of challenging behaviour.

In conclusion, until further independent research data supporting GT are obtained its use cannot be justified. However, the debate provoked by this controversial issue has perhaps led to a broadening of perspectives regarding the elimination of severe behaviour problems exhibited by people with severe or profound learning difficulties.

Rationale for the book

The interventions discussed above are examples of some of the controversial treatments which have emerged during the growth of the field of special education. Currently in the field of special education there are several interventions and diagnoses which are controversial in terms of claims that are made about their validity or effectiveness. The information available on these topics tends to be disparate in that it consists of books and articles written by proponents as well as published research concerning their validity. The aim of this book is to review the literature on each topic and comment on the current state of the art of each in a way which is accessible to teachers, other professionals and parents.

Therefore, this book will consider the rationale and research evidence in support of the major controversial issues currently receiving attention in the field of special education. It is based on a course of lectures developed by the senior author over the past 5 years and delivered to students on Diploma and Masters degree courses on special education. The book is therefore of relevance to all teachers and other professionals who are concerned with the education of children with SEN, including teachers in mainstream and special schools. It is particularly relevant to training courses for teachers of children with SEN and on courses on SEN within Masters and Doctoral degree programmes. It will also be of interest to educational psychologists, therapists and other professionals working in the field of special education. Finally, it is intended that the book will be of use to parents who may be considering choosing one of the controversial treatments for their child with SEN.

Outline of the book

Format of each chapter

Each chapter will cover a similar format which, in most cases, will be as follows:

- the historical development of the diagnosis or treatment will be outlined
- the definition of terms will be discussed
- the rationale of the diagnosis or treatment will be considered
- the diagnosis or treatment will be described
- typical applications of the approaches will be discussed
- research evaluations will be described and the results analysed
- conclusions will be reached about the state of the art of each diagnosis or treatment
- implications for practitioners and for further research will be discussed
- reference to sources of further information on each diagnosis or treatment will be made.

Topics covered

The first part of the book will address three controversial diagnoses: autism, dyslexia and attention deficit hyperactivity disorder (ADHD). Specifically the chapters will focus on:

- *Autism* – Does it exist as a distinct form of disability?
- *Dyslexia* – Can it be distinguished from other forms of reading difficulty?
- *ADHD* – Is there such a syndrome?

The second part of the book will address two controversial system-wide interventions: inclusion and exclusion. Specifically the chapters focus on:

- *Inclusion of children with SEN in mainstream schools* – Is it currently justified?
- *Exclusion of children from schools* – Whose needs are being met?

The third part of the book will address three controversial group interventions: conductive education, instrumental enrichment and peer tutoring. Specifically the chapters focus on:

- *Conductive education* – Are the claims made for its effectiveness justified?
- *Instrumental enrichment* – Is it the answer to raising standards in schools?
- *Peer tutoring* – Does it make a difference?

The fourth part of the book will address three controversial individual interventions: Irlen lenses, facilitated communication and reading recovery.

Specifically, the chapters focus on:

● *Coloured lenses and overlays* – Do they improve the ability of some children to read?
● *Facilitated communication* – Is it fact or fantasy?
● *Reading Recovery* - Does it work and is it cost-effective?

Finally, the concluding chapter will summarise findings from the above chapters along with implications for practitioners and for future research in special education.

References

Ahlgren, D. (1994) 'Sign language as the first language'. In Ahlgren, D. and Hyltenstam, K. (eds) *Bilingualism in Deaf Education*. Hamburg: Signum-Verl, pp. 55–60.

Allen, T., Rawlings, B. and Remington, E. (1993) 'Demographic and audiological profiles of deaf children in Texas with cochlea implants', *American Annals of the Deaf*, **138** (3), 260–66.

American Academy of Pediatrics (1983) 'The Doman–Delacato treatment of neurologically handicapped children', *Exceptional Parent*, **13** (5), 40–43.

Bailey, J. S. (1992) 'Gentle Teaching: Trying to win friends and influence people with euphemism, metaphor, smoke and mirrors', *Journal of Applied Behavior Analysis*, **25** (4), 879–83.

Bochner, S. (1977) 'Doman–Delacato and the treatment of brain-injured children', *Australian Journal of Mental Retardation*, **4** (7), 4–7.

Brasel, K. and Quigley, S. (1977) 'The influence of certain language and communication environments in early childhood on the development of language in deaf individuals', *Journal of Speech and Hearing Research*, **20**, 95–107.

Bridgman, G. (1977) *A Comparative Study of Children on Doman–Delacato and Special School Programmes*. Paper presented at the New Zealand Psychological Society Conference, Auckland, July, 1977.

Caselli, M. (1983) 'Communication to language: deaf children's and hearing children's development compared', *Sign Language Studies*, **39**, 113–44.

Conrad, R. (1979) *The Deaf Schoolchild*. London: Harper and Row.

Cummins, R. A. (1987) 'The ideas of Doman and Delacato: Not just false but historically contrived', *Australian Psychologist*, **22** (1), 86–87.

Cummins, R. A. (1988) *The Neurologically-Impaired Child: Doman–Delacato Techniques Re-appraised*. London: Croom Helm.

Cummins, R. A. (1992) 'Coma arousal and sensory stimulation: An evaluation of the Doman–Delacato approach', *Australian Psychologist*, **27** (2), 71–77.

Delacato, C. H. (1966) *Neurological Organization and Reading*. Springfield, Ill: Charles C. Thomas.

Doman, G. (1974) *What To Do About Your Brain Injured Child*. Garden City, NJ: Doubleday.

Emerson, E. (1990) 'Some challenges presented by severe self-injurious behaviour', *Mental Handicap*, **18**, 92–98.

Fredericks, H. D. B. (1969) *A Comparison of the Doman–Delacato Method and*

Behavior Modification Method upon the Co-ordination of Mongoloids. Report to the Oregon State System of Education, Monmouth, Oregon.

Geers, A. and Moog, J. S. (1992) 'The Central Institute for the Deaf Cochlea Implant Study; A progress report', *Journal of Speech-Language Pathology and Audiology,* **16** (2), 129–40.

Glynn, T. (1985) 'Providing a context for gentle teaching', *Mental Handicap in New Zealand,* **9** (4), 21–23.

Hyde, M. B. and Power, D. J. (1992) 'The receptive communication abilities of deaf students under oral, manual and combined methods', *American Annals of the Deaf,* **137** (5), 389–98.

Jacobson, J. W., Mulick, J. A. and Schwartz, A. A. (1995) 'A history of facilitated communication: Science, pseudoscience and antiscience', *American Psychologist,* **50** (9), 750–65.

Jones, R. S. P. and McCaughey, R. E. (1992) 'Gentle teaching and applied behavior analysis: A critical review', *Journal of Applied Behavior Analysis,* **25** (4), 853–67.

Kershner, J. R. (1967) *An Investigation of the Doman–Delacato Theory of Neuropsychology as it Applies to Trainable Mentally Retarded Children in Public Schools.* Report for the Pennsylvania State Department of Public Instruction, Harrisburg, Pennsylvania.

Lewis, V. (1987) *Development and Handicap.* Oxford: Blackwell.

Lynas, W. (1994) 'Choosing between communication options in the education of deaf children', *Journal of the British Association of Teachers of the Deaf,* **18** (5), 141–53

McGee, J. (1985) 'Gentle Teaching', *Mental Handicap in New Zealand,* **9** (3), 13–24.

McGee, J. (1992) 'Gentle Teaching's assumptions and paradigm', *Journal of Applied Behavior Analysis,* **25** (4), 869–72.

McGee, J. J., Menolascino, F. J., Hobbs, D. C. and Menousek, P. E. (1987) *Gentle Teaching: A Non-aversive Approach to Helping Persons with Mental Retardation.* New York: Human Sciences Press.

MacKay, D. N., Gollogly, J. and McDonald, G. (1986) 'The Doman–Delacato treatment methods: Principles of neurological organisation', *British Journal of Mental Subnormality,* **62**, 3–19.

Mashie, S. N. (1995) *Educating Deaf Children Bilingually.* Washington, DC: Gallaudet University Pre-College Programs.

Mason, D. and Ewoldt, C. (1996) 'Whole language and deaf bilingual-bi-cultural education – naturally!' *American Annals of the Deaf,* **141** (4), 293–98.

Mudford, O. C. (1995) 'Review of the Gentle Teaching data', *American Journal on Mental Retardation,* **99** (4), 345–55.

National Association of the Deaf (1990) *Cochlea Implants in Children.* Position paper of the NAD. Silver Spring, MD: National Association of the Deaf.

Oliver, M. (1996) *Understanding Disability: From Theory to Practice.* Basingstoke: Macmillan.

Rose, D. E., Vernon, M. and Pool, A. F. (1996) 'Cochlea implants in prelingually deaf children', *American Annals of the Deaf,* **141** (3), 258–61.

Sacks, O. (1989) *Seeing Voices.* London: Pan.

Schlesinger, H. (1986) 'Total communication in perspective'. In Luterman, D. (ed.) *Deafness in Perspective.* London: Taylor and Francis.

Singh, N. N. (ed.) (1997) *Prevention and Treatment of Severe Behavior Problems: Models and Methods in Developmental Disabilities.* Pacific Grove, CA: Brooks/Cole.

Twomey, D. and Dyar, D. (1995) 'Nottingham paediatric team charts progress in cochlea implant programme', *Human Communication*, **August/September**, 11–13.

Vernon, M. and Alles, C. D. (1994) 'Issues in the use of cochlea implants with prelingually deaf children', *American Annals of the Deaf*, **139 (5)**, 485–91.

I Controversial Diagnoses

2 Autism: Does it Exist as a Distinct Form of Disability?

Diagnosis

Kanner (1943) first provided a clear account of the syndrome of 'infantile autism', describing a distinct group of children different from other recognised clinical populations. Since this time the diagnosis of autism has undergone much evolution and controversy, a detailed account of which can be found in Schreibman (1988). Over the years autism has been considered a variety of things including a mental illness, an emotional disurbance, a personality disorder, a communication disorder, a mental handicap, a social communication disorder, a developmental disability and, more recently, an information processing problem or a sensory perceptual problem (Williams, 1996). Professionals, therefore, have a variety of views regarding autism despite the fact that many of them agreed on the same identifiable symptoms for diagnosis.

Three main sets of diagnostic criteria have been used. Rutter (1978) proposed criteria based on a compilation of research findings which included onset before the age of 30 months, impaired social development which is not due to the child's impaired intellect, delayed and deviant language development and insistence of preservation of sameness. The National Society for Autistic Children (NSAC) proposed criteria based on clinical observation and professional consensus (given in Ritvo and Freeman, 1978). There was some overlap with Rutter's criteria but also some marked differences. The NSAC emphasises developmental delays and sensory abnormalities rather than insistence of sameness. The American Psychiatric Association (1987) in DSM-III-R specified criteria based on a consensus of clinical impressions. It classified autism with the Pervasive Developmental Disorders (PDD), which cover children and adults with lifelong difficulties in social and communicative skills beyond those accounted for by general delay (Rutter and Schopler, 1992), and it described the syndrome in explicit behavioural terms.

The fact that three different sets of diagnostic criteria have been used in the past and that diagnosis has not been applied in a consistent manner has led to a very heterogeneous population of autistic children who vary widely in both the manifestation of the disability and the level of severity of the disorder. This has also led to confusion within the field of autism (Schreibman, 1988).

At present the two most commonly used sets of diagnostic criteria are the ICD-10 (World Health Organisation, 1992) and the DSM-IV (American Psychiatric Association, 1994). Both these systems specify three areas of deficit for a diagnosis of autism:

1. Communication.
2. Social development.
3. Restricted and repetitive behaviours and interests.

Both require the recognition of some type of abnormality before the age of 36 months. Currently autism continues to be classified as a Pervasive Developmental Disorder and, although this has recently been criticised, there appears to be no appropriate alternative at present (Lord and Rutter, 1994).

Aarons and Gittens (1992) highlight the problems of diagnosis and recognition and describe the present situation as 'fraught with muddle and confusion'. They believe that a descriptive approach to diagnosis is essential for the full extent of the autistic continuum to be recognised and they welcome the move away from the 'all or nothing approach' to the existence of autistic features previously held by many clinicians. Williams (1996) supports the view that there is no single condition called autism.

In practice, however, in many cases of children exhibiting autistic behaviour often no diagnosis is made and the presence of autism is strongly denied. The child's development may not be sufficiently delayed and there is often a failure to recognise the child's social impairments. Many health visitors and GPs, have never met an autistic child and may miss the signs which are present, diagnosing instead slow development, deafness or over anxious parents (Humphreys and Ramm, 1987). This prolongs the period of bewilderment and isolation and delays intervention. Aarons and Gittens (1992) suggest that many of the problems with diagnosis could be alleviated if there was greater training for professionals and more up to date knowledge in this field. This view is supported by Humphreys and Ramm (1987), Williams (1996) and by the National Society for Autistic Children.

Prevalence

Humphreys and Ramm (1987) state that the core syndrome affects 2.5 children in 10,000 with boys outnumbering girls by between 3:1 and 4:1. The most quoted prevalence, however, is that of Lotter (1966) who gave a rate of 4.5 per 10,000 which included the classic syndrome and those with many autistic features. This figure is supported by Wing and Gould (1979) who also give a figure of 21 in 10,000 when the criteria are broadened to include those with the social impairments characteristic of autism, regardless of mental or physical disabilities. The National Society for Autistic Children suggests the prevalence rate to be 4 or 5 in 10,000 for classic cases, rising to 17 in 10,000 for closely related conditions requiring similar services. More recently, however, when the full spectrum of the disorder is included, figures given are as high as 23 in 10,000 (Aarons and Gittens, 1992). These figures, however, include those with Asperges syndrome who are now defined as a separate Pervasive Developmental Disorder (American Psychiatric Association, 1994; World Health Organisation, 1992). This term refers to individuals without cognitive delay who have severely impaired social understanding and reciprocity, pragmatic difficulties and unusual, limited interests. The exact nature of Asperges syndrome and its relation to autism is unclear (Lord and Rutter, 1994). Lord and Rutter suggest that it may be better to use other terms such as atypical autism for those who do not fulfil the full criteria for autism.

Schreibman (1988) emphasises that prevalence rates are unreliable because of the inconsistency of diagnosis. Also, whilst autism appears to be found all over the world, most of the figures for the prevalence rates come from studies undertaken in America.

Recognition

Social deficits

A study by Wing and Gould (1979) led them to believe that the core deficit in autistic children is social in nature and there now appears to be some general agreement that it is the profound and pervasive impairment in social behaviour which characterises children with autism and is the most handicapping feature (Volkmar, 1987). Many writers have indicated that abnormal social and emotional behaviours are primary to the diagnosis (Denkla, 1986; Fein et al., 1986; Wing and Gould, 1979). The most characteristic aspect of these social deficits are difficulties in reciprocal social interaction and the ability to form relationships (Siegel et al., 1989). In the pre-school years these children are characterised by a lack of interest in other children, unusual eye contact and a limited range of facial expression (Lord, 1993) and they also have minimal involvement with their parents. This failure to develop social behaviour is also evident in their lack of peer contact and interactive play (Rutter, 1978). They usually avoid play situations with peers and, if in the same area, will engage in solitary activity. Their preference for being alone continues to be evident as they grow older (Schreibman, 1988). Despite the fact that healthy social attachment and responsiveness is grossly deficient autistic children do engage in some social behaviour. They often relate to people as objects and may form strong attachments to inanimate objects, such as vacuum cleaners (Schreibman, 1988).

Even those with minimal or no developmental delay are characterised by a lack of interest in forming friendships, lack of responsiveness to subtle social cues and continued interest in being alone. They remain, therefore, social isolates and may say or do socially inappropriate things and are therefore not accepted by their peer group. However great the intellectual capability, therefore, the lack of social skills is an enormous and wide-ranging handicap which affects every aspect of their lives (Aarons and Gittens, 1992). Lord and Rutter (1994), however, emphasise that most autistic children do not show deficits in all of these areas and that many of them may exhibit behaviours for brief periods or in particular situations that seem surprisingly social.

Communication

Although autism is characterised by delayed language acquisition it is the deviant quality of communication that is most specific to autistic individuals. It is often the child's failure to acquire language that first alerts the parents that something is wrong (Schreibman, 1988). Approximately 50% never develop functional speech (Rutter, 1978) and those who speak characteristically display language that is qualitatively different from that of normal children and children with other language disorders (Bartak *et al.*, 1977; Ricks and Wing, 1975; Rutter, 1978; Wing, 1976).

Autistic children do not engage in reciprocal conversation and their questions are only connected with their pre-occupations. Speech is repetitious or more of a monologue than a socially directed communication (Lord and Rutter, 1994). They often engage in non-communicative echoing of words and phrases which they have heard (Fay, 1969), sometimes repeating things sometime later. Other language characteristics include reversing pronouns (Ricks and Wing, 1975; Rimland, 1964; Rutter, 1978) and typically the child will refer to him or herself as 'you' or by name. Their comprehension may be severely impaired (Ricks and Wing, 1975) and they may repeat certain sounds, words or phrases over and over again with no apparent intent to communicate. Abnormalities of pitch, stress, rhythm and intonation and the making up of words are also characteristic.

Essentially the problems centre around the use of language (Aarons and Gittens, 1992) and when speech develops it has a lack of or unusual social quality (Tager-Flusberg and Anderson, 1991). The child fails to engage successfully in interactive communication. Aarons and Gittens (1992) consider that to focus solely on the linguistic features, without regard to the child's mode of being is inadequate and simplistic. They state that delay in language acquisition must be considered in the light of the autistic child's lack of motivation to communicate and they advocate that the presence of autism, no matter how mild or subtle, must be recognised. They list 18 deviant aspects of speech and language, but what is distinctive is that these reflect the cognitive and social impairments of the disorder.

Restricted and repetitive interests and behaviours

Stereotyped behaviours and interests are the third characteristic feature of autism. Spontaneous, flexible and imaginative play is rare and young children display limited, rigid play patterns (Rutter, 1978; Schreibman and Mills, 1983; Wing, 1976). It is more noticeable in older pre-school children, who may become preoccupied with a specific part of a toy or attached to unusual objects. Older, less retarded children often develop complex routines with objects which they act out over and over again (Le Couteur *et al.*, 1989). They sometimes engage in compulsive rituals, the intensity of which can be very strong (Rutter, 1978; Schreibman, 1988). As they mature they may become upset if daily routines are not followed to the letter or if trivial aspects of the environment are changed. As time goes on the behaviour patterns become habitual and present difficult management problems to the extent that family life is severly disrupted (Aarons and Gittens, 1992).

Repetitive, persistent stereotyped behaviour that seems to serve no other purpose than to provide sensory or kinaesthetic feedback (e.g. Lovaas *et al.*, 1971; Rincover, 1978) is often viewed as one of the defining features of autism (Rimland, 1964). It may include rhythmic body rocking, jumping, head bobbing and arm or hand flapping (Le Couteur *et al.*, 1989). This behaviour appears to be extremely important to the child and therefore interferes with the child's responsiveness to the acquisition of more normal behaviour (Koegel *et al.*, 1974; Lovaas *et al.*, 1971). It often renders them oblivious to their surroundings and can be a major obstacle to treatment. Some children injure themselves deliberately, especially the most retarded. The most common forms of self-injury are head banging or self-biting of hands and fingers which vary in intensity (Rumsey *et al.*, 1985; Rutter and Lockyer, 1967).

Relationship with other disorders

Researchers have noted the apparent overlap between autism and other childhood disorders (Rimland, 1964; Rutter, 1978; Schreibman and Charlop, 1987; Schreibman and Mills, 1983). Schreibman (1988) outlines the overlaps with mental retardation, childhood schizophrenia, developmental aphasia, pervasive developmental disorder and environmental deprivation.

Many autistic children show a wide range of non-specific problems, such as temper tantrums, found in a wide range of psychiatric conditions (as well as in many normal children). However, systematic comparison between autistic children and children with other psychiatric syndromes (after matching for age, sex and IQ) have confirmed that there are features of social relationships, language and play that are distinctive of autism (Rutter, 1978).

Diagnosis is based on a pattern of deficits and there is, therefore, a need to determine which behaviours can be accounted for by alternative explanations and then whether the remaining features of the child's behaviour fit best with autism or another disorder (Rutter, 1985). It is important, therefore, that its relationship with other disorders is recognised.

Mental handicap

Kanner (1943) believed that autistic children possessed normal intelligence and that it was their deficits in other areas which made them appear developmentally delayed. Most recent data, however, suggest that the majority of autistic children are mentally retarded (Schreibman, 1988) and that impaired cognitive ability is a feature shared by both these disorders. According to Ritvo and Freeman (1978) research estimates indicate that approximately 60% of autistic children have measured IQs below 50, 20% between 50 and 70 and 20% of 70 or above. Epidemiological studies show that 2–4 children in every 10,000 have autism, but if severe mental handicap with autistic features is included in the diagnosis the rate rises to as high as 20 in 10,000. Schreibman (1988) also points out that, although the National Autistic Society describes autism as a mental handicap, a small number of autistic individuals are not intellectually handicapped in the normal sense. IQ, however, is the single most powerful predictor of outcome in autism and the close association between autism and mental handicap cannot be ignored (Lord and Rutter, 1994).

Both autistic children and children who would receive a primary diagnosis of mental handicap show poor intellectual ability which persists throughout their life (Rutter, 1978) and many mentally handicapped children demonstrate behaviours typically seen in autistic children, such as self-stimulatory behaviours and attention deficits (Wing, 1976). There are, however, several characteristics which differentiate the two diagnoses. These are summarised by Schreibman (1988) as follows:

1. Many mentally handicapped children tend to exhibit appropriate social behaviour in comparison with the social deficits found in those with autism.
2. Mentally handicapped children are often communicative and, although their abilities to communicate may be limited, the intent and motivation are apparent. This contrasts with autistic children who may acquire adequate linguistic structures and even do well in certain language tests, but may still fail to engage successfully in interactive communication (Aarons and Gittens, 1992).
3. Autistic children have normal physical development whereas mentally handicapped children do not. The delays in acquisition of motor skills so often seen in mentally handicapped children are seldom seen in autistic children (Schreibman and Mills, 1983).

4. The pattern of intellectual impairment is different in the two groups. Handicapped children show impairment in a wide range of functioning, whereas autistic children display a more variable pattern of intellectual functioning. Autism tends to be associated with a distinctive cognitive pattern, with visual spatial skills greatest and verbal abstraction and conceptualisation skills weakest (Venter et al., 1992). It is important also to note that a significant minority of autistic individuals have unusual cognitive skills, such as an exceptional ability in drawing or mathematical calculations, as well as deficits (Rimland, 1964). These are often referred to as autistic savants, as illustrated in the popular film *Rainman*.

It is interesting to note that Williams (1996), an autistic person herself, states that the system of functioning of mentally retarded individuals is as alien to her as is the functioning of non-autistic individuals.

Childhood schizophrenia

Although childhood schizophrenia and autism share sustained impairment in social relations, resistance to changes in the environment, speech abnormalities and constricted or inappropriate affect, it is generally not difficult to distinguish schizophrenia from autism (Dykens et al., 1991). Differences which allow for differential diagnosis include the later onset of schizophrenia, a family history of mental illness, poor physical health, poor motor performance, higher IQ than are typically found in autistic children, periods of remission and relapse, higher levels of language skills and the presence of delusions and hallucinations (Rimland, 1964; Wing, 1976).

Other pervasive developmental disorders

The term Pervasive Developmental Disorder refers to children and adults who have severe lifelong difficulties in social and communicative skills beyond those accounted for by general delay (Rutter and Schopler, 1992). Both diagnostic systems (ICD-10 and DSM-IV) identify other Pervasive Developmental Disorders, including Rett's syndrome, Disintegrative Disorder and Asperges syndrome, as separate disorders. Waterhouse et al. (1996) found significant IQ and behaviour differences between autistic children and those with other Pervasive Developmental Disorders.

Rett's syndrome can produce autistic like behaviours in young children (Hagberg et al., 1983), but as these children get older motor and mental handicaps increase and social interest may appear to increase within the limits of the profound mental handicap. Differential diagnosis, therefore, is not usually very difficult after the age of 4 or 5 years (Olsson and Rett, 1987, 1990). Within Disintegrative Disorder behavioural changes include social withdrawal, loss of communication and stereotyped behaviours similar to those of autism. However, the disorder differs in the loss of motor and self-help skills and lack of complex stereotyped behaviours. There is currently some controversy about how Asperges syndrome compares to autism without mental handicap. It includes individuals with severe social impairments and behaviour much like those seen in autism but who are not mentally handicapped or even language delayed (Lord and Rutter, 1994) and therefore show milder symptoms, less restricted interests, fewer odd behaviours and have a better prognosis. Whether the differences between autism and Asperges syndrome are quantitative or qualitative has yet to be established.

Environmental deprivation

Children who have experienced severe neglect show language delay, abnormal social behaviour and sometimes odd habits and stereotyped behaviours (Ornitz and Ritvo, 1976; Lord and Rutter, 1994). They do not, however, show the peculiar language and communication difficulties and avoidance of social contact of autistic children. They also demonstrate marked improvement in an enriched environment (Ornitz and Ritvo, 1976).

Receptive-expressive language disorders

There is a rare group of children with severe receptive language disorders who exhibit some echolalia, social impairment and sometimes limited imaginative play but, although they often fail to understand language properly, they are usually attentive and responsive to others (Donaldson, 1995). They also do not show the stereotyped behaviours seen in autism and have a more normal intelligence.

Aetiology

The complexity of this disorder, the different emphasis theorists have placed on different aspects of the disorder and the lack of a definite cause has led to a proliferation of theories regarding its aetiology (Schreibman, 1988; Trevarthen et al., 1996).

Social environment

A number of aspects of the social environment have been implicated in the cause of the disorder. Originally, observations made by Kanner led to the belief that parents were at fault for providing insufficient warmth and affection. Following this there was a proliferation of theories implicating the family environment, including family breakdown, parental personality, breakdown of the bonding process between mother and child and insufficient stimulation (Cox *et al.*, 1975; Ward, 1970). Some writers have suggested theories based on learning principles with severe behavioural deficits attributed to faulty conditioning history (Ferster, 1961) whilst others suggest that it is the interaction between a biologically or psychologically susceptible child and parental psychopathology which is important (Kanner, 1949).

The reliability and validity of many of these early studies, however, is in question. More recent and methodologically sound studies (Freeman and Ritvo, 1984; Koegel *et al.*, 1983; Schopler and Reichler, 1971) provide evidence that parents of autistic children do not differ from those of normal children or those from other clinical populations on measures of personality and social interaction. It is also reasonable to assume that any lack of responsiveness by the parents may be a reaction to the child's behaviour (Rimland, 1964; Rutter, 1968; Schopler and Reichler, 1971) – a fact which many studies appear to have overlooked.

Any belief that parents were at fault has now been discredited by both research and clinical experience (Aarons and Gittens, 1992). It should be noted, however, that parental anxiety may aggravate the child's problems thereby reducing their ability to cope. Systematic research has failed to support any role of the psychosocial environment in the development of autism (Lord and Rutter, 1994) and, despite claims to the contrary (Gillberg, 1992), twin studies suggest that environmental factors play no more than a minor aetiological role (Rutter, 1991; Rutter *et al.*, 1993).

Cognitive deficits and abnormalities

Cognitive deficits and abnormalities have been studied in a number of areas, including deficits in information processing, perceptual and attention behaviours, intellectual impairment and language deficits (such as Hermelin and O'Connor, 1970; Tilton and Ottinger, 1964). Frith (1989) believes that autism is caused by a fundamental cognitive deficit that prevents prediction of the behaviour of other people. This explanation makes sense of the pragmatic difficulties typical of their language deficits and provides the key to understanding their conversational disabilities. More recently, a new kind of cognitive theory has become popular and proponents describe the autistic child as lacking a normally developed 'theory of mind' with the main feature being an inability to attribute beliefs to others (Baron-Cohen, 1989, 1990; Baron-Cohen *et al.*, 1985; Happe, 1994; Leslie and Frith, 1988). There are hypotheses about the possible neurobiological basis of deficits in information processing and attention in autism (Bailey *et al.*, 1996). Williams (1996) in her personal account of autism states that the problems are essentially to do with information processing with other behaviours being a result of the way the child compensates for this. Work on cognitive deficits and abnormalities has been extensive and wide ranging, but Bailey *et al.* (1996) conclude that basic deficits have yet to be established. They discuss the various theories relating to cognitive deficits and whether they can explain the clinical symptoms of the disorder. They stress the need to broaden the focus of investigations to encompass all characteristics of the disorder. Despite this, some writers, including Rutter (1983), have argued that a cognitive deficit is the basis of autism and that the importance of emotional disorder has been exaggerated.

Organic aetiologies

All of the evidence now available strongly indicates that the causes of autism are biological (Aarons and Gittens, 1992) and recent emphasis in research has been placed on organic causes for autism because of the increasing evidence of an organic basis for the disorder and because of the increased technology available to investigate such factors. Three sources of organic factor have been implicated: those associated with pregnancy and birth, genetic factors and viruses.

Pregnancy and birth: There is generally a high incidence of pre-natal problems in children with autism compared with their siblings and normal children (Nelson, 1991; Tsai, 1987). A list of factors implicated is given by Tsai (1987). Research suggests that obstetric factors can occasionally serve as causes of autism, but that this only accounts for a small number of cases.

Genetic factors: Over the years autism has been associated with a number of genetic disorders (Folstein and Rutter, 1988; Reiss *et al.*, 1986; Smalley, 1991; Smalley *et al.*, 1988) and, more recently, investigators have looked at specific gene structure (Bailey *et al.*, 1993; Bolton and Rutter, 1990; Cohen *et al.*, 1989; Gillberg and Wahlstrom, 1985; Wolff *et al.*, 1989). This is a relatively new field, however, and studies so far have been inconclusive. Twin studies to date (Folstein and Rutter, 1977; Rutter *et al.*, 1993; Steffenburg *et al.*, 1989) indicate that a strong genetic component may be present and family genetic studies (Folstein and Rutter, 1988; Piven *et al.*, 1992; Ritvo *et al.*, 1985; Smalley *et al.*, 1988) suggest a rate of autism in siblings of 3%. Bailey *et al.* (1996) review genetic studies comprehensively and conclude that a strong genetic component exists, that a pattern of interacting genes results in the overall clinical picture and that autism might include genetically distinct subvarieties.

Viruses: Recent research has also indicated that certain viruses may be implicated in the cause of autism (Aarons and Gittens, 1992).

The brain

Aarons and Gittens (1992) conclude that brain damage or dysfunction is present in autism in all its manifestations and that the wide range of presenting features suggest multiple neurological deficits. In nearly every case of autism, when appropriate techniques are available, evidence of abnormality in the brain can be found (Aitken, 1991; Gillberg, 1988, 1992; Schore, 1994; Steffenburg, 1991; Trevarthen and Aitken, 1994). It appears this developmental disorder originates in the failure of the cerebral systems that regulate a child's motivation for learning meanings in communication (Trevarthen et al., 1996). No consistent abnormalities appear in brain scans of subjects with primary autism (Prior et al., 1984) but magnetic resonance imaging (MRI) research (Courchesne, 1995) confirms histo-anatomical findings that parts of the cerebellum and brain stem are underdeveloped. Evidence of neurochemical abnormalities, mainly from studies on the use of medication saw raised levels of urinary serotonin in 30% of cases, but neurochemical findings are as yet inconclusive (Bailey, 1993; Cook, 1990; Elliot and Ciaranello, 1987) and the case for a neurochemical basis for autism has not yet been substantiated. All of the available evidence supports the conclusion that autism is caused by abnormal brain development that begins before birth but which may not demonstrate its effects in behaviour until the end of infancy, when the child should be beginning to develop meaningful language (Trevarthen et al., 1996).

In summary, there is no conclusive proof for the support of any one of these theories and Schreibman (1988) suggests that a search for a single aetiology may be fruitless. The variation in results, heterogeneity of the population and the possible existence of subgroups within the autistic population suggest that multiple aetiologies may be responsible. Aarons and Gittens (1992) suggest that for autism to develop brain damage has to occur in the setting of a genetic predisposition, that the cause is likely to be heterogeneous, ensuing when a number of possibly quite common factors coincide, and it is the coincidence that is rare and makes autism uncommon. Humphreys and Ramm (1987) suggest that a variety of influences (viral, autoimmune or genetic) can upset nervous system development at an early stage and shift the process from a normal course to an autistic one.

Bailey et al. (1996) thoroughly examine the present knowledge on the genetic, neuropsychological and neurobiological components of autism and discuss how these different levels of research may be integrated. They indicate that the few attempts to put forward conceptual causal models which integrate findings across all levels have been unsatisfactory and stress that this must be a research goal if we are to understand autism fully.

Assessment

Rigorous assessment of autism is a multi-faceted, multi-disciplinary process which involves determining the presence of the behavioural characteristics associated with the disorder, eliminating alternative explanations for the child's behaviour, establishing the child's baseline cognitive functioning and then selecting from different diagnoses (Lord and Rutter, 1994). Both Lord and Rutter and Schreibman (1988) advocate the use of a combination of parental and teacher reports, observation and standardised assessment. Traditional tests, however, are of limited value in assessing children suffering from such severe deficits (Schreibman and Charlop, 1987). For this reason a number of specifically designed instruments have been developed for the autistic population, including clinical interview, observational data, behaviour checklists, observation schemes and an emphasis on behavioural assessment (Schreibman, 1988). Aarons and Gittens (1992) provide a checklist and handbook, for use by professionals, outlining what to look for and how to interpret their findings within a structured framework with a developmental base. It outlines a number of key areas of the child's development on which to focus.

The initial step in the assessment process is usually a clinical interview with the parents. The Autistic Diagnostic Interview – Revised (Le Couteur *et al.*, 1989) is a semi-structured standardised interview for parents or carers which is based on the DSM-IV and ICD-10 diagnostic criteria, but which requires a professional to have some training to be able to implement it. Schreibman and Charlop (1987) provide a comprehensive list of the information which may be gathered from a clinical interview and which includes developmental history, social behaviour, speech development, self-stimulatory or self-injurous behaviour, affect, insistence in maintenance of sameness, isolated skills and behaviour problems both at home and at school. Lord and Rutter (1994) emphasise that whilst a variety of formats may be appropriate for the clinical interview what is important is that the clinician has a framework into which to put the information which is gathered from the interview.

An observation session is essential to assess the child's behaviour in a different setting and with an unfamiliar person in addition to establishing the reliability of parental information. Several behaviour checklists and observational schemes have been developed and a range of those available is detailed in Schreibman (1988). Schreibman states that these have the advantage of providing uniformity in the information gathered and that they can be used without the family being present. She stresses, however, that it is important that these are not used in isolation, but in conjunction with other assessment procedures.

The presence of sufficient behavioural characteristics indicative of autism may lead to a diagnosis of autism but this alone does not provide sufficient information to identify the most appropriate treatment for specific children, or to make predictions about their prognosis (Schreibman and Charlop,

1987). Schreibman and Koegel (1981) and Lovaas *et al.* (1973) have developed a more specific structured observational assessment for this purpose. Williams (1996) emphasises that autistic individuals are a 'mixed bag' and the need to assess their individual needs and to deal specifically with each underlying problem. She states that there is a danger that by stereotyping these individuals they will not get the treatment that they need. She advocates that teachers and professionals acquire knowledge and training as they are unaware of the underlying problems, how to recognise them and what to do about them and are unable to tell one type of autism from another.

Treatment

The goals of treatment are outlined by Lord and Rutter (1994) as:

1. Fostering social and communicative development.
2. Enhancing learning and problem solving.
3. Decreasing behaviours that interfere with learning and access to opportunities for normal experiences.
4. Helping families to cope.

These goals need to be broken down into more specific and immediate aims to work with them practically. Lord and Rutter (1994) also stress the importance of linking treatment goals to the developmental level of the child.

Methods of treatment

Medication
There have been large advances in the drug treatment of autistic children over the last two decades; but, despite this, no specific treatment has been adequately substantiated and many have potentially negative side-effects (Gadow, 1992; Riddle *et al.*, 1991; Schreibman, 1988). Trevarthen *et al.* (1996) and Lord and Rutter (1994) provide detailed accounts of the wide variety of the drugs which have been used. Some may have helpful effects on a limited range of behaviours (Rumsey *et al.*, 1985), but there is no evidence that any 'treat' autism or that they are more effective than any other forms of treatment (Campbell *et al.*, 1987; Schreibman, 1988; Sloman, 1991; Trevarthen *et al.*, 1996). Lord and Rutter (1994) believe that it is unlikely that drug treatment will ever replace the need for psychological and empathic forms of intervention (a view supported by Trevarthen *et al.*, 1996). They suggest, however, that the careful use of medication has a place in the treatment of some individuals when it is combined with other forms of treatment. However, some writers, such as Sloman (1991), doubt that there is any value at all in using drugs with those who are autistic.

Therapy

A wide range of therapies (including speech, occupational, physical, music and psychotherapy) are available and their appropriateness depends on the individual deficits and needs of the child. Most autistic children benefit from some focused training in communication and some from help with motor skills and social skills (Mesibov, 1984; Williams, 1989). Having reviewed the research on psychotherapy (e.g. Rutter and Bartak, 1973) the National Institute of Mental Health (1975) concluded that psychotherapy with autistic children has not proved effective and is unlikely to do so. Trevarthen *et al.* (1996), however, argue that – in a modified form and with the recognition that autism is a real pathology of the mind – psychotherapy can give the therapist enhanced insight into a child's confusions and fears and can lead to constructive education to increase the child's awareness and capacity to regulate feelings.

Behavioural treatment

Autism can be viewed as a syndrome of behaviours. Therefore, once the functional relationship of these behaviours with the environment has been identified treatment proceeds by manipulating those aspects of the environment which affect them. The literature documenting the effectiveness of this type of approach and its successful application to a wide range of behaviours of autistic children is extensive (Carr, 1985; Schreibman, 1988). This approach has had a major impact on the management of difficult behaviours, the acquisition of self-help skills and educational treatment of autistic children. However, limits of likely outcomes and of the maintenance and generalisation of changes are now recognised (Lord, 1984; Lovaas *et al.*, 1973). Some studies have reported that an unusually intensive behavioural treatment beginning at a very young age leads to major gains for many children (e.g. Lovaas, 1987; McEachin *et al.*, 1993), but these results have yet to be replicated and the methodology employed in these studies has been criticised (Lord and Rutter, 1994).

Education

There has been an intensive research effort directed at the development of effective education for these children (e.g. Koegel *et al.*, 1982; Wilcox and Thompson, 1980). Lord and Rutter (1994: 584) state that:

> Education has been by far the most powerful source of improvement for autistic children and adolescents in the last 50 years.

Important developments in this field are outlined by Schreibman (1988). These include the development of comprehensive functional curricula which take into account communication and the cognitive and social aspects of the disorder, the provision of teachers specially trained in the needs of autistic children, research into the design of classrooms for autistic children and the transition of autistic children from more to less restricitve environments.

It is important to remember that all autistic children are different, that they vary in their academic ability and their behaviour and that they need to be individually assessed. Early placement in a playgroup or nursery is recommended (Aarons and Gittens, 1992; Schreibman, 1988) thereby providing social experiences and allowing the child's difficulties to be clarified. It is likely that the majority of autistic children will require special educational needs provision (Lord and Rutter, 1994) but many of the brighter ones can manage in mainstream school with classroom assistance and special needs help at least for a while (Aarons and Gittens, 1992). Schreibman (1988) claims that after an intensive educational programme many can make the transition into less structured settings in mainstream schools. There are few interpretable data, however, comparing different degrees of integration with autistic children (Lord and Rutter, 1994). Parents should always consider the schools available and ascertain for themselves which is the most suitable for their child as this depends on both their academic ability and their behaviour (Aarons and Gittens, 1992). Lord and Rutter (1994) suggest that the policy of educating the child in the least restrictive environment is reasonable, but that this environment may not be easy to find. Success seems to depend on whether the programme is well structured, positive in attitude and able to cope with the individual needs of the child (Harris et al., 1990; Strain, 1983). This view is supported by Trevarthen et al. (1996) and Aarons and Gittens (1992) who stress that the ethos of the school and the interest and attitude of its staff are important.

The importance of early intervention to minimise secondary behavioural difficulties such as entrenched rituals which interfere with the learning process cannot be over-stressed (Trevarthen et al., 1996). Delay in diagnosis due to the lack of awareness of primary health care professionals or denial that autism exists therefore can only exacerbate the child's difficulties. Communication in infancy and pre-school ages offers the best model for the kind of one-to-one teaching that autistic children respond to best. Trevarthen et al. (1996) give details of early intervention programmes presently in use.

Limited generalisation of treatment effects may occur if the intervention is conducted in only one environment. It is important, therefore, to involve parents in any programme of intervention. Trevarthen et al. (1996) state that any educational provision for the autistic child, however expert, must be child and family based, involving the parents as collaborators with teachers as it is the parents or carers who have the key position particularly in the early stages of this learning.

Family support

Family support may take a variety of forms including teaching management techniques (e.g. Harris, 1984; Koegel et al., 1982), emotional support, practical help such as finding respite services and providing information regarding local and national resources such as support groups. Lord and Rutter (1994) stress that it is important to remember that different families may require different kinds of support and that families vary with what they are able to cope with. It is important, therefore, to encourage each family to work out their own solution to their difficulties. Williams (1996) comments that parents often feel robbed of control by professionals. She reviews a wide range of treatments from an autistic person's perspective. She notes that many treatments show a lack of understanding of the underlying problems associated with autism either by addressing the symptoms rather than the cause or by focusing on helping the individual cope with a problem rather than dealing with it.

Prognosis

Autism is a lifelong disorder and scarcely any adults with autism achieve complete normality (Lord and Rutter, 1994). All those with autism, however, are different and therefore so is their prognosis. The most important prognostic indicators with respect to social functioning and academic attainment are the child's language ability, cognition level and level of adaptive functioning (Howlin and Rutter, 1987; Lord and Schopler, 1989; Lotter, 1978; Rutter, 1970; Rutter et al., 1992; Venter et al., 1992). The overall level of behavioural disturbance (particularly aggression and pervasive, intrusive repetitive behaviours) is also important for prognosis (Venter et al., 1992). The age of the child is important with regard to treatment effectiveness. Clearly, the earlier the treatment the greater the benefits.

Those children with a severe developmental delay will require supervised living and working situations throughout their life and this can be obtained within a variety of day and residential settings. Some autistic individuals are able to function in local authority residential homes in a group setting with supervision and support. More able autistic individuals may be able to attend courses for children with special needs at Further Education Colleges or residential courses which promote independence. The prognosis for complete independence, however, is limited (Lord and Rutter, 1994) and even the most able, despite adequate intelligence and acquisition of useful skills, usually fail to survive in the world of work because of their social impairment. They need help finding and keeping jobs and coping with responsibilities and social demands (Rutter et al., 1992). It is noted that there are few placements which are able to harness the skills of these individuals whilst at the same time coping with their difficulties (Aarons and Gittens, 1992). As Lord and Rutter (1994) note, however, good services (education, family support and behavioural interventions) make a real difference in social outcome but they do not remove the basic handicaps (Howlin and Rutter, 1987).

Conclusion

There is no doubt that autism – characterised by profound social deficits, deviant communication and restricted and repetitive interests and behaviours – exists and that it is a pervasive and severely disabling disorder. Research over the past decade has led to increased knowledge with regard to its prevalence and course and the cognitive and social deficits involved. Studies indicate that multiple aetiologies are responsible, that brain damage or dysfunction is present and that there is a strong genetic component to the disorder. There has been increasing refinement in the classification of autism and, most importantly, ongoing improvement in the methods of educating autistic children. However, research needs to be broadened to take account of all the characteristics of the disorder rather than to focus on specific aspects. Only in this way will a full understanding of the disorder be achieved.

Successful treatment and education depends on early diagnosis and intervention. The overlap of symptoms with a number of other disorders means that diagnosis must be achieved through a comprehensive multi-disciplinary assessment and by a process of eliminating all possible alternatives. No two autistic individuals are alike and assessment needs also to be specific enough to take account of their individual needs. There needs to be a recognition of the diverse nature of the disorder to avoid stereotyping and inapproprate treatment. Autism is relatively rare and because of its low incidence many professionals have had little opportunity to either observe or study the disorder. There is a tendency, therefore, to under-diagnose. Professionals working directly with children such as health visitors and teachers require greater awareness of the diagnostic criteria for autism, its overlap with other conditions and training in its recognition.

Specialist educational resources in a wide range of settings need to be available so that the needs of autistic children can be met in the least restrictive environment. Whilst there is no cure for autism access to appropriate educational facilities can significantly affect the quality of life for these individuals.

References

Aarons, M. and Gittens, T. (1992) *The Handbook of Autism: A Guide for Parents and Professionals*. London: Routledge.

Aitken, K. J. (1991) 'Examining the evidence for a common structural basis to autism', *Developmental Medicine and Child Neurology*, **33**, 1015–20.

American Psychiatric Association (1987) *Diagnostic and Statistical Manual of Mental Disorders* (3rd edn.). Washington, DC: American Psychiatric Association.

American Psychiatric Association (1994) *Diagnostic and Statistical Manual of Mental Disorders* (4th edn. DSM-IV). Washington, DC: American Psychiatric Association.

Bailey, A. J. (1993) 'The biology of autism', *Psychological Medicine*, **23**, 7–11.

Bailey, A. J., Bolton, P., Butler, L. *et al.* (1993) 'Prevalence of the fragile X anomaly amongst autistic twins and singletons', *Journal of Child Psychology and Psychiatry*, **34**, 673–88.

Bailey, A., Phillips, W. and Rutter, M. (1996) 'Autism: towards an integration of clinical, genetic, neuropsychological and neurobiological perspectives', *Journal of Child Psychology and Psychiatry*, **37(1)**, 89–126.

Baron-Cohen, S. (1989) 'The autistic child's theory of mind: a case of specific developmental delay', *Journal of Child Psychology and Psychiatry*, **30**, 285–98.

Baron-Cohen, S. (1990) 'Autism: a specific cognitive disorder of "mind-blindness"', *International Review of Psychiatry*, **2**, 81–90.

Baron-Cohen, S., Leslie, A. and Frith, U. (1985) 'Does the autistic child have a theory of mind?' *Cognition*, **21**, 37–46.

Bartak, L., Bartolucci, G. and Pierce, S. J. (1977) 'A preliminary comparison of phonological development in autistic, normal and mentally retarded subjects', *British Journal of Disorders of Communication*, **12**, 137–47.

Bolton, P. and Rutter, M. (1990) 'Genetic influences in autism', *International Review of Psychiatry*, **2**, 65–78.

Campbell, M., Perry, R., Small, A. and Green, W. (1987) 'Overview of drug treatment in autism'. In Schopler, E. and Mesibov, G. B. (eds) *Neurobiological Issues in Autism*. New York: Plenum Press, pp. 341–52.

Carr, E. G. (1985) 'Behavioural approaches to language and communication'. In Schopler, E. and Mesibov, G. B. (eds) *Communication Problems in Autism*. New York: Plenum Press, pp. 38–54.

Cohen, I. L., Vietze, P. M., Sudhalter, V, Jenkins, E. C. and Brown, W. T. (1989) 'Parent–child diadic gaze patterns in fragile X males and non-fragile X males with autistic disorder', *Journal of Child Psychology and Psychiatry*, **30**, 845–56.

Cook, E. H. (1990) 'Autism: review of neurochemical investigation', *Synapse*, **6**, 292–308.

Courchesne, E. (1995) 'New evidence of cerebellar and brainstem hypoplasia in autistic infants, children and adolescents: The MRI imaging study by Hashimoto and colleagues', *Journal of Autism and Developmental Disorders*, **25**, 19–22.

Cox, A., Rutter, M., Newman, S. and Bartak, L. (1975) 'A comparative study of infantile autism and specific developmental receptive language disorder: II. Parental charcteristics', *British Journal of Psychiatry*, **126**, 146–59.

Denkla, M. B. (1986) 'New diagnostic criteria for autism and related behavioural disorders – guidelines for research protocol', *Journal of the American Academy of Child Psychiatry*, **25**, 221–24.

Donaldson, M. L. (1995) *Children with Language Impairments: An Introduction*. London: Jessica Kingsley.

Dykens, E., Volkmar, F. and Glick, M. (1991) 'Thought disorder in high functioning autistic adults', *Journal of Autism and Developmental Disorders*, **21**, 291–302.

Elliot, G. and Ciaranello, R. (1987) 'Neurochemical hypotheses of childhood psychoses'. In Schopler, E. and Mesibov, G. B. (eds) *Neurobiological Issus in Autism*. New York: Plenum Press, pp. 245–62.

Fay, W. H. (1969) 'On the basis of autistic echolalia', *Journal of Communication Disorders*, **2**, 38–47.

Fein, D., Pennington, B., Markowitz, P., Braverman, M. and Waterhouse, L. (1986) 'Towards a neuropsychological model of autism: Are the social deficits primary?'

Journal of the American Academy of Child Psychiatry, **25**, 198–217.

Ferster, C. B. (1961) 'Positive reinforcement and behavioural deficits of autistic children', *Child Development*, **32**, 437–56.

Folstein, S. and Rutter, M. (1977) 'Infantile autism: A genetic study of 21 twin pairs', *Journal of Child Psychology and Psychiatry*, **18**, 297–321.

Folstein, S. and Rutter, M. (1988) 'Autism: familial aggregation and genetic implications', *Journal of Autism and Developmental Disorders*, **18**, 3–30.

Freeman, B. J. and Ritvo, E. R. (1984) 'The syndrome of autism: Establishing the diagnosis and principles of management', *Pediatric Annals*, **13**, 284–305.

Frith, U. (1989) *Autism: Explaining the Enigma*. New York: Blackwell.

Gadow, K. D. (1992) 'Pediatric psychopharmacotherapy: A review of recent research', *Journal of Child Psychology and Psychiatry*, **33**, 153–97.

Gillberg, C. L. (1988) 'The neurobiology of infantile autism', *Journal of Child Psychology and Psychiatry*, **29**, 257–66.

Gillberg, C. L. (1992) 'The Emanuel Miller memorial lecture 1991: Autism and autistic-like conditions: sub-classes among disorders of empathy', *Journal of Child Psychology and Psychiatry*, **33**, 813–42.

Gillberg, C. L. and Wahlstrom, J. (1985) 'Chromosome abnormalities in infantile autism and other childhood psychoses: a population study of 66 cases', *Developmental Medicine and Child Neurology*, **27**, 293–304.

Hagberg, B., Aicardi, J., Dias, K. and Ramos, O. (1983) 'A progressive syndrome of autism, dementia, ataxia and loss of purposeful hand use in girls: Rett's syndrome: report of 35 cases', *Annals of Neurology*, **14**, 471–79.

Happe, F. (1994) 'Annotation: current psychological theories of autism: the "theory of mind" account and rival theories', *Journal of Child Psychology and Psychiatry*, **35 (2)**, 215–29.

Harris, S. L. (1984) 'Intervention planning for the family of the autistic child: a multi-level assessment of the family system', *Journal of Marital and Family Therapy*, **10**, 157–66.

Harris, S. L., Handleman, J. S., Kristoff, B., Bass, L. and Gordon, R. (1990) 'Changes in language development among autistic and peer children in segregated and integrated pre-school settings', *Journal of Autism and Developmental Disorders*, **20**, 23–31.

Hermelin, B. and O'Connor, N. (1970) *Psychological Experiments with Autistic Children*. New York: Pergamon Press.

Howlin, P. and Rutter, M. (1987) *Treatment of Autistic Children*. Chichester: John Wiley.

Humphreys, A. and Ramm, S. (1987) 'Autism: the isolating syndrome', *Special Children*, October 14, 16–19.

Kanner, L. (1943) 'Autistic disturbances of affective contact', *Nervous Child*, **2**, 217–50.

Kanner, L. (1949) 'Problems of nosology and psychodynamics of early infantile autism', *American Journal of Orthopsychiatry*, **19**, 416–26.

Koegel, R. L. and Covert, A. (1972) 'The relationship of self-stimulation to learning in autistic children', *Journal of Applied Behaviour Analysis*, **5**, 381–87.

Koegel, R. L., Firestone, P. B., Kramme, K. W. and Dunlap, G. (1974) 'Increasing spontaneous play by suppressing self-stimulation in autistic children', *Journal of Applied Behaviour Analysis*, **7**, 521–28.

Koegel, R. L., Russo, D. C. and Rincover, A. (1977) 'Assessing and training teachers in the generalised use of behaviour modification with autistic children', *Journal of Applied Behaviour Analysis*, **10**, 197–205.

Koegel, R. L., Schreibman, L., Britten, K. R., Burke, J. C. and O'Neill, R. E. (1982) 'A comparison of parent training to direct clinic treatment'. In Koegel, R. L., Rincover, A. and Egel, A. L. (eds) *Educating and Understanding Autistic Children*, San Diego, CA: College Hill Press, pp. 260–79.

Koegel, R. L., Schreibman, L., O'Neill, R. E. and Burke, J. C. (1983) 'The personality and family interaction characteristics of parents of autistic children', *Journal of Consulting and Clinical Psychology*, **51**, 683–92.

Le Couteur, A., Rutter, M., Lord, C., Rios, P., Robertson, S., Holdgafer, M. and McLennan, J. D. (1989) 'Autism Diagnostic Interview: A semi-structured interview for parents and caregivers of autistic persons', *Journal of Autism and Developmental Disorders*, **19**, 363–87.

Leslie, A. M. and Frith, U. (1988) 'Autistic children's understanding of seeing, knowing and believing', *British Journal of Developmental Psychology*, **6**, 315–24.

Lord, C. (1984) 'The development of peer relations in children with autism'. In Morrison, F. J., Lord, C. and Keating, D. P. (eds) *Applied Developmental Psychology*, Vol. 1. New York: Academic Press, pp. 165–229.

Lord, C. (1993) 'Complexity of social behaviour in autism'. In Baron-Cohen, S., Tager-Flusberg, H. and Cohen, D. (eds) *Understanding Other Minds: Perspectives from Autism*. Oxford: Oxford University Press, pp. 292–316.

Lord, C. and Rutter, M. (1994) 'Autism and pervasive developmental disorders'. In Rutter, M. and Hersov, L. (eds) *Child and Adolescent Psychiatry: Modern Approaches*. Oxford: Blackwell Scientific, pp. 569–93.

Lord, C. and Schopler, E. (1989) 'The role of age at assessment, developmental level, and test in the stability of intelligence scores in young autistic children', *Journal of Autism and Developmental Disorders*, **19**, 483–99.

Lotter, V. (1966) 'Epidemiology of autistic conditions in young children. I. Prevalence', *Social Psychiatry*, **1**, 124–37.

Lotter, V. (1978) 'Follow-up studies'. In Rutter, M. and Schopler, E. (eds) *Autism: A Reappraisal of Concepts and Treatment*. New York: Plenum Press, pp. 475–95.

Lovaas, O. I. (1987) 'Behavioural treatment and normal educational and intellectual functioning in young autistic children', *Journal of Consulting and Clinical Psychology*, **55**, 3–9.

Lovaas, O. I., Litrownik, A. and Mann, R. (1971) 'Response latencies to auditory stimuli in autistic children engaged in self-stimulatory behaviour', *Behaviour Research and Therapy*, **9**, 39–49.

Lovaas, O. I., Koegel, R., Simmons, J. Q. and Long, J. S. (1973) Some generalisation and follow up measures on autistic children in behaviour therapy', *Journal of Applied Behaviour Analysis*, **6**, 131–66.

McEachin, S. J., Smith, T. and Lovaas, I. O. (1993) 'Long-term outcome for children who receive early intensive behavioural treatment', *American Journal of Mental Retardation*, **97** (4), 359–91.

Mesibov, G. B. (1984) 'Social skills training with verbal autistic adolescents and adults: a program model', *Journal of Autism and Developmental Disorders*, **14**, 395–404.

National Institue of Mental Health, Research Task Force (1975) *Research in the Service of Mental Health*. Rockville, Maryland.

Nelson, K. (1991) 'Prenatal and perinatal factors in the etiology of autism', *Pediatrics*, **87**, 761–66.

Olsson, B. and Rett, A. (1987) 'Autism and Rett syndrome: behavioural investigations and differential diagnosis', *Developmental Medicine and Child Neurology*, **29**, 429–41.

Olsson, B. and Rett, A. (1990) 'A review of the Rett syndrome with a theory of autism', *Brain and Development*, **12**, 11–15.

Ornitz, E. M. and Ritvo, E. R. (1976) 'The syndrome of autism: A critical review', *American Journal of Psychiatry*, **133**, 609–21.

Piven, J., Nehme, E., Simon, J., Barta, P., Pearlson, G. and Folstein, S. E. (1992) 'Magnetic resonance imaging in autism: measurement of the cerebellum, pons and fourth ventricle', *Biological Psychiatry*, **31**, 491–504.

Prior, M. R., Tress, B., Hoffman, W. L. and Boldt, D. (1984) 'Computed tomography study of children with classic autism', *Archives of Neurology*, **431**, 482–84.

Reiss, A. L., Feinstein, C. and Rosenblum, K. N. (1986) 'Autism and genetic disorders', *Schizophrenia Bulletin*, **12**, 724–28.

Ricks, D. M. and Wing, L. (1975) 'Language, communication and the use of symbols in normal and autistic children', *Journal of Autism and Childhood Schizophrenia*, **5**, 191–222.

Riddle, M. A., King, R. A., Hardin, M. T., Scahill, L., Ort, S.I., Chappell, P., Ramusson, A. and Leckman, J. (1991) 'Behavioural side-effects of fluoxetine in children and adolescents', *Journal of Child and Adolescent Psychopharmacology*, **1**, 193–98.

Rimland, B. (1964) *Infantile Autism*. New York: Appleton-Century-Crofts.

Rincover, A. (1978) 'Variables affecting stimulus-fading and discriminative responding in psychotic children', *Journal of Abnormal Psychology*, **87**, 541–53.

Ritvo, E. R. and Freeman, B. J. (1978) 'National Society for Autistic Children definition of the syndrome of autism', *Journal of Autism and Childhood Schizophrenia*, **8**, 162–67.

Ritvo, E. R., Freeman, B. J., Mason-Brothers, A., Mo, A. and Ritvo, A. M. (1985) 'Concordance for the syndrome of autism in 40 pairs of afflicted twins', *American Journal of Psychiatry*, **142**, 74–77.

Rumsey, J. M., Rapoport, M. D. and Sceery W. R. (1985) 'Autistic children as adults: psychiatric, social and behavioural outcomes', *Journal of the American Academy of Child Psychiatry*, **24**, 465–73.

Rutter, M. (1968) 'Concepts of autism: A review of research', *Journal of Child Psychology and Psychiatry*, **9**, 1–25.

Rutter, M. (1970) 'Autistic children: infancy to adulthood', *Seminars in Psychiatry*, **2**, 435–50.

Rutter, M. (1978) 'Diagnosis and definition'. In Rutter, M. and Schopler, E. (eds) *Autism: A Reappraisal of Concepts and Treatment.*. New York: Plenum Press, pp. 85–104.

Rutter, M. (1983) 'Cognitive deficits in the pathogenesis of autism', *Journal of Child Psychology and Psychiatry*, **26**, 193–214.

Rutter, M. (1985) 'Infantile autism and other pervasive developmental disorders'. In Rutter, M. and Hersov, L. (eds) *Child and Adolescent Psychiatry: Modern Approaches*. Oxford: Blackwell Scientific, pp. 545–66.

Rutter, M. (1991) 'Autism as a genetic disorder'. In McGuffin, P. and Murray, R. (eds) *The New Genetics of Mental Illness*. Oxford: Heinemann Medical, pp. 225–44.

Rutter, M. and Bartak, L. (1973) 'Special educational treatment of autistic children:

A comparative study. II. Follow-up findings and implications for services', *Journal of Child Psychology and Psychiatry*, **14**, 241–70.

Rutter, M. and Lockyer, L. (1967) 'A five to fifteen year follow-up study of infantile psychosis. I. Description of sample', *British Journal of Psychiatry*, **113**, 1169–82.

Rutter, M. and Schopler, E. (1992) 'Classification of pervasive developmental disorders: some concepts and practical considerations', *Journal of Autism and Developmental Disorders*, **22**, 459–82.

Rutter, M., Mawhood, L. and Howlin, P. (1992) 'Language delay and social development'. In Fletcher, P. and Hale, D. (eds) *Specific Speech and Language Disorders in Children*. London, Whurr Publishers, 63–78.

Rutter, M., Bailey, A., Bolton, P. and Le Couteur, A. (1993) 'Autism: syndrome definition and possible genetic mechanisms'. In Plomin, R. and MaClearn, G. E. (eds) *Nature, Nurture and Psychology*. Washington, DC: APA Books, pp. 269–84.

Schopler, E. and Reichler, R. J. (1971) 'Developmental therapy by parents with their autisitc child'. In Rutter, M. (ed.) *Infantile Autism: Concepts, Characteristics and Treatment*. London: Churchill-Livingstone, pp. 206–27.

Schore, A. N. (1994) *Affect Regulation and the Origin of Self: The Neurobiology of Emotional Development*. Hillsdale, NJ: Erlbaum.

Schreibman, L. (1988) *Autism*. California: Sage Publications.

Schreibman, L. and Charlop, M. H. (1987) 'Autism'. In Van Hasselt, V. B. and Hersen M. (eds) *Psychological Evaluation of the Developmentally and Physically Disabled*. New York: Plenum.

Schreibman, L. and Koegel, R. L. (1981) 'A guideline for planning behaviour modification programs for autistic children'. In Turner, S. M., Calhoun, K. S. and Adams, H. E. (eds) *Handbook of Clinical Behaviour Therapy*. New York, John Wiley and Sons.

Schreibman, L. and Mills, J. I. (1983) 'Infantile autism'. In Ollendick, T. J. and Hersen, M. (eds) *Handbook of Child Psychopathology*. New York: Plenum.

Siegel, B., Vukicevic, J., Elliot, G and Kramer, H. (1989) 'The use of signal detection theory to assess DSM-III-R criteria for autistic disorder', *American Academy of Child and Adolescent Psychiatry*, **28**, 542–48.

Sloman, L. (1991) 'Use of medication in pervasive developmental disorders', *Psychiatric Clinics of North America*, **14**, 165–82.

Smalley S. (1991) 'Genetic influences in autism', *Psychiatric Clinics of North America*, **14**, 125–39.

Smalley, S., Asarnow, R. and Spence, M. (1988) 'Autism and genetics: a decade of research', *Archives of General Psychiatry*, **45**, 958–61.

Steffenburg, S. (1991) 'Neuropsychiatric assessment of children with autism.: A population-based study', *Developmental Medicine and Child Neurology*, **33**, 495–511.

Steffenburg, S., Gillberg, C., Helgren, L., Anderson, L., Gillberg, L., Jakobsson, G. and Bohman, M. (1989) 'A twin study of autism in Denmark, Finland, Iceland, Norway and Sweden', *Journal of Child Psychology and Psychiatry*, **30**, 405–16.

Strain, P. S. (1983) *The Utilisation of Classroom Peers as Behaviour Change Agents*. New York: Plenum Press.

Tager-Flusberg, H. and Anderson, M. (1991) 'The development of contingent discourse ability in autistic children', *Journal of Child Psychology and Psychiatry*, **32**, 1123–34.

Tilton, J. R. and Ottinger, D. R. (1964) 'Comparison of the toy play behaviour of autistic, retarded and normal children', *Psychological Reports*, **15**, 967–75.

Trevarthen, C. and Aitken, K. (1994) 'Brain development, infant communication, and empathy disorders: Intrinsic factors in child mental health', *Development and Psychopathology*, **6**, 599–635.

Trevarthen, C., Aitken, K., Papoudi, D. and Robarts, J. (1996) *Children with Autism: Diagnosis and Interventions to Meet their Needs*. London: Jessica Kingsley Publications.

Tsai, L. (1987) 'Pre-, Peri-, and Neo-natal factors in autism'. In Schopler, E. and Mesibov, G. B. (eds) *Neurobiological Issues in Autism*. New York: Plenum Press, pp. 179–89.

Venter, A., Lord, C. and Schopler, E. (1992) 'A follow up study of high functioning autistic children', *Journal of Child Psychology and Psychiatry*, **33**, 489–507.

Volkmar, F. (1987) 'Social development'. In Cohen D. and Donnellan, A. (eds) *Handbook of Autism and Pervasive Developmental Disorders*. New York: John Wiley, pp. 41–61.

Ward, A. J. (1970) 'Early infantile autism: diagnosis, etiology and treatment', *Psychological Bulletin*, **73**, 350–62.

Waterhouse, L., Morris, R., Allen, D., *et al.* (1996) 'Diagnosis and classification in autism', *Journal of Autism and Developmental Disorders*, **26 (1)**, 59–86.

Wilcox, B. and Thompson, A. (eds) (1980) *Critical Issues in Educating Autistic Children and Youth*. US Department of Education, Office of Special Education, November.

Williams, D. (1996) *Autism: An Inside-Out Approach*. London: Jessica Kingsley.

Williams, T. (1989) 'A social skills group for autistic children', *Journal of Autism and Developmental Disorders*, **19**, 143–56.

Wing, L. (1976) 'Diagnosis, clinical description, and prognosis'. In Wing, L. (ed.) *Early Childhood Autism: Clinical, Educational and Social Aspects* (2nd edn). Oxford: Pergamon Press, pp. 15–48

Wing, L. and Gould, J. (1979) 'Severe impairments of social interaction and associated abnormalities in children: epidemiology and classification', *Journal of Autism and Developmental Disorders*, **9**, 11–29.

Wolff, P., Gardner, J., Paccia, J. and Lappen, J. (1989) 'The greeting behaviour of fragile X males', *American Journal of Mental Retardation*, **93**, 406–11.

World Health Organisation (1992) *The ICD-10 Classification of Mental and Behavioural Disorders: Clinical Descriptions and Diagnostic Guidelines*. Geneva: World Health Organisation.

3 Dyslexia – Can it be Distinguished from Other Forms of Reading Difficulty?

> Learning disabilities are a significant problem because they affect about five per cent of children. Yet, despite decades of discussion and research, we still don't know enough about how to deal with the problem and there is ignorance and controversy at every level, including both theory and practice. We don't yet know what works best, nor do we know what works for whom.
>
> (Beale, 1995: 275)

Sadly, the picture of confusions painted by the above quotation is perhaps the only certain element in the dyslexia field. That is, dyslexia is a subject about which much is written but little is agreed. The most cursory glance at the literature reveals disagreements, inconsistencies and discrepancies related to the incidence, aetiology, definition, identification and remediation of the problem. This chapter will first present the historical background to the debate about dyslexia, with reference to current research. It will then look at definitions and consider the problems of identifying who is, and who is not, dyslexic. The chapter will provide an overview of the major remediation techniques used, and the implications of the research on remediation for educational practice will be considered.

Historical perspective

The word 'dyslexia' has its origins in both Latin and Greek. The Latin *dys* means 'difficult' and *legere* means 'to read'. The Greek *lexis* or the Latin *legein* mean 'speech' or 'to speak'. Dyslexia, therefore, literally means difficulty with reading and speaking. Initially, dyslexia came under the broad umbrella of the medical disorders known as aphasias which referred to difficulties with language in its many forms. Although the word was used to describe a loss of speech, aphasia grew to encompass not only difficulties with spoken and receptive language but also problems with learning to read and write (Richardson, 1992).

From the early nineteenth century, the medical profession has been describing various types of aphasias which were the results of injuries to the brain. Neurologists believed that each type of aphasia could be related to specific locations in the brain. In 1810, this idea that certain functions related to localised areas of the brain was put forward by Franz Gall (Miles and Miles, 1990) and although his work fell into disrepute due to his study of the mind related to the bumps on a person's head, this localisation theory continued to find support. An autopsy, carried out on a patient who had lost the power of speech, revealed 'a profound but accurately circumscribed lesion of the posterior third of the second and third frontal convolutions' (Head, 1926: 25). This area of the brain became known as 'Broca's area' after the French surgeon, Pierre Paul Broca, who first described it. However, the notion that something as complex as speech could be located in one spot was, even then, considered simplistic.

Loss of the ability to read, despite the retention of adequate sight, speech and intellect, was identified by a German physician, Kussmaul, in 1878. He referred to this condition as 'word blindness' which remains a synonym for dyslexia. Later, in 1887, the word dyslexia was probably first used by the German ophthalmologist, Berlin, to describe patients who were having difficulties reading because of cerebral disease. Thus the word dyslexia was first used to refer to a specific acquired aphasia (Richardson, 1992).

The first references in the medical literature about congenital word blindness (developmental dyslexia) are to be found in the work of Hinshelwood and Kerr in 1895 and Morgan in 1896 (Miles and Miles, 1990; Pumfrey and Reason, 1991). Morgan published a case description of a boy named 'Percy F.' who, despite being one of the brightest pupils in his class, had extreme difficulties in reading, writing and spelling. Kerr published similar descriptions of children who were experiencing problems with reading and writing but who had no other apparent cognitive difficulties. This has remained the central focus of the dyslexia debate; the unaccountable discrepancy between a child's intellectual ability and his or her severe difficulties in learning to read, write and spell.

Confusions arise whenever the terms dyslexia, word blindness, specific developmental dyslexia, specific learning difficulty or learning disability (to list but a few labels) are mentioned. Hinshelwood was concerned that the term 'word blindness' was being used to describe anyone who was unable to learn to read and write and that it was unjust to group together children whose difficulties were specific to reading and writing only, with pupils whose difficulties were due to a general lack of ability. Because he believed that children with word blindness had defective development of the visual memory centre, Hinshelwood advocated a multisensory method of teaching which would appeal to as many cerebral centres as possible (Miles and Miles, 1990). This has remained the most widely endorsed method of remediation for dyslexia.

This notion, that dyslexia was the result of deficits in visual processing, has, however, not been substantiated. Although there is data suggesting that dyslexics may have deficits in the transient visual pathway, replication in rigorous investigations have failed to confirm this. 'Therefore, it is unclear at this point whether or not visual deficits are an important contributing factor to dyslexia' (Catts, 1996: 15).

Much of what Hinshelwood and his contemporaries recognised about dyslexic pupils was given prominence by an American psychiatrist, Samuel Orton, in the 1920s. Like Hinshelwood, he viewed developmental dyslexia as a condition which often ran in families and was found more often in boys than girls. Orton also noted that a conflicting laterality of hand and eye seemed to occur more often in dyslexics. He also recognised the difficulties some dyslexic pupils encounter with letter reversals, the sequencing of letters within words, and correct sequencing of syllables within spoken words. He, too, advocated a multisensory approach to the remediation of these problems. Orton hypothesised that these confusions arose from conflicting images of visual symbols as interpreted by the right and left hemispheres of the brain. This idea, that distinguishing these mirrored images could be a problem for some children whose brain development was slower than normal, has since been challenged:

Children with reading problems are no more prone to mirror image reversals when they read letters, words and sentences than other children are, and the same goes for writing. Direct comparisons even between poor and normal readers of the same age (and mental age) show no difference in the proportion of 'reversal' errors that the two groups of children make.

(Bryant and Bradley, 1985: 24)

Despite the movement away from a visually based deficit in later literature, Orton continues to be respected for the systematic teaching programme which he and Anna Gillingham pioneered and for his sympathetic consideration of the distress caused by developmental dyslexia to so many children (Miles and Miles, 1990).

Neuroanatomical analysis has shown that there are differences to be found in the brains of dyslexic people. Dyslexics have long been considered to have better conceptual reasoning abilities or 'right brain' strengths than their abilities to read, write and spell which have been related to their 'left brain' weaknesses. Technological advances have made it possible to study brain morphology. Post-mortem studies, computed tomography and magnetic resonance imaging techniques have shown that the brains of many dyslexics deviate from the normal asymmetry of the cerebral hemispheres. Although the study of the human brain is extending neuroanatomical and neurophysiological understanding of dyslexia, the picture is still far from complete. However, it would seem that differences often found in the brain morphology of dyslexic people are related to areas known to affect language development (Riccio and Hynd, 1996).

Research suggests that developmental dyslexia presents a separate pathophysiology from that of acquired dyslexia which often accompanies accidental brain damage (Benson and Geschwind, 1969; Gross-Glenn et al., 1991). Consistent patterns of brain anomalies in both adult and child dyslexics indicate that such patterns of brain development are long-standing rather than an indication of immature brain development (Riccio and Hynd, 1996). The more researchers discover about the functions of areas of the brain the more it becomes apparent that these areas are inextricably linked and that simplistic views of left and right hemispheric influences upon the reading and writing processes are inadequate. It may be that we should emphasise '. . . the interaction of the left and right hemispheres in fluent reading rather than a deficit in one hemisphere or the other.' (Hynd *et al.*, 1987)

As will be apparent from the above look at the historical background to dyslexia, the research crosses several fields of expertise including education-alists, psychologists, linguists and the medical profession.

Although our understanding of dyslexia is developing, there remains much that is not known conclusively and even more about which there is disagreement.

Concepts, classifications and definitions of dyslexia

One of the principal difficulties which arise when trying to define dyslexia is the wide range of terms used to describe the condition. As many as forty-two terms have been listed from the literature by Hinson and Kelly (1986) and 'thirty-two definitions were counted in a recent report' (Ogilvy, 1994: 55). When there is no one label used consistently by all researchers nor one single, universally accepted definition of the condition, it is near impossible to compare research studies which use different terminology and do not make clear what they mean by the terms they are using.

In the UK, the terms specific learning difficulty, developmental dyslexia and dyslexia are the ones most commonly used by different groups to describe children who have long-standing difficulties in reading, writing and spelling. In America, the same problems are referred to as 'learning disabilities'. The desire to distinguish children with the above labels from other poor readers has motivated research over many years and has produced widely differing results and points of view. Labels and descriptions come and go but still there is no one definition which is acceptable to all. Researchers struggle to prove unequivocally that a discrete category of children exists, that they have a distinct aetiology and that they can be identified by unique characteristics which set them apart from other poor readers. Argument rages on over terms such as dyslexia, which many consider are used to describe an unproven condition:

> . . . 'dyslexia' carries with it so many empirically unverified connotations and assumptions that many researchers and practitioners prefer to avoid the term.
>
> (Stanovich, 1994: 579)

The definition of specific developmental dyslexia suggested by the World Federation of Neurology in 1968 is closely related to many of the definitions offered by other institutions to the present day (Pumfrey and Reason, 1991; Hammill, 1990). Their definition was:

> A disorder manifested by difficulty in learning to read despite conventional instruction, adequate intelligence and socio-cultural opportunity. It is dependent upon fundamental cognitive disabilities which are frequently of constitutional origin.
>
> (Critchley, 1970: 11)

The above definition has been criticised for raising more questions than it solves. For example, what constitutes 'conventional instruction'? What is 'adequate intelligence'? Are we saying that dyslexia, considered to have hereditary factors, only affects those of average or high intelligence? Surely not. The Code of Practice (1994) makes it clear that any pupil, regardless of IQ, whose performance in reading, writing, spelling, or numeracy is markedly below what the teacher would expect compared with their oral skills, can be said to have a special educational need which must be addressed.

If dyslexia is a developmental condition it seems unacceptable to exclude from its ranks pupils with low socio-economic backgrounds or IQs below the average level. Rutter *et al.* (1970) found that children who present marked difficulties in learning to read, in contrast to their scores on intelligence tests, are more commonly found in large families living in deprived areas. The Code of Practice should make it possible to identify such children early in their school lives and give them the additional support they need.

In the above definition, the phrase, 'fundamental cognitive disabilities', although vague, does suggest the possibility of identifying pupils by a list of observable disorders. Although no one list is accepted by all interested parties, the difficulties experienced by pupils who have specific learning difficulties are usually considered to include:

- clumsiness;
- difficulties in sequencing tasks such as reciting the days of the week or months of the year;
- difficulties with perception of spacial relationships;
- disorders in language;
- bizarre spelling;
- disordered temporal orientation;
- confusion over left and right;
- directional confusion manifested by the reversal of letters, e.g. b/d, u/n, p/q and problems arising from cross laterality.

The suggestion that a child could be identified as having specific learning difficulties from such a list of possible weaknesses may be better than using a criterion of exclusion, such as in the definition above but it is still less than satisfactory, since there is no agreed number of weaknesses required to confirm a diagnosis of dyslexia. The Bangor Dyslexia Test (Miles, 1983) assesses pupils in relation to some of the above difficulties in order to identify dyslexia. This, and tests like it, continue to be used despite research which suggests that many of these deficits are present in all young or inexperienced readers. Many teachers continue to associate pupils' tendencies to confuse 'b' and 'd' with a dyslexic profile despite evidence to suggest that all poor readers exhibit such problems (Bryant and Bradley, 1985). Such tests can therefore only be used as tentative screening devices. For this reason, perhaps, Badian (1996) was unable to distinguish between dyslexic and 'garden-variety' poor readers aged 6–7 years although she did identify a distinctive, more discrepant group of older dyslexic pupils, aged 8–10 years for whom there was support for dyslexia as a phonological deficit. However, Bryant and Impey (1986) found that the reading patterns of some developmental dyslexics who were classified as phonological dyslexics and morphemic dyslexics were not distinguishable from those of 'normal' 10-year-old readers.

The Code of Practice (DfE, 1994: para. 3:61) also contains a list of deficits associated with dyslexia and the behavioural difficulties which can arise due to the frustrations experienced by pupils with specific learning difficulties. Schools are required to take note of clumsiness, significant difficulties of sequencing or visual perception, memory problems and significant delays in language functioning. The Code requires schools to keep meticulous records of pupils' progress, the specific difficulties mentioned above, behaviour problems as well as the 'extreme discrepancies between attainment in different core subjects' mentioned earlier. Such records, supported by standardised tests, should lead to the development of appropriate Individual Education Plans which should meet the needs of each pupil, whatever their IQ.

The literature reviews and studies which compare 'dyslexic' with 'non-dyslexic' pupils are numerous (for example: Frith, 1981; Miles and Haslum, 1986; Snowling, 1985; Tansley and Panckhurst, 1981). The weaknesses inherent in such studies have been listed by Presland (1991) and are, in brief:

1. That the various features used to define dyslexia are distributed fairly randomly between children with reading difficulties and quite commonly among children without such difficulties.
2. That children at an early stage of development, and dyslexics, present the same reading behaviours.
3. That studies of unstable ocular dominance and reading and spelling behaviours which showed differences in dyslexic and non-dyslexic groups have not been successfully replicated (Bruck, 1988; Newman *et al.*, 1985).
4. That dyslexics fall into more than one group, each presenting 6 different difficulties.
5. That children's reading strategies, and hence the kinds of errors they make, are determined to a considerable extent by the methods of instruction they have received (Barr, 1975).

In the face of such criticisms, it is easy so see why there exists such confusion in the minds of teachers and parents. A behaviourally based, highly structured approach to teaching reading used by Collette-Harris and Minke (1978) resulted in 'so much progress on perceptual tests used to identify the dyslexics that they no longer meet the criteria for being labelled in this way' (Presland, 1991: 217).

Perhaps if such studies, instead of being used to dismiss dyslexia, were successfully replicated, the methods they adopted could benefit many children and enhance the approaches at present available to support these pupils.

The Education Acts of 1981 and 1993 use the umbrella term, 'a child with learning difficulties', making no specific reference to dyslexia, but the 'Code of Practice on the Identification and Assessment of Special Educational Needs' (DfE, 1994) does give guidelines on a definition of children with 'specific learning difficulties (for example Dyslexia)':

> Some children may have significant difficulties in reading, writing, spelling or manipulating numbers, which are not typical of their general level of performance.
>
> (DfE, 1944: para. 3:60)

This reinforces the discrepancy definition of dyslexia which compares pupils' reading abilities with their expected potential in relation to their IQ score. Because specific learning difficulties are included in the Code of Practice as one type of special educational need, many psychologists have moved from a position of not wishing to distinguish between pupils with reading difficulties and those with dyslexia, to the present time, when more and more children are being diagnosed as dyslexic by the discrepancy model. The British Dyslexia Association and the Dyslexia Institute take every opportunity to keep the issue of dyslexia in the minds of the public. Therefore, parents of children who have reading, writing or spelling difficulties have high expectations of receiving additional support for their children by achieving the label 'dyslexic' for them. If the difficulties encountered by pupils labelled as dyslexic are merely an extreme form of problems on a continuum encountered by all poor readers then it seems less than fair to allocate the lion's share of additional resources to the few, rather than dealing with the wider issues of teaching children to read. Every child should have the best possible support and appropriate teaching methods to reach their full potential in the essential skills of reading, writing, spelling and numeracy. Children whose attainment in language skills does not match their observed potential in other areas deserve to have their educational needs met especially since to ignore these needs can lead to frustration, lack of self-esteem and ultimately to behavioural problems.

There are, however, weaknesses in the discrepancy definition since it assumes that a low IQ score automatically means a child will be a poor reader but there is evidence that this is not always the case (Siegel, 1992). There may be many reasons why a child has difficulties in learning to read.

Stanovich (1986) suggested that because children who find reading difficult spend less time reading they are 'less likely to gain the knowledge required by the verbal items of ability tests' (Frederickson and Reason, 1995). Also, an IQ score may vary over time for several reasons, sometimes depending upon the particular test applied and as a result of the sort of remedial teaching being given:

> Disabled children not exposed to an intensive remedial programme showed significant decreases in IQ scores over a period of 18 months whereas a similar group receiving intensive remediation showed significant improvements in IQ scores.
>
> (Frederickson and Reason, 1995: 198)

Siegel (1988) found that although, compared with normal readers, disabled readers were far poorer on word recognition, non-word reading and discrimination of real and non-words, this performance did not vary significantly in relation to IQ levels. The assumption that 'poor readers of high aptitude – as indicated by IQ test performance – were cognitively different from poor readers of low aptitude and that they had a different aetiology', would seem to be questionable; yet those of us who teach are aware of a group of pupils whose difficulties in learning to read baffle us and who, despite their obvious abilities in other areas orally, we know will become progressively less able to access the curriculum due to their lack of basic literacy skills:

> Without the development of adequate listening, speaking, reading, writing and spelling skills, the national curriculum cannot be delivered to pupils.
>
> (Pumfrey, 1991: 223)

The over-prescriptive nature of the National Curriculum makes it difficult to give these pupils the degree of repetition and over-learning they require whilst still allowing them full access to the rest of the curriculum. Pupils who are withdrawn from school to attend privately funded centres for specialist teaching cannot easily take their full part in the curriculum.

This does not seem to bring us any closer to a definition or clear classification of dyslexia. Perhaps the developmental approach to the classification of reading difficulties as suggested by Frith (1985) may be useful (see also Snowling, 1991). Considering the stages through which readers progress on the road to reading competence, Frith labels pupils at the level at which they begin to experience difficulties. Children who fail to progress from the initial stage of reading which is visually based (a look-and-say stage) to be able to decode words and use letter-sound connections, would be classified as phonological dyslexics. From this stage, reading becomes an automatic function and does not rely upon regular word patterns alone. Children who cannot progress to this stage would be called developmental dysgraphics, too dependent upon letter sounds and patterns. Frith describes those who progress through these stages to become competent readers but who cannot transfer these skills to their spelling ability as having a specific difficulty, 'group B' spellers. If this model of identification were adopted, it might make it easier to help children by teaching them strategies which can advance their skills. Perhaps identifying the difficulties the child is experiencing and organising appropriate remediation might eliminate the need for a dyslexia label. However, this would clearly require a degree of retraining for many class teachers in the early identification of reading difficulties and specific remedial techniques which may support such pupils.

Remediation

If one particular method of remediation proved to be essential and successful for those pupils diagnosed as dyslexic as opposed to the treatment required by other poor readers, Presland suggests that this 'would constitute evidence for the concept' (Presland, 1991: 218). The special educational intervention believed to be needed by dyslexic children involves 'withdrawing the child for individual, direct, structured teaching' (Riddell *et al.*, 1992). The structured approaches advocated are phonetic and multi-sensory, which use the senses on vision, touch, hearing and movement, and incorporate the fundamental strategies of over-learning and repetition (Ogilvy, 1994). Specific procedures of a most formal, step-by-step nature are typically used in withdrawal settings and specialist centres, for example the Alpha to Omega Programme (Hornsby and Shear, 1976). Studies related to the implementation and effectiveness of such programmes for dyslexic pupils produce variable results and long-term benefits remain in doubt. Specific approaches to spelling, e.g. Simultaneous Oral Spelling (Gillingham and Stillman, 1956), have proved to be effective but are equally effective for poor spellers, whether they are dyslexic or not (Bradley, 1981). As yet, there is little evidence that specific programmes designed for dyslexics are any less effective for 'garden-variety' poor readers or that these programmes are substantially different from other remedial programmes in common use:

> Their common characteristics – phonic, 'structured, sequential, cumulative and thorough' – do not even distinguish them clearly from LEA specialist remedial teaching.
>
> (Presland, 1991: 218)

Since evidence suggests that any reader who is experiencing difficulties would benefit from the above approaches it is difficult to identify dyslexia through a specific and essentially unique remediation procedure (Siegel, 1989; Stanovich, 1991; Tansley and Panckhurst, 1981).

However, recent research is moving from a purely IQ discrepancy based identification towards a recognition of the importance of phonological coding in the development of reading skill. Poor readers with and without IQ discrepancy have difficulty reading pseudo words which has been linked to their inability to break words into sound patterns:

This pseudo word deficit in a reading-level match is one of the most distinctive indicators of the reading disabled phenotype.

(Stanovich, 1994: 586)

Because of the phonological difficulties found to underlie the reading difficulties of many children some researchers have described dyslexia as a developmental language disorder. From this viewpoint, the main deficit in dyslexia:

appears to be a problem in phonemic segmentation or phoneme awareness skills which causes the primary symptom in dyslexia, a deficit in the phonological coding of written language.

(Pennington, 1989: 90)

A phonographic method of teaching reading and spelling, THRASS, (Teaching Handwriting Reading and Spelling Skills) has been incorportated into the programmes of some private dyslexia clinics recently and has also had a remarkable impact upon reading and comprehension skills in the schools that have used the programme (Davies and Ritchie, 1996). This multisensory approach can be used in a highly structured manner for dyslexic pupils but can be equally beneficial for all pupils in a more flexible fashion. It is based upon the 44 sounds of spoken English as opposed to the conventional 26 letters of the alphabet.

There needs to be far more carefully controlled research into the effectiveness of the different remedial approaches to discover which elements best support individual pupils' weaknesses. Programmes, such as Reading Recovery (Clay, 1985) which endeavour to identify and support each child's strengths and weaknesses may well embody ideas which could help some dyslexic pupils. One of the features advocated by Connor (1994: 118) in his review of intervention strategies was 'maximal exposure to meaningful and enjoyable reading (real reading)'. The same author reminds us of the vital part played by parents in children's learning and projects related to the effectiveness of parental involvement in children's reading are numerous. Projects employing parents in the use of Paired Reading or Pause, Prompt and Praise techniques have brought positive results and cannot be dismissed from any consideration of the strategies that may be helpful to children who are experiencing difficulties in learning to read. Since the problems of poor readers and dyslexics alike are heterogeneous in nature:

... it is inappropriate to seek a unitary remedial approach or to suggest that a diagnosis of dyslexia would presuppose a teaching approach that is different in kind from approaches commonly used among children with reading difficulties.

(Connor, 1994: 119)

We need to tailor programmes and strategies to meet each pupil's needs.

Catts (1996: 14) writes that it is unlikely that humans are 'biologically predisposed to read and write and that in some individuals this predisposition is disrupted'. Since written language entered the evolutionary arena relatively late in mankind's development it is more likely that:

> reading is dependent on biological mechanisms that serve other primary functions for humans . . . it would follow that the disorder that we have come to call dyslexia is a result of disruptions in these mechanisms.
>
> (Catts, 1996: 15)

There is a growing body of research which suggests that children who have difficulty appreciating sounds within words often have problems learning to read. Projects aimed at developing these phonological awareness skills in young children have been claimed to deter reading failure (Lundberg, Frost and Peterson, 1988). Research by Cornwall (1992) found that phonological awareness was a significant predictor of success in reading, writing and spelling. This study attempted to control for age, socio-economic status, behaviour problems and intelligence.

If children's success in reading is heavily influenced by their ability to hear individual sounds within words and to segment words into sound bites then perhaps we need to be looking more closely at the language development of young children:

> Children who could have been identified at early ages continue to fail. Their spoken language problems evolve into written language problems. Some of these children are not evaluated until they reach middle or high school.
>
> (Greene, 1996: 51)

We come back to the original question. Can dyslexia be distinguished from other forms of reading difficulty? It would seem from research that regardless of IQ level, children who have difficulty in phonological processing are likely to experience difficulties in learning to read, write and spell. It would seem that the majority of poor readers, whether they be defined as dyslexic or as mere 'garden-variety' poor readers have, as their chief deficit, a weakness in their ability to process words phonologically. Does this mean that we can no longer differentiate between poor readers and dyslexics? Are there areas in which these two groups differ? If phonological processing were the only requirement for good reading skill then the term dyslexia would need to be applied to the majority of poor readers irrespective of their IQ level. Reading, however, requires many more skills than those needed to 'bark at print', as any primary teacher knows only too well. Higher order reading skills include forward and backward cueing, a recognition of the value and relevance of punctuation, an understanding of semantic and syntactic rules and the ability to interpret and predict. So, it may be that within the group of poor readers who all share a deficit in phonological processing, there may be an identifiable group of pupils who differ from other poor readers in that they possess higher order language skills:

> Dyslexics, who by most definitions have normal IQs, typically demonstrate normal higher-level language abilities.
>
> (Catts, 1996: 19)

The above researcher suggests that an expanded language-based view of reading difficulties which considers both phonological and higher-order language skills might make it easier to match remediation to pupil needs. Since there is some evidence to suggest that it is possible to identify children who are likely to have difficulties learning to read and write before they enter school, early intervention could reduce the number of children who become distressed by reading failure if the issues of language development were targeted pre-school (Badian, 1994).

Implications

It is difficult to demonstrate, from present research evidence, a clearly defined and unique group of pupils whose reading difficulties set them apart from other poor readers. The chief implication of such a situation is to suggest that far more emphasis is needed upon the identification of individual reading difficulties and studies to determine which remedial approaches work best for which pupils.

There is a desperate need for more and better teacher training and in-service training in the area of basic literacy and numeracy especially in relation to the needs of pupils who experience difficulties. Many class teachers feel inadequately prepared to identify and assess pupils who have serious problems in learning to read, write and spell.

In a world of ever-reducing funding for special educational support it is vital that as many children as possible are identified early and given the sort of support that will avoid their becoming the subject of reading failure at a later date when expensive remediation will be required. Recent legislation and the publicity machines of groups such as the British Dyslexia Association have raised parents' expectations in relation to the provision for pupils with learning difficulties. However, this raised expectation has not been supported by additional financial resources. Many parents are demanding statements of special educational needs for their children whilst the funds for meeting such demands remain limited and finite. It is an unhappy situation which allows the more vocal and articulate parents to achieve resources which may be equally needed by other pupils. Although, as has been stated above, children from deprived backgrounds have a greater tendency to experience reading difficulties it is the middle-class parents who more often win additional support for their children (Riddell *et al.*, 1992). Ogilvy (1994) suggests that the controversy over specific learning difficulties has two chief outcomes. Firstly, that by focusing attention upon within-child deficits other important factors are overlooked: the child's family, the teaching, the curriculum and the school's policies and organisation, all of which affect the child's learning. Secondly:

> that the emphasis on remediation detracts from the broader issue of preventing reading failure in all children.
>
> (Ogilvy, 1994: 63)

Conclusions

Whether or not dyslexia exists as a discrete condition which can be separated from other poor readers would seem to be of less importance than the matter of how we can best support and alleviate the difficulties of all those who struggle with reading, writing, spelling and numeracy. There is clear evidence that early identification can reduce the risk of reading failure and that it is possible to identify those children who are likely to have difficulties. Perhaps we should not be continuing to put:

> emphasis upon demonstrating the existence of a dyslexic condition at the expense of seeking to link assessment with intervention . . . instead assessment should be directed towards finding the most effective way of helping any given child rather than towards providing for a purportedly special group of children who share a dyslexic label.
>
> (Connor, 1994: 131–132)

References

Badian, N. A. (1994) 'Preschool prediction: Orthographic and phonological skills, and reading', *Annals of Dyslexia*, **44**, 3–25.

Badian, N. A. (1996) 'Dyslexia: a validation of the concept at two age levels', *Journal of Learning Disabilities*, **29 (1)**, 102–12.

Barr, R. (1975) 'The effects of instruction on pupil reading strategies', *Reading Research Quarterly*, **10 (4)**, 555–82.

Beale, I. L. (1995) 'Learning disabilities: current status and future prospects', *Journal of Child and Family Studies*, **4 (3)**, 267–77.

Benson, D. F. and Geschwind, N. (1969) 'The alexias'. In Vinken, P. J. and Bruyn, G. W. (eds) *Handbook of Clinical Neurology*, Vol. 4. Amsterdam: North-Holland.

Bradley, L. (1981) 'The organisation of motor patterns for spelling: An effective remedial approach for backward readers', *Developmental Medicine and Child Neurology*, **23**, 83–91.

Bruck, M. (1988) 'The Word Recognition and Spelling of Dyslexic Children', *Reading Research Quarterly*, **23 (5)**, 51–69.

Bryant, P. and Bradley, L. (1985) *Children's Reading Problems*. Oxford: Blackwell.

Bryant, P. and Impey, L. (1986) 'The similarities between normal readers and developmental and acquired dyslexics', *Cognition*, **24**, 121–37.

Catts, H. W. (1996) 'Defining dyslexia as a developmental language disorder: An expanded view', *Topics in Language Disorders*, **16 (2)**, 14–29.

Clay, M. (1985) *The Early Detection of Reading Difficulties* (3rd edn). Auckland: Heinemann

Collette-Harris, M. and Minke, K. A. (1978) 'A behavioral experimental analysis of dyslexia', *Behavior Research and Therapy*, **16 (4)**, 291–95.

Connor, M. J. (1994) 'Dyslexia (SpLD): assessing assessment', *Educational Psychology in Practice*, **10 (3)**, 131–40.

Cornwall, A. (1992) 'The relationship of phonological awareness, rapid naming, and verbal memory to severe reading and spelling disability', *Journal of Learning*

Disabilities, **25**, 532–38.

Critchley, M. (1970) *The Dyslexic Child.* London: Heinemann.

Davies, A. and Ritchie, D. (1996) *THRASS: Teaching Handwriting, Reading and Spelling Skills Special Needs Pack.* London: Collins.

Department for Education (1994) *The Code of Practice on the Identification and Assessment of Special Edicational Needs.* London: HMSO.

Frederickson, N. and Reason, R. (1995) 'Discrepancy definitions of specific learning difficulties', *Educational Psychology in Practice*, **10** (4), 195–205.

Frith, U. (1981) 'Experimental approaches to dyslexia: An introduction', *Psycholgical Research*, **43**, 97–109.

Frith, U. (1985) 'Beneath the surface of developmental dyslexia'. In Patterson, K. E., Marshall, J. C. and Coltheart, M. (eds) *Surface Dyslexia.* London: Routledge and Kegan Paul.

Gillingham, A. and Stillman, B. W. (1956) *Remedial training for children with specific disability in reading, writing and penmanship.* Cambridge: Educators Publishing Service.

Greene, J. F. (1996) 'Psycholinguistic assessment: The clinical base for identification of dyslexia', *Topics in Language Disorders*, **16** (2), 45–72.

Gross-Glenn, K., Duara, R., Barker, W. W., *et al.* (1991) 'Positron emission tomographic studies during serial word-reading by normal and dyslexic adults', *Journal of Clinical and Experimental Neuropsychology*, **13**, 531–44.

Hammill, D. D. (1990) 'On defining learning disabilities: an emerging consensus', *Journal of Learning Disabilities*, **23** (2), 74–84.

Head, H. (1926) *Aphasia and Kindred Disorders of Speech:* London, Macmillan.

Hinson, M. and Kelly, A. (1986) 'Specific learning difficulties: One Local Educational Authority's approach in practice', *Support for Learning*, **2**, 19–28.

Hornsby, B. and Shear, F. (1976) *Alpha to Omega.* London: Heinemann.

Hynd, G. W., Hynd, C. R., Sullivan, H. G. and Kingsbury, T. B. (1987) 'Regional cerebral blood flow in developmental dyslexia: Activation during reading in a surface and deep dyslexic', *Journal of Learning Disabilities*, **20**, 294–300.

Lundberg, I., Frost, J. and Peterson, O. P. (1988) 'Effects of an extensive program for stimulating phonological awareness in preschool children', *Reading Research Quarterley*, **23** (3), 263–84.

Miles, E. (1983) *Bangor Dyslexia Test.* Cambridge: Learning Development Aids.

Miles, T. R. and Haslum, M. N. (1986) 'Dyslexia: Anomaly or normal variation', *Annals of Dyslexia*, **36**, 103–17.

Miles, T. R. and Miles, E. (1990) *Dyslexia: A Hundred Years On.* Buckingham: Oxford University Press.

Newman, S. P., Wadsworth, J. F., Archer, R. and Hockly, R. (1985) 'Ocular dominance, reading, and spelling ability in school children', *British Journal of Ophthalmology*, **69** (3), 228–32.

Ogilvy, C. M. (1994) 'What is the diagnostic significance of Specific Learning Difficulties?' *School Psychology International*, **15** (1), 55–68.

Pennington, B. F. (1989) 'Using genetics to understand dyslexia', *Annals of Dyslexia*, **39**, 81–93.

Presland, J. (1991) 'Explaining away dyslexia', *Educational Psychology in Practice*, **6** (4), 215–21.

Pumfrey, P. D. (1991) 'Identifying and alleviating Specific Learning Difficulties: issues and implications for LEAs, professionals and parents', *Educational*

Psychology in Practice, **6** (4), 222–28.

Pumfrey, P. D. and Reason, R. (1991) *Specific Learning Difficulties (Dyslexia): Challenges and Responses.* Windsor: NFER-Nelson.

Riccio, C. A. and Hynd, G. W. (1996) 'Neuroanatomical and neurophysiological aspects of dyslexia', *Topics in Language Disorders,* **16** (2), 1–13.

Richardson, S. O. (1992) 'Historical perspectives on dyslexia', *Journal of Learning Disabilities,* **25**, 40–47.

Riddell, S., Duffield, J., Brown, S. and Ogilvy, C. (1992) *Specific Learning Difficulties: Policy, Practice and Provision.* Unpublished Report to the Scottish Office Education Department, Department of Education, University of Stirling.

Rodgers, B. (1983) 'The identification and prevalence of specific reading retardation', *British Journal of Educational Psychology,* **53**, 369–73.

Rutter, M. and Yule, W. (1975) 'The concept of specific reading retardation', *Journal of Child Psychology and Psychiatry,* **16**, 181–97.

Rutter, M., Tizard, J. and Whitmore, K. (eds) (1970) *Education, Health and Behaviour.* London: Longmans.

Siegel, L. S. (1988) 'Evidence that IQ scores are irrelevant to the definition and analysis of reading disability', *Canadian Journal of Psychology,* **42**, 201–15.

Siegel, L. S. (1989) 'IQ is irrelevant to the definition of learning disabilities', *Journal of Learning Disabilities,* **22**, 469–78.

Siegel, L. S. (1992) 'An evaluation of the discrepancy definition of dyslexia', *Journal of Learning Disabilities,* **25**, 618–29.

Snowling, M. J. (1985) *Children's Written Language Difficulties.* Windsor: NFER-NELSON.

Snowling, M. J. (1991) 'Developmental reading disorders', *Journal of Child Psychology and Psychiatry,* **32** (1), 49–77.

Stanovich, K. (1986) 'Matthew effects in reading', *Reading Research Quarterly,* **21**, 360–407.

Stanovich, K. E. (1991) 'Discrepancy definitions of reading disability: has intelligence led us astray?', *Reading Research Quarterley,* **26** (1), 7–29.

Stanovich, K. (1994) 'Annotation: Does Dyslexia Exist?', *Journal of Child Psychology and Psychiatry,* **35** (4), 579–95.

Tansley, P. and Panckhurst, J. (1981) *Children with Specific Learning difficulties: A Critical Review.* Windsor: NFER-Nelson.

Yule, W. and Rutter, M. (1985) 'Reading and other learning difficulties'. In Rutter, M. and Hersov, L. (eds) *Child and Adolescent Psychiatry: Modern Approaches.* Oxford: Blackwell pp. 444–64.

4 Attention Deficit Hyperactivity Disorder – Is it a Distinct Disorder and a Useful Concept?

Introduction

Research into Attention Deficit Hyperactivity Disorder (ADHD) has expanded over the last 20 years and it has become one of the most studied and most well known of the childhood psychiatric disorders. Increasingly it is recognised as a serious, developmentally disabling and prevalent condition which affects individuals in childhood and often through into adult life. ADHD, however, is a complex disorder and, despite the attention it has received more recently, many controversial issues still surround it. The discussion here focuses on whether ADHD can be regarded as a distinct disorder and whether it is a useful concept for professionals faced with helping children who show the behavioural symptoms of hyperactivity, impulsivity and inattentiveness.

Brief history

Medical attention was first focused on hyperactivity at the beginning of the 1900s by Still and Tredgold, and until the 1960s it was accepted that the condition was due to brain damage, that the prognosis was poor and that the only effective treatment was placement in classrooms with minimal stimulation or within special residential centres. During the 1960s the focus changed from brain damage to deficient brain mechanisms as the most likely cause. Treatments included stimulant medication and psychotherapy. Research blossomed in the 1970s and by the end of this decade poor attention and impulse control were seen as equally important to, if not more important than, hyperactivity in explaining the difficulties of these children. Environmental causes of the disorder, such as diet and management of behaviour by parents, were also implicated. This led to alternative treatments, such as dietary intervention, behaviour modification programmes and parent training programmes. In the 1980s the increase in research on ADHD continued and attempts were made to develop more specific diagnostic criteria and to distinguish its diagnosis from that of other disorders. Increasing interest was placed on motivational factors and reinforcement mechanisms as a core difficulty. By the end of the 1980s ADHD was thought to be a developmentally handicapping condition with a strong biological or hereditary predisposition. Its severity, its relationship with other disorders and its outcome are now thought to be dependent on the social environment and treatment is thought to require multiple methods, each effective for different aspects of the disorder. A more detailed history is provided by Barkley (1990).

Diagnosis

Professional opinion as to how the problems of hyperactivity and attention deficit should be conceptualised and understood has been divided and there has been a lack of general agreement with regard to diagnostic criteria. One of the problems is that a number of different disciplines may be involved in the diagnosis. Taylor (1985) comments that it is not even clear whether the proponents of different positions are even talking about the same children. However, more recently there has been an increasing appreciation of the heterogeneity of the problems subsumed within the diagnosis and this has led to reappraisal of the components of the disorder.

The American diagnosis, given in the most recent edition of the *Diagnostic and Statistical Manual of Mental Disorders* (DSM IV), lists nine characteristics of inattention and nine characteristics of hyperactivity/impulsivity with at least six of these 18 behaviours having to be shown in both class and freeplay for a diagnosis to be made (American Psychiatric Association, 1993). It is the number of symptoms rather than their severity which is required for diagnosis. In the DSM IV classification individuals with symptoms primarily of inattention are designated as ADHD 'predominantly inattentive type'; those with symptoms primarily of hyperactivity/impulsivity are designated as ADHD 'predominantly hyperactive/impulsive type'; and those with significant symptoms in both categories are designated as ADHD 'combined type'. In addition, there are three further prerequisites for diagnosis:

1. That symptoms are shown before the age of 7 years.
2. That symptoms are present for at least 6 months.
3. That symptoms are present in school, home and social settings.

A different system of classification, the *International Classification of Diseases* (ICD-10) published by the World Health Organisation (1990), is used in Europe. The European definition of ADHD is not as broad as the American one and the focus is on hyperactivity rather than inattention (although this view is changing more recently in Europe). Both classification systems acknowledge that the degree of pervasiveness of the symptoms may be particularly important in indicating the severity of the disorder. However, the European definition requires pervasiveness across situations for the diagnosis to be made, thereby severely restricting the diagnosis of the disorder. Whereas the American definition uses it simply to rate the severity of the disorder (Barkley, 1990), Cooper and Ideus (1995) consider that there are only technical differences and that more recently a wider diagnosis has also been advocated by some writers in the UK.

The terminology associated with ADHD has undergone many changes over the last 50 years. It should be noted that in the DSM III (American Psychiatric Association, 1980) the disorder was called Attention Deficit Disorder (ADD) because, at that time, some researchers believed that inattention was the central deficiency. Symptoms were placed in the three broad categories of inattention, impulsivity and hyperactivity and ADD with hyperactivity and ADD without hyperactivity could be diagnosed. Throughout this text both these categories are encompassed within the term ADHD and hyperactivity and inattentiveness differentiated where appropriate.

Prevalence

Diagnostic confusion is highlighted by the vast apparent differences in the prevalence rates of ADHD between the USA and Britain. Figures in Britain are given as 1 in 1000 (or 0.1%) (Rutter *et al.*, 1970) and in the USA as 5% (Miller *et al.*, 1973). ADHD cannot be strictly defined and precisely measured and, therefore, its true incidence cannot accurately be determined. Kohn (1989; cited in Barkley, 1990) uses this to challenge the existence of ADHD as a disorder. Barkley (1990), however, states that the prevalence rates for any psychiatric disorder cannot be accurately determined. He argues that the prevalence rates for ADHD will depend greatly on how it is defined, the population studied, the location and the degree of agreement among parents, teachers and professionals. Kohn also argues that if so many children demonstrate the characteristic behaviours of ADHD it cannot be right to label them as having a disorder. Within the diagnostic criteria, however, there is a requirement that the behavioural characteristics of ADHD must be developmentally inappropriate for the children's age before they can be considered as clinically meaningful (American Psychiatric Association, 1987).

Is ADHD a valid disorder?

To be classified as a distinct disorder it must be shown that the major features of ADHD are related, that it is distinct from other disorders, that there is a common aetiology and a similar course and outcome for those with the disorder and that the symptoms predict different responses to certain treatments.

The major features of ADHD

The relatively weak or insignificant correlation between the measures of hyperactivity, inattention and impulsivity – the major behaviours associated with the disorder – have often been used to provide evidence against its existence as a distinct disorder (Barkley, 1990). Barkley suggests, however, that these findings may have more to do with the way in which we define these problems in ADHD children and with the measures used to assess these behaviours. He refers to a number of studies which factor analyse parent or teacher ratings of ADHD symptoms and which show that they are interrelated to such an extent that they may be combined into a single dimension of hyperactivity. Rutter (1989) points out that it may still be clinically useful to recognise a disorder despite a lack of relationship between its components, provided that there are common aetiologies and a similar development and outcome.

Distinction from other disorders

The main problem in classification of ADHD as a distinct disorder and its diagnosis is that several different kinds of disorder are often present together and they interact in complex ways.

Learning disabilities

Barkley (1990) estimates that 25–50% of children with ADHD have at least one type of learning difficulty in either reading, maths or spelling. Kavanagh (1994) estimates that about 40% of children with ADD have at least one type of learning disability in either reading, maths or oral or written language. There is also evidence that there are strong links with speech and language disorders (Love and Thompson, 1988; Shelton and Barkley, 1994). The approach used to define learning disabilities will, however, greatly affect the outcome of such studies. Many of the American diagnostic symptoms for inattentiveness are similar to those of children with pragmatic language disorders; thus children with a primary difficulty in inattention will, inevitably, resemble those with learning difficulties. Wood and Felton (1994), however, comment that reading disability and ADD must be recognised as two distinct disorders, which can occur together and can interact, but are not causally linked. Lowenthal (1994) concludes that the relationship between ADHD and Learning Disabilities is still unclear.

Emotional and behavioural disorders

The distinction between hyperactivity and emotional and behavioural disorders, particularly Conduct Disorder, is a more complex problem. It is so common for the two to be intertwined that many have doubted the value of making a distinction and have taken the view that Conduct Disorder and ADHD are synonymous (Taylor, 1994). Cooper and Ideus (1995) highlight the considerable overlaps between ADHD and other conditions in the UK which would be categorised under the heading of emotional and behavioural difficulites. This is supported by Barkley's (1994) research showing high percentages of ADHD children with emotional and behavioural difficulties, such as defiant behaviour, Conduct Disorder and Emotional Disorder. Cooper and Ideus (1995) go further and suggest that a significant proportion of children in Britain labelled emotionally and behaviourally disturbed are children with ADHD.

Hinshaw (1987), however, reviewed rating scale studies and found a considerable consensus that hyperactivity and Conduct Disorder are separate factors, although there was a high correlation between them. Studies show that children with both problems usually begin with hyperactivity which develops rapidly into a Conduct Disorder or an Oppositional Defiant Disorder if it is not treated early enough (Barkley *et al.*, 1990; Lyon, 1994). Wodrich (1994) suggests several possible reasons for this relationship. He suggests that hyperactivity may be a primer for Conduct Disorder, that there may be a single cause for both disorders or that both may have an association with chronic failure. Taylor (1994) believes that hyperactivity is one of the routes into Conduct Disorder, with family adversity helping to determine whether the route is followed. Kavanagh (1994) supports this view, describing ADHD as one of the most common and debilitating disorders among school-age children and one which exacerbates their other difficulties. Lyon (1994) suggests that it is the low self-esteem and the vicious negative cycle of failure experienced by ADHD children which may lead to other disorders.

Taylor (1994) stresses that clinicians must be wary regarding the confusion between ADHD and Conduct Disorder because the implications of the two diagnoses are vastly different.

Barkley (1990) describes the evidence for the distinction of ADHD from other disorders as conflicting. Many studies often compare subjects having more than one disorder with others having more than one disorder, rather than pure cases. When subjects have been more carefully selected differences between ADHD and other disorders have been more significant.

Aetiologies

It is agreed that multiple aetiologies may lead to ADHD and that there is no single set of causes for the disorder (Barkley, 1990; Cooper and Ideus, 1995; Hinshaw, 1994; Wodrich, 1994). There is a wide and complex array of influential factors, which are biological, psychological and social in nature and which can interact in complex and different ways. The pattern of causes and associations is not the same in all cases (Johnston, 1991). Over the last decade considerable research has been done into the causes of ADHD; although often studies are methodologically difficult, findings have been inconsistent and many studies lack replicability. The problems are mainly due to the presence of different disorders within the same individual. The majority of the research is correlational, with no direct evidence of causality; therefore, great care needs to be taken in interpreting most of the results (Barkley, 1990).

Genetic factors

For many years studies have shown higher rates of hyperactivity in the biological relatives of ADHD children as compared with those of normal children or those of adopted hyperactive children, although many of these studies have been criticised for their methodology (Barkley, 1990). Findings show that between 20% and 32% of children with ADHD also have a parent or sibling with the disorder. More recently a study by Goodman and Stevenson (1989) – the largest study of twin pairs to date – gave an estimate for the disorder of 30–50% hereditary, thus suggesting that genetic factors play a significant role in the causation of the disorder. The current scientific consensus is, therefore, that ADHD is principally an inherited condition and that there is a biological predisposition to the disorder (Wodrich, 1994).

Environmental factors

The study by Goodman and Stevenson (1989) showed that common environmental factors – such as poverty, family lifestyle, pollution or diet – accounted for between 0% and 30% in the variance of ADHD symptoms. This provides an argument against any theory attributing hyperactivity to entirely environmental factors. There is little, if any, evidence that ADHD can arise purely out of social or environmental factors, although the condition may be exacerbated by them (Barkley, 1990).

(a) Diet

A study by Feingold (1975) first introduced the idea that diet may be an influential factor in ADHD; however, more recent carefully controlled studies comparing control and experimental diets showed little or no effect (Conners et al., 1976). There are some single case studies which suggest that a change of diet has a beneficial effect. Barkley (1990) reviews the research in this field in more detail and concludes that there is little evidence to support a change of diet for most children with ADHD.

(b) Lead

Studies so far show a weak association between levels of lead in the bloodstream and ADHD symptoms (Thomson et al., 1989). More research,

however, is needed and there is presently no basis to assume that lead inges-
tion is a primary cause of ADHD.

(c) Family and social factors

It has been shown that parents of ADHD children are more likely to give
commands and be negative towards their children than other parents
(Cunningham and Barkley, 1979). Barkley (1990) suggests, however, that
this is a response to the demands of living with a child with ADHD rather
than a cause of it. Some associated problems, such as Conduct Disorder,
may, however, be influenced by factors such as parenting. Wodrich (1994)
concludes that family and social influences may exacerbate ADHD, but do
not make a significant contribution to the occurrence of symptoms.

Brain differences

Less than 5% of children with ADHD have evidence of actual brain damage
such as head trauma, brain infection etc. (Barkley, 1990; Wodrich, 1994).
Wodrich states that although brain injury may cause symptoms of hyperactivity, impulsivity and inattention, the child's condition is usually recognised
as distinct from ADHD disorder. More subtle brain injuries, such as birth-
related brain injury, have only shown a weak association with the later development of ADHD.

The work of Zametkin et al. (1990) and other smaller scale studies suggest that a deficiency in neurotransmitters in the areas of the brain involved
in response inhibition, attention and sensitivity to rewards and punishments
may characterise at least some individuals with ADHD. Definite differences
in the central nervous system have been found, although their exact nature is
yet to be determined. Neurological studies suggest that the irregular metabolism of brain chemicals contributes directly to the behaviour patterns seen in
children with ADHD.

Shaffer and Greenhill (1979) question the value of the concept of ADHD
on the basis of a lack of common aetiologies which would direct the clinician to the underlying psychopathology or neurophysiology. Many investigators, however, take an interactional view of causality and consider ADHD to
be the final common pathway of various antecedent variables which include
both biological and psychosocial factors (Weiss and Hechtman, 1993).

Development and outcome

Weiss and Hechtman (1993) conclude from their studies that about half of
hyperactive children grow out of their symptoms and half continue to be disabled to a varying extent by continuing symptoms in adulthood. At the age
of three overactivity is a good predictor of the presence of Conduct Disorder
in later childhood (Campbell, 1987). Barkley et al. (1990) found that a major

outcome was the development of aggressive and anti-social behaviour and delinquency. The findings of Weiss and Hechtman (1993), however, suggests that few ADHD children grow up to be serious adult offenders, although there may be a small sub-group who have more negative outcomes and who need to be identified early for successful treatment. All studies of outcome show that the symptoms of the original syndrome diminish in adolescence, but low self-esteem, poor school performance and poor peer relations are continuing problems for these children (Weiss and Hechtman, 1993). There is some evidence that early, prolonged, multiple intervention may prevent the negative self-esteem so often seen in these children (Satterfield *et al.*, 1981). Berry *et al.* (1985) also found that children with ADHD 'predominantly inattentive type', whilst less visible than those who are predominantly hyperactive, are a high-risk group for both school and social failure.

Weiss and Hechtman (1993) review developmental and outcome studies and highlight their similar findings which agree on fundamental outcome issues. In their opinion, the empirical evidence leads to the conclusion that a syndrome of hyperactivity exists.

Taylor (1994), however, concludes that research has not yet established whether hyperactivity should be considered a disorder or a risk factor. He explains that a risk factor would imply that ADHD would affect psychological development adversely at all levels of severity, whilst a disorder implies that only those above a certain threshold are vulnerable to later problems in social adjustment. The idea of a disorder also implies that it compromises later development even without the presence of other problems, while a risk factor may affect later development only if it is combined with other problems.

Assessment and treatment

There are specific implications for the identification, treatment and education of children whose inattention and restlessness affect their development. The complexity and variety of problems exhibited by these children demand separate assessment and separate treatment measures (Barkley, 1990; Cooper and Ideus, 1995; Taylor, 1994a; Wodrich, 1994).

Assessment
In the assessment of children with ADHD it is important to differentiate between primary and secondary symptoms and to be certain that symptoms are not due to other difficulties, such as learning difficulties. The overlap with other disorders has to be acknowledged and a whole picture gained through a multi-modal assessment which enables the difficulties of ADHD children to be assessed separately (Lyon, 1994).

Various forms of assessment are used to gain information from different sources. The absence of one source of information can limit the accuracy of the assessment. Assessment measures include behaviour checklists, rating scales, observations within various settings and interviews with parents, teachers and the child. These assessment methods are discussed more fully in Barkley (1990) and in Wodrich (1994). In order to determine the child's educational needs measures of ability, achievement and behaviour are also required.

Assessment ratings, however, often result in non-specific diagnoses because of the confounding of ratings by the presence of other disorders (Montague *et al.*, 1994) and there is a need for better methods of differential diagnosis and assessment (Lowenthal,1994).

Treatment

Practitioners have become increasingly aware that children with ADHD require a multiple treatment plan based on their individual needs (Goldstein and Goldstein, 1990). Lowenthal (1994), Johnston (1991) and Ahonen *et al.* (1994) all support this view stating that a single approach is not effective in treating the disorder. Erk (1995), for example, argues that for clients in whom inattentiveness is the predominant feature their unique symptoms and needs need to be recognised and interventions matched accordingly.

Medication

It has been suggested that, used properly, medication (stimulants such as Ritalin) can be safe and highly effective in treating children with ADHD (Barkley, 1990). Lyon (1994) suggests that 80% of ADHD children respond favourably to medication. Maximum effectiveness occurs within 1–1½ hours and begins to wear off after 4 hours and repeat doses are necessary. When effective there is rapid improvement in overactivity, distractibility and impulsivity. This results in an improvement in both behaviour, short-term learning, social skills and self-esteem, typically within 3–6 months of beginning treatment. Wodrich (1994), however, states that medication should only be given on the basis of a thorough assessment. He emphasises the need for continual monitoring of its effects and the fact that medication is not effective in treating other aspects of behaviour which may be related to ADHD, such as Conduct Disorder. Wodrich gives details of the possible side-effects of medication, such as sleep disturbance, irritability and rebound hyperactivity, although he comments that too much emphasis has been placed on the side-effects, which are, he considers, quite rare.

There is, however, no evidence to date for the long-term effectiveness of medication and Barkley (1990) suggests that treatments other than medication are required to maximise the chances of long-term improvement. Cooper and Ideus (1995) support this view and stress that medication may help other psychological treatments to work in more severe cases and that medication alone does not lead to long-term improvement in academic performance, social behaviour and emotional development.

Behaviour modification

Barkley (1990) and Taylor (1994) highlight the lack of persistence for tasks with little intrinsic appeal or minimal immediate consequences by children with ADHD. Shaping behaviour through targeting certain behaviours and the use of reward and punishment can result in improvement because a lot of the ADHD child's difficulties lie in their behaviour. Barkley (1990) stresses, however, that behaviour modification techniques do not alleviate the problems of attention deficit and hyperactivity. For this reason, they are not effective alone, but may help enormously in conjunction with other treatments, especially if the child also has Conduct Disorder or Oppositional Defiant Disorder.

Cooper and Ideus (1995) suggest that teachers need to be more skilled in this area. The success of behaviour modification techniques in school often depends on frequent monitoring of the child's behaviour, being able to give immediate feedback and being able to provide back-up consequences on a consistent basis. Techniques may, therefore, require practical modification in mainstream schools. Despite some success, however, generalisation and maintenance of treatment gains with behaviour modification have not been realised in practice and Barkley (1990) stresses that the problems of ADHD children are so pervasive and so durable that they require individualised, broad-based and long-term intervention.

Classroom management techniques

Hyperactivity is often relative to the situation (Johnston, 1991) and much can be done by teachers within the classroom environment to help children with ADHD. Examples include: changing the seating arrangements so that a child is less distracted; having clear classroom rules; changing the nature of tasks; or incorporating breaks to suit a child's concentration span. The research in this field is reviewed by Barkley (1990) and both Barkley and Wodrich (1994) provide a range of ideas for improving the classroom environment for children with ADHD. The importance of classroom management is also supported by Dalston (1995).

Professional counselling and psychotherapy

Counselling and psychotherapy are more long-term strategies which can be used to enhance the self-esteem and the self-awareness of the individual and provide them with alternative strategies for coping with their difficulties (Erk, 1995). Erk believes that improving the self-esteem of the client with ADHD 'predominantly inattentive type' through counselling should be the main aim for these children because they have often experienced years of frustration, failure and rejection. Family counselling may also be used to help the family to come to terms with the disorder, to cope effectively and to deal with issues of attitudes towards the child and towards treatment (Erk, 1995). Dalston (1995) stresses the part that family therapy can play in preventing a negative cycle of behaviour from developing within the family.

Social skills training

Children with ADHD are at a high risk of peer rejection because their impulse and judgement deficits lead them to have difficulties with relationships (Wodrich, 1994). This can lead to low self-esteem, loneliness and depression. Erk (1995) argues that this is especially so for children with ADHD 'predominantly inattentive type' and he views social skills training and education as essential for these childrren. Barkley (1990) describes a three-stage model for social skills training in detail. He advocates long-term, multi-faceted programmes where consideration is given to the generalisation of skills to the normal environment or where active efforts are made to promote a change in peer status. He stresses that parents, teachers and peers need to be involved in order to create meaningful change.

Self-help

It is recognised that children with ADHD have poor self-regulation of behaviour. Teaching self-control and self-evaluation through meta-cognitive training techniques has been advocated by Dalston (1994) and by Ahonen *et al.* (1994).

Acceptance

The reactions of others, which can lead to a vicious cycle of failure, often determine the way that the behaviour of a child with ADHD develops (Taylor, 1994). Encouraging acceptance of the child, therefore, especially in parents and teachers, can be beneficial.

Parental involvement

Parental involvement is advocated by most writers in this field (Barkley, 1990; Dalston, 1994; Lyon, 1994; Wodrich, 1994). Increasing parental competence has a positive effect on children's behaviour (Goldstein and Goldstein, 1990). Barkley (1990) describes a counselling and training programme for parents which incorporates the provision of knowledge about ADHD, opportunity for discussion and training in behaviour modification techniques. Many parents have such difficulties in managing their child that they seek help themselves. Programmes which are used to help the child need to be reinforced in the home for maximum effectiveness.

Educational support

Children with ADHD exhibit a wide range of problems in the classroom setting ranging from being disorganised to being disruptive. As well as behaviour problems, they often have attendant academic problems. There is a great need, therefore, for effective school interventions. In some cases small classes with a well-trained teacher may be effective, but for more severe cases it may be necessary to provide special educational services or provide a special educational placement. ADHD children may end up with support from a variety of specialist services because of their associated difficulties.

Presently, however, in both the USA and the UK a child cannot qualify for special educational support on the grounds of ADHD alone; they can only qualify on the basis of their associated difficulties, such as Learning Disability or Emotional or Behavioural Disorder.

Dietary intervention

Although present research indicates that diet has little effect on the symptoms of ADHD children, parents of ADHD children often experiment with it. Taylor (1985) suggests that, whilst one should not encourage a change of diet, professionals should support parents who choose to experiment with it.

The variety of treatment strategies outlined above reflect the complex and varied nature of the difficulties of children with ADHD. Different strategies affect different problems and effective treatment, therefore, needs to be guided by a thorough and accurate assessment of all the child's difficulties and continual monitoring of the effects of different interventions. Accurate diagnosis and early intervention are essential to prevent secondary problems (Lowenthal, 1994; Lyon, 1994). Lyon argues for the need for teachers to have more training in the recognition of ADHD to be able to diagnose the condition. Collaboration between different professionals is necessary for effective multi-modal treatment to be planned (Barkley, 1990; Cooper and Ideus, 1995; Lyon, 1994; Taylor, 1994). Lyon (1994) states that experience, training and research evidence indicate that most children with ADHD can be effectively helped when teachers, psychologists and parents work closely together. Wodrich (1994) concludes that school is probably the best place to begin intervention for ADHD.

Conclusion

Research on ADHD has expanded greatly over the last 20 years. Ideas about how ADHD is viewed have, therefore, changed rapidly and there has been much controversy in this field. The major classification schemes for psychiatric disorders (DSM IV and ICD-10) recognise ADHD as a distinct disorder and the clinical picture has widespread agreement amongst investigators and clinicians. Diagnostic criteria have become more specific and with more recent general agreement more refined tests to evaluate whether ADHD is a distinct disorder can now be undertaken.

At present, however, the evidence supporting the view that ADHD is a distinct disorder is still largely inconclusive. Research into some aspects of ADHD suggest that there is a distinction, whereas research into other aspects suggest that it is not clear. The relationship between the major components of ADHD (hyperactivity, impulsivity and inattention) is still uncertain because the outcome of studies is confounded by the way in which these problems are defined and the measures used to assess them. It has been suggested, however, that it may be clinically useful to recognise the disorder despite a lack of relationship between its components provided that there are common aetiologies and a similar development and outcome. Research into causality has been complicated by the interaction of the large number of factors, differing in nature, which have been implicated. More recently, however, it is generally agreed that there is a large hereditary component to the disorder and that other factors, such as the family and social environment, may exacerbate a child's difficulties but are not a primary cause. Irregular metabolism of brain chemicals contribute directly to the behaviour patterns seen in ADHD children, but the exact nature of this has not yet been determined. Some investigators question the lack of common aetiologies, whilst others accept an interactional view with ADHD being the final common pathway of a variety of factors. Studies of development and outcome share some general agreement and indicate that the presence of ADHD symptoms can be a predictor of certain outcomes. However, it is unclear whether this is evidence for the classification of ADHD as a distinct disorder or a risk factor.

The relationship between ADHD and other disorders, particularly Conduct Disorder, is a complex one. Children with ADHD frequently have other disorders, such as learning disabilities and emotional and behavioural disorders. Many writers have emphasised the overlap between ADHD and emotional and behavioural disorders. There is an increasing body of evidence suggesting that ADHD symptoms can develop into a Conduct Disorder, although the reason for this has not been definitely established. The implications of the two diagnoses, however, are vastly different. Children with ADHD have pervasive, long-term difficulties which require a broad-based, long-term, multi-modal treatment plan based on their individual needs. As Taylor (1985: 434) states:

> The heterogeneity of the problems of hyperactive children means that diagnostic formulation and assessment should start from the recognition that hyperactivity is present, not stop with it.

The specific and practical implications for the assessment, treatment and education of children who exhibit behaviours of inattentiveness and hyperactivity imply that it is both valid and beneficial to recognise ADHD as a distinct disorder. At the same time, its relationship with associated disorders must also be recognised. ADHD children often receive support from a variety of specialist services because of their associated problems. At the present time, however, a child cannot qualify for educational support within the SEN Code of Practice (DfE, 1994) on the grounds of ADHD alone and, in this sense, ADHD is not a recognised disorder. Children, therefore, who have ADHD without associated learning or emotional and behavioural problems are unlikely to have their needs recognised or addressed, yet they may have significant difficulites in a number of areas. Children who have ADHD and learning or emotional and behavioural difficulties may receive help, but only for these associated problems. The more pervasive and disabling nature of their difficulties may remain unrecognised and untreated. Given their recognition, however, there is much that teachers can do within the classroom to help ADHD children. The complex nature of their problems necessitates early intervention, before associated problems have developed, and close collaboration between the various professionals who are often involved is essential. Only in this way can effective treatment be planned.

References

Ahonen, T., Luotoniemi, A., Nokelainen, K., Savelius, A. and Tasola, S. (1994) 'Multimodal intervention in children with attention-deficit hyperactivity disorder', *The European Journal of Special Needs Education*, **9**(2), 168–81.

American Psychiatric Association (1980) *Diagnostic and Statistical Manual of Mental Disorders* (3rd edn). Washington, DC: APA.

American Psychiatric Association (1987) *Diagnostic and Statistical Manual of Mental Disorders* (3rd edn., revised). Washington, DC: APA.

American Psychiatric Association (1993) *Diagnostic and Statistical Manual of Mental Disorders* (4th edn.). Washington, DC: APA.

Barkley, R. A. (1990) *Attention-Deficit Hyperacivity Disorder: A Handbook for Diagnosis and Treatment*. New York: Guildford Press.

Barkley, R. A. (1994) 'It's not just an attention disorder', *Attention! The Magazine of Children and Adults with Attention Deficit Disorders*, **2**, 22–27.

Barkley, R. A., DuPaul, G. J. and McMurray, M. B. (1990) 'Comprehensive evaluation of attention deficit disorder with and without hyperactivity as defined by research criteria', *Journal of Consulting and Clinical Psychology*, **58**, 775–89.

Berry, C. A, Shaywitz, S. E. and Shaywitz, B. A. (1985) 'Girls with attention deficit disorder: a silent minority. A report on cognitive and behavioural characteristics, *Pediatrics*, **76**(5), 801–9

Campbell, S. B. (1987) 'Parent-referred problem 3-year-olds: Developmental changes in symptoms', *Journal of Child Psychology and Psychiatry*, **28**, 835–45.

Conners, C. K., Goyette, C., Southwick, D., Lees, J. M. and Andrulonis, P. A. (1976) 'Food additives and hyperkinesis', *Pediatrics*, **58**, 154–66.

Cooper, P. and Ideus, K. (1995) 'Is attention deficit disorder hyperactivity a Trojan Horse?' *Support for Learning*, **10** (1), 29–33.

Cunningham, C. E. and Barkley, R. A. (1979) 'The interactions of hyperactive and normal children with their mothers during free play and structured task', *Child Development*, **50**, 217–24.

Dalston, S. (1995) 'Helping Phil keep still', *ATL Report*, **17** (5), 12–13.

DfE (1994) *The Code of Practice on the Identification and Assessment of Special Educational Needs*. London: HMSO.

Douglas, V. I. (1983) 'Attention and cognitive problems'. In Rutter, M. (ed.) *Developmental Neuropsychiatry*. New York: Guildford Press, pp. 280–329.

Erk, R. R. (1995) 'The conundrum of Attention Deficit Disorder', *Journal of Mental Health Counselling*, **17** (2), 131–45.

Feingold, B. (1975) *Why Your Child is Hyperactive*. New York: Random House.

Goldstein, S. and Goldstein, M. (1990) *Managing Attention Disorders in Children*. New York: Wiley.

Goodman, R. and Stevenson, J. (1989). 'A twin study of hyperactivity: II. The aetiological role of genes, family relationships and perinatal adversity', *Journal of Child Psychology and Psychiatry*, **30**, 691–709.

Hinshaw, S. R. (1987) 'On the distinction between attention deficits/hyperactivity and conduct problems/aggression in child psychopathology', *Psychological Bulletin*, **101**, 443–63.

Hinshaw, S. R. (1994) *Attention Deficit Disorders and Hyperactivity in Children.* Thousand Oaks, CA: Sage.

Johnston, R. B. (1991) *Attention Deficits, Learning Disabilities and Ritalin: A practical guide.* London: Chapman and Hall.

Kavanagh, J. F. (1994) 'ADD and its relationship to spoken and written language', *Topics in Language Disorders*, **14 (4)**, v–viii.

Love, A. J. and Thompson, M. G. G. (1988) 'Language disorders and attention deficit disorders in young children referred for psychiatric services', *American Journal of Orthopsychiatry*, **58**, 52–63.

Lowenthal, B. (1994) 'Attention deficit disorders: Characteristics, assessment and interventions', *European Journal of Special Needs*, **9 (1)**, 80–90.

Lyon, J. (1994) 'Hope for the hyperactive', *Times Educational Supplement*, **21 October**.

Miller, R. G., Palkes, H. S. and Stewart, M. A. (1973) 'Hyperactive children in suburban schools', *Child Psychiatry and Human Development*, **4**, 121–27.

Montague, M., McKinney, J. D. and Hocutt, A. (1994) 'Assessing students for attention deficit disorder', *Intervention in School and Clinic*, **29 (4)**, 40–42.

Rutter, M. (1989). 'Attention deficit disorder/hyperkinetic syndrome: Conceptual and research issues regarding diagnosis and classification'. In Sagvolden, T. and Archer, T. (eds) *Attention Deficit Disorder: Clinical and Basic Research.* Hillsdale, NJ: Erlbaum, pp. 1–24.

Rutter, M., Graham, P. and Yule, W. (1970) *A Neuropsychiatric Study in Childhood.* London: Heinemann.

Satterfield, J. H., Satterfield, B. T. and Cantwell, D. P. (1981) 'Three year multimodality treatment study of 100 hyperactive boys', *Journal of Pediatrics*, **98**, 650–55.

Shaffer, D. and Greenhill, L. (1979) 'A critical note on the predictive validity of "the hyperactive syndrome" ', *Journal of Child Psychology and Psychiatry*, **20**, 61–72.

Shelton, T. L., and Barkley, R. A. (1994) 'Critical issues in the assessment of attention deficit disorders in children', *Topics in Language Disorders*, **14 (4)**, 26–41.

Taylor, E. A. (1985) 'Syndromes of attention deficit and overactivity'. In Rutter, M., Taylor, E. A. and Hersov, L. (eds) *Child and and Adolescent Psychiatry: Modern Approaches.* Oxford: Blackwell, pp. 424–43.

Taylor, E. (1994a) 'Syndromes of attention deficit and overactivity'. In Rutter, M., Taylor, E. and Hersov, L. (eds) *Child and Adolescent Psychiatry: Modern Approaches.* Oxford: Blackwell, pp. 285–307.

Taylor, E. (1994b) 'Hyperactivity as a special educational need', *Therapeutic Care and Education*, **3 (2)**, 130–44.

Thomson, G. O. B., Raab, G. M., Hepburn, W. S., Hunter, R., Fulton, M. and Laxen, D. P. H. (1989) 'Blood lead levels and children's behaviour – results from the Edinburgh lead study', *Journal of Child Psychology and Psychiatry*, **30**, 515–28.

Weiss, G. and Hechtman, L. T. (1993) *Hyperactive Children Grown Up.* New York: Guildford Press.

Wodrich, D. L. (1994) *Attention Deficit Hyperactivity Disorder: What Every Parent*

Wants to Know. London: Paul Brooks Publishing.

Wood, F. B. and Felton, R. H. (1994) 'Separate linguistic and attention factors in the development of reading', *Topics in Language Disorders*, **14 (4)**, 42–57.

World Health Organisation (1990) *International Classification of Diseases* (10th edn.). Geneva: WHO.

Zametkin, A. J., Nordahl, T. E., Gross, M., *et al.* (1990) 'Cerebral glucose metabolism in adults with hyperactivity of childhood onset', *New England Journal of Medicine*, **323**, 1361–66.

II Controversial System-Wide Interventions

5 Integration of Children with Special Educational Needs into Mainstream Schools – Inclusion or Delusion?

> The history of the twentieth century for disabled people has been one of exclusion. The twenty-first century will see the struggle of disabled people for inclusion go from strength to strength. In such a struggle, special, segregated education has no role to play.
>
> (Oliver, 1996: 94)

> ... full inclusion can provide only an illusion of support for all students, an illusion that may trick many into jumping on the bandwagon ... special education is in danger of riding the bandwagon called "full inclusion" to its own funeral.
>
> (Kauffman and Hallahan, 1995: ix–x)

These two quotations highlight a major controversy in the field of special education at present: the move to promote the inclusion, or integration, of all children with special educational needs (SEN) into mainstream schools. In recent years there has been an increasing trend towards the inclusion of children with SEN into ordinary school placements. Some writers have suggested that such inclusion should be regarded as a 'right' of all children with SEN (Kirkaldy, 1990; Oliver, 1996). Others have warned that widespread adoption of inclusive models will lead to a deterioration in the education provided for many children with SEN, as well as the eventual demise of the field of special education itself (Kauffman and Hallahan, 1995; Welton, 1989).

This chapter reviews the relevant literature and discusses the extent to which current views on inclusion have evolved through the development of policy, theory, research and practice. It attempts to evaluate the extent to which inclusion is a worthwhile goal for special education or whether its proponents are really deluding themselves and others into thinking that it will lead to more effective education for children with SEN.

The terms inclusion, integration and mainstreaming are typically used synonymously to refer to a variety of non-segregated settings and also to a process of increasing participation in mainstream education (Booth, 1992). The evolution of educational policy with regard to such inclusion will be considered first, followed by a discussion of developments in theory, research, and finally, practice.

Policy

In order to appreciate recent developments in special education it is necessary to briefly recall the historical evolution of the field. The early history of special education began in the second half of the eighteenth century with the opening of facilities for children with hearing and visual impairments. This was followed several decades later by the establishment of institutions for people with mental handicaps and physical disabilities (Cole, 1989; Hurt, 1988). These facilities were all provided on a segregated basis in line with the philosophies in vogue at that time regarding people who differed from the norm.

When school attendance became compulsory in many Western countries around the end of the nineteenth century this resulted in an increased awareness of pupils in ordinary schools who experienced considerable difficulties in learning. Attempts to identify these pupils in the early twentieth century led to the development of individual tests of ability, later to be called IQ tests. This was followed by the appointment of child psychologists to identify such children and the establishment of special classes and schools to provide appropriate education for them.

The first half of the twentieth century saw increasing provision of special classes and schools for children with SEN throughout the Western world. Thus the history of special education is very much tied up with the emergence of special segregated facilities, followed some time later by the provision of specialist training for staff (Cole, 1989).

In the 1950s and 1960s studies were conducted in the USA to evaluate the effectiveness of special classes for children with 'educable mental retardation' (Kirk, 1964). Results were generally equivocal and there was no clear overall superiority of either special class or ordinary class placement. Special classes appeared more beneficial socially while pupils in regular classes were sometimes better off academically.

However, there were considered to be serious methodological problems with most studies, especially in the use of comparison groups matched only for age and IQ. These tended to bias results in favour of integrated placements, since children who were placed in special classes typically had greater academic and behavioural problems than their peers with similar IQs who remained in ordinary classes (Madden and Slavin, 1983).

Also, special education at this time was notable for the inadequacy of specialist training and the inappropriateness of curricula (Cruickshank, 1974). Despite these factors the outcome of this debate was the formation of increasingly negative views about special classes amongst those involved in special education.

Very influential in this development was Dunn's (1968: 8) article criticising special classes. Dunn reviewed the efficacy studies and concluded that, '... retarded pupils make as much progress in the regular grades as they do in special education'. However, Kauffman and Hallahan (1995) have drawn attention to the fact that Dunn's recommendations for change were based on a special class population in the USA selected using an earlier definition of educable mental retardation which ranged up to an IQ of 85. Whereas, from 1973 onwards, an upper IQ limit of 70 was used in determining special class placement. They point out that Dunn mainly argued against the use of special classes for students in the IQ range 70–85. His article has therefore been wrongly cited in support of criticism of special classes for children with IQs in the 50–70 range, which is the typical range of IQ scores used to identify children with moderate learning difficulties in the UK.

Another criticism of special classes, which emerged in the USA, was that they promoted racial segregation, since ethnic minorities, especially blacks, were often substantially over-represented in such classes. Following the civil rights movement in the USA in the 1960s this became increasingly unacceptable.

Legislation which emerged in the USA in 1974 and in the UK in 1976 encouraged the integration of children with SEN into ordinary schools but did not mandate it. The UK legislation appeared 2 years before the publication of the Warnock Report (DES, 1978) suggesting that the decision to encourage increased integration came, not from the careful deliberations of the Warnock committee, but from the Department of Education and Science. When it was published the Warnock Report defined three levels of integration: locational, social and functional. In locational integration children with SEN are educated on the same site as other children and in social integration they also share some out-of-classroom activities with them. In functional integration pupils with SEN are educated in the same classrooms as their non-disabled age peers.

However, the Warnock Committee side-stepped the debate regarding the advantages and disadvantages of integration and simply re-affirmed the requirements of the 1976 Act. These were that, subject to certain criteria, pupils with SEN were to be educated in ordinary schools in preference to special schools. The four criteria were:

● that this was in accordance with parental wishes;
● that the child's educational needs could be met in the ordinary school;
● that it would be consistent with efficient use of resources;
● that it would not detract from the education of the SEN child's classmates.

However, despite the clear stipulation of these criteria in the 1981 Education Act, several Local Education Authorities in England subsequently developed special education policies which involved progression towards a situation in which all children with SEN would be integrated into their local primary and secondary schools (e.g. Humberside County Council, 1988). Such policies have also been adopted in many parts of the world including several countries in Europe (O'Hanlon, 1993), in New Zealand (Wilton, 1994), in some states in Australia (Slee, 1995), in some regions of Scotland (Henderson, 1991), in some states in the USA (Katsiyannis *et al.*, 1995) and in some provinces in Canada (Shaw, 1990).

In a programme broadcast on national television in 1987, Mary Warnock stated that such a policy would be more expensive to implement than existing arrangements, particularly in the transition phases. She noted, however, that LEAs were intending to make these changes within existing levels of resources. Further, she suggested that if such integration was to occur without the provision of adequate resources, then children with SEN would be worse off than if they remained in the segregated facilities which were scheduled for closure. Later, in a television programme transmitted in January 1992, she stated that, although the 1981 Act encouraged schools to integrate children with SEN, 'it was recognised that there would always be a need for special schools'. This effectively counters the widely espoused myth that a major aim of the Warnock Report was to increase levels of integration in mainstream schools greatly and to close special schools (see also Warnock, 1992).

Concern expressed in the press by Baroness Warnock about the effectiveness of SEN provision in mainstream schools (Warnock, 1992) was supported by an influential report carried out by the Audit Commission and HMI (DES, 1992) which was critical about many aspects of SEN provision. Pressure on Government from these sources along with that from various parent and professional organisations concerned with children with SEN was compounded by concern about demands from parents for increasing numbers of children to be statemented. These events led to the enactment of the 1993 Education Act and the *Code of Practice* for SEN (DfE, 1994a) which accompanied it.

The *Code of Practice* (DfE, 1994a), while making the point that the needs of most children with SEN can be met within mainstream schools, takes a moderate stance on the integration issue by emphasising the importance of having a continuum of SEN provisions to meet a continuum of needs. This continuum of provision ranges from segregated special schools, through special classes, to mainstream school placements. The stance which the *Code* takes on the need for a continuum supports the philosophy on which the current range of SEN provision is based in most countries, including the UK.

However, some writers (e.g. Booth, 1994) have openly criticised the *Code of Practice* for recognising the need for a continuum of SEN provision rather than adopting the philosophy of inclusive education and promoting the integration of all children with SEN into mainstream schools and classes.

The policy of the major professional organisation in the field of special education in the UK, the National Association of Special Educational Needs (NASEN), has been one of general support for the *Code of Practice* along with considerable enthusiasm for the concept of inclusion. However, professional and parent organisations in the USA have been overwhelmingly critical about the trend towards full inclusion. Only the Association for Persons with Severe Handicaps has given inclusion its unqualified support. In contrast, the organisations which support a continuum of placement options include the Council for Exceptional Children, American Foundation for the Blind, the Council for Learning Disabilities, American Society for Deaf Children, National Association for Gifted Children, American Federation of Teachers, and the National Association of School Psychologists (Borthwick-Duffy, Palmer and Lane, 1996; Kauffman and Hallahan, 1995).

Despite the clear balance of policy guidelines and statements in favour of maintaining a continuum of SEN provision, the literature on including all children in ordinary schools has been growing rapidly in the last few years. Some examples of this literature will now be discussed along with some recent criticisms of inclusive ideologies.

Theory

In recent years, promotion of the concept of 'full inclusion', which involves all children with SEN being catered for in mainstream schools, has led to many publications which have focused on strategies for its implementation. For example, in the USA, Gartner and Lipsky (1989) have proposed an alternative to the continuum of SEN provision which has been a widely accepted model for the delivery of special education services for many years (Deno, 1970). They suggest that, instead of the severity of SEN determining the degree of segregation necessary, it would determine the amount and range of services provided to children, who would all be integrated. That is, children with mild SEN would receive a low level, those with moderate SEN a higher level, and those with severe SEN the highest level, of support and resources, in their integrated settings.

Alper and her colleagues (Alper and Ryndal, 1992; Wisniewski and Alper, 1994) have suggested a number of guidelines for implementing inclusion. They have suggested that, in order to bring about inclusion, a systematic approach is required involving five stages: developing networks; assessing resources; reviewing options; installing specific inclusion strategies; and providing a system of feedback and self-renewal. The specific strategies they put forward include: flexible grouping; peer tutoring; buddy systems; alternative teacher roles; and computer assisted instruction. Another suggested approach has been that of 'Neverstreaming' (Slavin, 1996). The main focus of this approach is on intensive early intervention which is continued into primary schools to ensure that 'nearly' all children remain in the mainstream.

A widely reported suggestion is that the techniques of co-operative learning (Johnson and Johnson, 1987; Self et al., 1991) can be used to educate children with SEN effectively in mainstream schools. Peer tutoring has also been widely suggested as a means of facilitating inclusion of children with learning difficulties into ordinary classes (see Chapter 9). Research supporting the effectiveness of peer tutoring in developing the literacy skills of students with learning difficulties has begun to appear (Simmons et al., 1995).

Stainback and Stainback (1990) have provided guidelines for teachers to establish classrooms in which every aspect of organisation and instruction are intended to create an environment in which individual differences are respected and children help each other to succeed. The Stainbacks have also been instrumental in promoting the concept of support networks as necessary components of effective integration. They have provided guidelines for programmes of staff development, and for the development of various strategies necessary for supporting children with SEN in mainstream classrooms. In a similar vein, Forest, Pearpoint and O'Brien (1996) have promoted various 'tools' which are intended to be used to facilitate effective inclusion. These include MAPS and PATH, which are creative action planning techniques designed to help individuals work towards more effective futures, as well as Circles of Friends whose aim is to build and enrich friendship networks among young people at school and in the community. However, there appears to have been little evaluation of the effectiveness of any of the above strategies in facilitating the integration of pupils with disabilities into mainstream schools.

A major innovation in the USA has been the development of the Adaptive Learning Environment Model (ALEM) which embodies effective teaching practices to facilitate successful integration of children with SEN into regular schools (Wang and Walberg, 1983). The components of the ALEM include:

- support services delivered by special educators in regular classes;
- curriculum based assessment;
- highly prescriptive teaching;
- individual educational plans;
- self-management of learning experiences;
- flexibility in arranging learning environments.

However, Fuchs and Fuchs (1988) have suggested that there is a lack of research evidence for the success of the ALEM system of integrating children into regular schools.

The most far-reaching theoretical development to emerge from the field of special education in recent years is the Regular Education Initiative (REI) (Reynolds, Wang and Walberg, 1987; Stainback and Stainback, 1984). The basis of the REI is the proposal that the regular education system should assume responsibility for the education of all children, including those with SEN. There would then be no need for a separate special education system, since the expertise and resources required for children with SEN would be delivered from within ordinary schools. However, the REI has come in for increasing criticism in recent years. Mostert (1991) asserts that the REI reflects a denial of the differences which profoundly affect children with disabilities who are placed in regular schools. He considers that such an approach will actually perpetuate or even exacerbate such differences. Further, he charges REI proponents with branding detractors as outcasts in need of conversion to the radical REI agenda. Hocutt, Martin and McKinney (1991) emphasise that appropriateness of educational programmes is more important than where students are educated and suggest that it is irresponsible to push ahead with inclusion without evaluating the outcomes of such projects. Kauffman (1991) suggests that the charges made by REI proponents have not been substantiated and that the REI is a product of the socio-political thinking associated with the Reagan–Bush administrations and is in reality more concerned with cost-cutting than improving practice.

In the, UK much of the recent literature on integration has focused on guidelines for developing whole-school policy and procedures for meeting SEN (Dean, 1989, 1996; Hegarty, 1993; Sayer, 1994). That is, writers have spelled out the roles and tasks which teachers need to fulfil, and the attitudes, skills and knowledge which they require to do this successfully. For example, procedures for identifying and assessing children with special needs are discussed, as are arrangements for meeting these needs in ordinary schools. Many of these guidelines have been incorporated in the *Code of Practice* (DfE, 1994a) and are becoming commonplace in schools.

Another emphasis in the UK literature has been the organisation of 'support teaching' (Davies and Davies, 1988; Garnett, 1988; Hockley, 1988). Throughout the 1980s and 1990s, in mainstream schools, there has been an increase in the use of in-class support teaching and a decline in the use of withdrawal groups and special classes. Withdrawing pupils from class for small group work on basic literacy skills or placing them in special classes or units has been seen as undesirable because of the isolation, possible stigma and loss of time following the mainstream curriculum (Lewis and Howell-Jones, 1991). Support teaching requires a change in the role of special educators from working directly with children with SEN to working with and supporting other teachers with such children in their classes which is a very different and perhaps more difficult task.

Following his extensive research on support teaching, Thomas (1992) reports that it is fraught with difficulties. Particularly problematic is the collaborative relationship required between support teacher and classroom teacher. This is the key to the success of support teaching but often falls down due to the limited time for liaison, lack of interpersonal skills on behalf of support teachers and the negative attitudes of many class teachers. Because of these factors support teaching is often found to be less effective than the use of withdrawal groups in facilitating progress. Evidence for this suggestion is provided by the results of recent studies which have compared the effectiveness of in-class support with withdrawal strategies for students with mild disabilities. Marston (1996) found that students who were withdrawn to a resource room to receive tuition in small groups made greater progress with reading than those who received only in-class support. Lingard (1994) has shown that intensive teaching in small groups is more effective than in-class teaching in accelerating progress in reading and spelling skills.

A more recent suggestion by Dyson (1990), akin to the REI in the USA, is that special needs co-ordinators in ordinary schools should become 'effective learning consultants.' Such consultants would be responsible for analysing and planning learning situations and managing resources in order to help teachers cater effectively for the individual differences in their classes (Jordan, 1994). The skills and knowledge used by such consultants would be mostly those needed for special needs work. However, their focus would not be specifically on children with SEN but on facilitating effective learning for children throughout the school. In a similar vein, Ainscow (1991, 1995) has written extensively from the perspective that the effectiveness of SEN provision is inextricably bound up with the school's effectiveness in optimising learning for all pupils. Ainscow therefore sees the necessary focus to be one of whole school improvement in which teachers are encouraged to critically reflect on establishing procedures for optimising the educational progress of all students. However, Lingard (1996) has criticised the suggestions of both Dyson and Ainscow on the basis that what they have proposed is idealistic and impractical. Lingard considers that by promoting these philosophical models of integration, these writers, along with other leading academics in the field of special education in the UK, have distracted attention away from other possible innovations designed to improve the effectiveness of education for children with SEN.

There has also been a recent increase in published criticisms of the inclusion movement in the USA. In their edited book entitled, *The Illusion of Full Inclusion: A Comprehensive Critique of a Current Special Education Bandwagon*, Kauffman and Hallahan (1995) have suggested that bandwagons also go to funerals and that, at present, special education is in danger of riding the bandwagon named 'full inclusion' to its own funeral! The stated aim of the book is to provide an informed discussion of the inclusion movement and to warn of the dangers of embracing the 'illusory rhetoric of full inclusion'. In one of the chapters it is suggested that the drive for full inclusion focuses attention on the process of education rather than educational outcomes, on mainstream curricula rather than functional curricula, on advocacy for programmes rather than advocacy for children, and on rhetoric rather than research evidence. Another chapter compares the inclusive school movement with that of the REI and concludes that – whereas an aim of the REI was to promote co-operation between special and general education – advocates of full inclusion aim to eliminate special education altogether. Another difference noted is that the REI had broad support both from advocates for children with high-incidence and low-incidence disabilities, whereas most of the proponents of full inclusion are mainly concerned with the education of children with severe intellectual disability. It is also suggested in the book that the inclusion movement emanates not so much from Dunn's critique of special classes as from an extension of civil rights issues to people with disabilities and from budget considerations, and concludes that such a combination of 'holiness and financial stress' is hard to counter.

Further criticism of the inclusion movement in the USA has come from

Borthwick-Duffy *et al.* (1996) and Little and Witek (1996) who suggest that the thinking of inclusion proponents is based more on emotion and philosophy than empirical evidence. These authors point out that the research evidence to date does not support a full inclusion model and therefore suggest that decisions about inclusion should be made on a case-by-case basis as is mandated by the current legislation in the USA.

Clearly there has been recent progress in the elaboration and dissemination of theoretical bases for effective inclusion practices, both in the USA and the UK. However, although this theory has been severely criticised it appears to have gone further towards inclusion than was apparently intended by government policies in both countries. Is this perhaps because of research evidence regarding the effectiveness of integration or because parents and teachers are overwhelmingly positive about inclusion?

Research

Effectiveness of integration

There have been several publications which have described integration projects in the UK (e.g. Bennett and Cass, 1989; Hegarty, Pocklington and Lucas, 1982; Jones, 1990). These have been mainly attempts to describe what is seen as good practice with regard to the inclusion of children with SEN in mainstream schools, rather than to evaluate the effectiveness of the provision. The few accounts which have included some form of evaluation have reported both positive and negative outcomes for the children (e.g. Beasley and Upton, 1989).

However, several reviews of the literature on the effectiveness of integration have been published in the 1980s. These have dealt mainly with the integration of children with mild to moderate learning difficulties since this has been the group on which the majority of research has focused. The major reviews will now be discussed in chronological order.

In the earliest review of the literature it was suggested that integration led to more favourable outcomes for children with learning difficulties but not for those with learning disabilities (e.g. dyslexia) and emotional or behavioural difficulties (Carlberg and Kavale, 1980).

In an extensive review Gottlieb (1981) addressed the four main reasons proposed by Dunn (1968), in his influential paper, why special classes for children with mild to moderate learning difficulties were not justified. These are as follows:

1. Achievement is greater in regular classes.
2. Such children are less stigmatised in ordinary classes.
3. Special classes increase racial segregation.
4. There is greater individualisation of the curriculum in ordinary classes.

Regarding the first point, Gottlieb concluded that there were no clear differences between segregated and integrated placements on academic achievement and on some aspects of social adjustment. However, there were consistent differences on social status, in favour of segregated placements. On the second point, he concluded that children with moderate learning difficulties who were integrated were more stigmatised and rejected by non-handicapped peers than their segregated age-mates. On the third point, he concluded that the data available suggested that mainstreaming practices were not rectifying the racial imbalances in classrooms. With regard to the fourth point, he reported on studies which found a low level of individualisation of teaching in both special and ordinary classes.

Madden and Slavin (1983) in their review focused on academic and social outcomes of integrated as compared with segregated placements. Most studies reviewed were considered methodologically flawed or demonstrated no significant differences. However, the results of a few methodologically adequate studies suggested that integration was more effective than special class placement when mainstream teachers were trained special educators who individualised the instruction they provided.

Zigler and Hodapp (1986) found from their review that children with mild to moderate learning difficulties did equally well on academic achievement in segregated and integrated settings. Also, that while integrated children exhibited higher levels of social skills, they were routinely stigmatised by their non-handicapped peers. Levels of racial segregation were found to be about equal in both settings. Integrated placements were found to cost less than segregated ones, but there was less individualisation of programmes than in segregated placements.

Chapman (1988) in his review found that integrated children had lower levels of self-esteem than children who were segregated.

Danby and Cullen (1988) reviewed the evidence for five educational assumptions inherent in the policy of integration. They found no support for the assumptions that educational efficacy, social benefits and reduced stigma would result for children with learning difficulties who were integrated. Regarding the assumptions of improved parent involvement and effects on non-handicapped peers, they found that so little research had been conducted that it was not possible to comment.

Lindsey (1989) considered the findings of previous reviews on educational achievement, social interaction and stigmatisation, and concluded that support for integration on empirical grounds was lacking.

Hornby (1992) summarised previous reviews of the research and concluded that they have generally failed to find support for the effectiveness of integration in attaining the goals espoused in its rationale. Apart from the lower cost of integrated placements, the reviews found little evidence that the goals of integration are being met. Thus it appears that greater educational attainment, increased social skills, reduced stigma, increased self-esteem, greater racial integration, improved parent involvement, and individualisation of instruction do not necessarily result from integrating children with moderate learning difficulties into ordinary classes.

Parent perceptions

It is clear from the above reviews that researchers have tended to investigate the effects of integration on pupil factors such as academic achievement, social skills, self-esteem and stigmatisation. Only a few studies have concerned themselves with consumer satisfaction; that is, the perceptions of parents, or their children, regarding the impact of integration.

McDonnell (1987) surveyed 253 parents of children with severe disabilities regarding their satisfaction with their children's educational placement. Of the 120 parents whose children attended special schools, 66% reported that their children had previously been in integrated settings. Of the 133 parents whose children attended classes integrated into mainstream schools, 73% had previously attended special schools. Results showed that there were no differences in levels of satisfaction with their children's current placement between parents of integrated and special school children. Both sets of parents reported high levels of satisfaction with the overall quality of their children's educational programme.

Simpson and Myles (1989) surveyed parents of children with learning and behavioural difficulties concerning their attitudes to mainstreaming. They found that 76% of parents were willing to support the integration of their children if certain specified resources were provided. Only 25% of the parents were willing to support mainstreaming without guarantees about these additional resources. Related to this finding, other researchers have reported that parents have expressed concern about the adequacy of teacher training and the effectiveness of instruction in integrated settings (Bailey and Winton, 1987).

Lowenbraun, Madge and Affleck (1990) surveyed parents to determine their satisfaction with placement of their mildly mentally handicapped children in integrated classrooms of typically 8 such children and 24 non-handicapped peers. They found that 88% of parents were satisfied with the placement, even though only 42% of them had initially requested it. However, they also found that parents of children who had previously been in resource room placements were slightly more satisfied with this arrangement than with their current integrated class placements.

Kidd and Hornby (1993) surveyed the parents of 29 pupils who transferred from special schools for pupils with moderate learning difficulties into mainstream schools. Fourteen months after the transfer they found that, overall, 65% of parents were satisfied with the transfer, as were 76% of the pupils. However, there was a clear difference between satisfaction rates of pupils integrated into units in mainstream schools as opposed to those placed in mainstream classes: 92% of parents of pupils placed in units were satisfied while this was the case for only 47% of parents of pupils placed in mainstream classes. A similar pattern of satisfaction was found for pupils.

With regard to parental satisfaction with segregated placements, Meyers and Blacher (1987) found that 70% of parents of children with severe and profound learning difficulties were either satisfied or very satisfied with their child's special education placements. Also, Kauffman (1991) reported that a Harris poll conducted in the USA in 1989 found that 77% of parents of children with disabilities were satisfied with the special education system.

To summarise, the findings of research on parent perceptions of segregated and integrated placements suggest that parents are neither overwhelmingly for or against the practice of integration. This reinforces the importance of maintaining a continuum of special education placements.

Teacher perceptions

It has been suggested that a key element in the effectiveness of integration must be the views of the personnel who have the major responsibility for implementing it: that is, teachers (Forlin, Douglas and Hattie, 1996). It is argued that teachers' beliefs and attitudes are critical in ensuring the success of inclusive practices since teachers' acceptance of the policy of inclusion is likely to affect their commitment to implementing it. It is also considered that they are in an excellent position to evaluate the impact of such practices on the children involved. It is not surprising, therefore, that, from the time when integration was first mooted, numerous studies of teachers' views on this issue have been conducted.

In a recent review of the research on teacher perceptions of inclusion Scruggs and Mastropieri (1996) analysed the results of 28 studies published between 1958 and 1995. The major finding was that, although on average 65% of teachers supported the general concept of inclusion, only 40% believed that this is a realistic goal for most children. Fifty-three per cent of teachers reported that they were willing to teach students with disabilities and 54% considered that such students could benefit from inclusion. However, only 33% of teachers believed that the mainstream classroom was the best place for students with disabilities and 30% suggested that they could have a negative effect on the classroom environment.

With regard to the ability of general educators to implement inclusion, only 28% thought there was sufficient time available and only 29% considered they had sufficient expertise. Seventy-one per cent of teachers considered that class size should be reduced in order to facilitate inclusion and the vast majority of teachers also considered that there were insufficient resources available to support inclusion.

An important finding was that there was no correlation between positive attitudes toward inclusion and date of publication, suggesting that teachers' views have not substantially changed over the years. The authors conclude by pointing out that the majority of studies have been conducted with primary school teachers. They cite several sources which suggest that secondary school teachers are generally less positive about inclusion. They therefore suggest that the findings of their review may present an overestimate of the level of positive views regarding inclusion among teachers overall.

Practice

> With changes in values and beliefs, the education of students with disabilities is being increasingly implemented in general education settings. While an increasing number of parents and professionals are calling for more inclusionary education, others are warning against the adoption of a single inclusionary model that limits the options available.
>
> (Katsiyannis, Conderman and Franks, 1995: 286)

Katsiyannis *et al.* (1995) recently conducted a survey of all states in the USA regarding their progress on inclusion. Thirty-three out of the 40 states which replied reported supporting inclusion pilot projects. Of these, 21 states provided information about the implementation of inclusion at the school district level. This ranged from 100% of school districts implementing inclusion in some states to only 1% of school districts in other states. The authors concluded that – although there is great variety in State policies and practices – the trend is one of acceleration in inclusion activity.

Concern about the increasing spread of inclusive practice in the USA led to a recent action research project, reported by Vaughn and Schumm (1995), which focused on the implementation of inclusive approaches in three primary schools in large urban areas. The authors worked with teachers, parents, administrators and governors at the schools over a 2-year period helping them to re-organise their provision for students with disabilities. The aims of the project were to develop more inclusive models of provision to meet these students' needs effectively. The authors concluded that for inclusion to be effective and therefore responsible rather than irresponsible and possibly damaging, inclusive practices needed to include nine components. These are:

1. Using the extent to which students with SEN make satisfactory academic and social progress in ordinary classes as the major criteria for considering alternative interventions – as opposed to insisting on mainstream class placement regardless of the academic and social progress of students.
2. Allowing teachers to choose whether or not they will be involved in teaching inclusive classes – as opposed to expecting all teachers, regardless of their attitudes towards inclusion or their expertise in teaching students with SEN, to teach inclusive classes.
3. Ensuring the provision of adequate human and physical resources – as

opposed to expecting reductions in the cost of provision through implementing inclusion.

4. Encouraging schools to develop inclusive practices tailored to the needs of the students, parents and communities they serve as well and to take into account the expertise of their own staff – as opposed to imposing inclusive models on schools without involving them in discussion.

5. Maintaining a continuum of services including withdrawal for small group teaching and placement in special education classrooms – as opposed to viewing full inclusion as the only alternative.

6. Continually monitoring and evaluating the organisation of provision to ensure that students' needs are being met – as opposed to sticking rigidly to one model of inclusion without ongoing evaluation to assess its effectiveness.

7. Ensuring ongoing professional development is available to all staff who need it – as opposed to not considering teachers' need for training in order to be able to implement inclusion.

8. Encouraging the development of alternative teaching strategies and means of adapting the curriculum to meet the specific needs of students with a wide range of ability – as opposed to exposing students with SEN to the same teaching and curriculum as other students.

9. Developing an agreed philosophy and policy on inclusion which provides guidance to teachers, parents and others – as opposed to imposing a policy of inclusion on schools without the opportunity for discussion.

The authors point out that these nine components of 'responsible inclusion' were put into practice in the three schools they worked with and were key factors in bringing about improvement in the effectiveness of provision for students with disabilities.

In the UK, surveys of levels of integration have been conducted by Swann. Despite finding little evidence for increased integration in an earlier study (Swann, 1985) a more recent survey by Swann (1991) has reported a trend towards increased integration of children with SEN into ordinary schools. This study found that, between 1982 and 1990, the numbers of children with SEN segregated into special schools decreased in 44 LEAs and in 15 of these the decrease was greater than 25%. However, levels of segregation increased in 15 LEAs, and in three of these the increase was greater than 25%. It is clear that, although there is considerable variation in levels of segregation amongst LEAs, the overall trend is one of increased integration.

A survey of integration practices in eight countries which was conducted in 1989 has found that the proportion of children with SEN, aged 6–17 years, who were not functionally integrated varied from 1.5% to 4.2% of the school population (Pijl and Meijer, 1991). England and Italy had the lowest levels of segregation (at 1.5%), while Belgium (3.5%), the USA (3.8%), Holland (3.9%) and West Germany (4.2%) had the highest levels. Sweden (at 2.0%) and Denmark (2.4%) had levels of integration in the middle of the range. The overall findings of the study indicated that in each of the countries at least 1.5% of children with SEN were not functionally integrated. That this is the case, even in Italy, where in principle special and regular education have been fully integrated since 1977, suggests that a policy of functional integration for all children with SEN is a goal which is very difficult to achieve in practice.

Turning to practice within the UK, a survey of pupils with SEN in ordinary schools in 38 LEAs found that the quality of teaching in approximately half of all lessons observed was less than satisfactory (HMI, 1989). This suggests that many of the ordinary school settings into which children with learning difficulties could be integrated are not conducive to meeting their special educational needs.

This is perhaps hardly surprising considering the limited amount of input on teaching pupils with SEN in initial teacher training courses in the UK (Garner, 1996) and the limited availability of in-service training (Miller and Garner, 1996). In fact, one of the most worrying aspects of the current situation in the field of special education in the UK, is recent arrangements for funding specialist training. These have led to drastically reduced levels of funding being available for providing such training. As a result, many of the 1-year full-time in-service courses in special education have closed and are being replaced by part-time modular courses, which are less costly (Hornby, 1990). Thus there is likely to be limited availability of special education expertise within the field of education in the foreseeable future. This means that children with SEN who are integrated into ordinary schools may not receive the specialist help they need.

Another difficulty for pupils with SEN who are integrated into mainstream schools has emerged following the implementation of the 1988 Education Act. As Visser (1993: 10) has stated, 'The positive effects of having a common curriculum have to be set against the imposition of one which in many respects is inappropriate'. Guidelines on pupils with SEN which followed the 1988 Act suggested that all children with SEN, including those with 'profound and multiple learning difficulties' should follow the National Curriculum (NCC, 1989a, b). Since the National Curriculum was originally designed without children with SEN in mind and may be inappropriate for many children with moderate and severe learning difficulties, this could have negative consequences for them (Stakes and Hornby, 1996). Although this guidance has been watered down in more recent publications (Dearing, 1993; NCC, 1993) with time set aside for, and more emphasis on, such things as life and social skills, the national curriculum still exerts a determining influence on the curriculum to which most children with learning difficulties are exposed.

Another aspect of the 1988 Act which is likely to work against children with SEN who are integrated into ordinary schools is Local Management of Schools (Russell, 1990). Following the 1988 Act there was a substantial increase in requests from schools and parents for formal assessments, and a significant rise in the number of statements resulting from such assessments (Evans and Lunt, 1993; Pyke, 1996). It appears that many schools are less willing to admit or retain children with SEN, unless they have a statement specifying the extra resources provided by the LEA, for fear of increasing their costs and lowering the assessment results which they are required to publish (Welton, 1989).

In reaction to the practice of education for children with SEN which followed the 1988 Act, Lady Warnock wrote, 'It is very generally agreed that the issuing of statements by LEAs has fallen into disarray. [and] there are thus increasing numbers of children in mainstream schools who urgently need help, if they are not to fall further and further behind' (Warnock, 1993: ix).

Given the above developments in the practice of education for children with SEN in the UK, it needs to be emphasised that many of the current changes, particularly as consequences of the 1988 Education Act, are working against the interests of many children with SEN who are integrated into ordinary schools. This has led to recent calls for a review of integration policies. Gardiner (1996) reported on a recent speech by the president of the Society of Education Officers in the UK in which a rethink of inclusion policies was proposed. It was suggested that 10 years earlier inclusion was widely considered to be the way forward but that with less money and the pressure of market-led services a less idealistic policy was needed. Such considerations have also led Fish and Evans (1995: 100) to suggest that:

> The current educational policy, rooted in economic competition and personal choice is not sympathetic to social integration and as a result, the integration of disabled children, young people and adults into schools and society receives less priority. A reappraisal of the concept of integration . . . is now necessary.

Conclusions

Although there have been considerable developments in the theory of providing integrated education to children with SEN it seems that the views of many special educators regarding such inclusion have gone well beyond the intentions of the government policies which initiated them. Also, there has been a lack of research evidence in support of the effectiveness of integration for children with SEN in ordinary schools. Currently held policies on inclusion have evolved mainly from espoused theory and examples of 'good practice' rather than implementation of the intentions of policy guidelines or research evidence regarding its effectiveness.

Some of the current changes in the practice of education in the UK, particularly those which have occurred as a consequence of the 1988 Education Act, are clearly working against the interests of many children with SEN who are integrated into ordinary schools, especially those with learning difficulties. Current policies, of promoting increased integration into ordinary schools of pupils with SEN, are therefore particularly inappropriate at the present time when the pressures on ordinary schools are having the effect of making them both less able and less willing to provide for children with SEN.

These conclusions suggest that proponents of inclusion are deluding themselves, and perhaps others, when they argue that greater inclusion will lead to more effective education for children with SEN.

It is therefore considered important that a realistic policy regarding inclusion is adopted and that ongoing evaluation of integration projects are conducted. Tizard (1978) has suggested that the four criteria for integration, stipulated in the Warnock Report and referred to earlier, provide a useful framework for designing evaluations of integration projects. Feedback from such evaluations would facilitate the improvement of future practice and provide evidence regarding the effectiveness of inclusion.

Until there is more evidence about the effectiveness of inclusion, less idealistic and more carefully considered policies regarding the integration of children with SEN need to be adopted. Few special educators would disagree with the suggestion that all children, including those with SEN, could be educated on the same site, that is, locationally integrated. Also that as much social integration as possible should be encouraged, for the benefit of all pupils. Special educators would also generally agree that many children with SEN can be successfully included in regular classes given a favourable school ethos, sufficient in-service training and adequate human and material resources.

The most important rights of people with SEN are probably the right to an appropriate education, and the right to be fully integrated into society. Inclusion in ordinary schools, or segregation into special classes or schools, is only defensible if it facilitates these two rights. Therefore, it is considered that the most productive approach is to adopt a policy for the education of children with SEN in the most integrated setting which meets Warnock's four criteria and Vaughn and Schumm's (1995) nine components of responsible inclusion. It is considered that this is the approach most likely to ensure effective education for these children and to facilitate maximum integration into the community when they leave school.

The conclusion of this analysis of the current state of theory, research and practice is that policies of increasing levels of integration for all children with SEN and of eventually including them all in their local schools should be abandoned. Instead the level of integration – either locational, social or functional – should be decided on the needs of each individual child and the exigencies of each situation.

As the 1981 and 1993 Education Acts require, the ability of the ordinary school setting to meet the needs of children with SEN proposed for integration should be carefully considered in each case, as should the likely effects on other children in the school, and the likely costs of adequately resourcing each placement. Most importantly, the wishes of parents must be respected and their right to make choices between the various options should be maintained.

To operate such a system it is necessary to maintain a range of special education provisions, along a continuum from special schools, through units in mainstream schools to ordinary class placements, similar to that which exists at present in most developed countries. Once the necessity for this is accepted then the focus of special educators can return to that of optimising the appropriateness of education for children with SEN rather than considering methods of achieving greater inclusion.

References

Ainscow, M. (ed.) (1991) *Effective Schools for All*. London: David Fulton.

Ainscow, M. (1995) 'Special needs through school improvement: School improvement through special needs'. In Clark, C., Dyson, A. and Millward, A. (eds) *Towards Inclusive Schools?* London: David Fulton, pp. 63–77.

Alper, S. and Ryndal, D. L. (1992) 'Educating students with severe handicaps in regular classes', *Elementary School Journal*, **92 (3)**, 373–87.

Bailey, D. B. and Winton, P. J. (1987) 'Stability and change in parents' expectations about mainstreaming', *Topics in Early Childhood Special Education*, **7 (1)**, 73–88.

Beasley, F. and Upton, G. (1989) 'Effectiveness of locational integration for children with moderate learning difficulties'. In Jones, N. (ed.) *Special Educational Needs Review* (Vol. 2). Lewes: Falmer Press, pp. 146–60.

Bennett, N. and Cass, A. (1989) *From Special to Ordinary Schools: Case Studies in Integration*. London: Cassell.

Booth, T. (1992) 'Integration, disability and commitment'. In Booth, T., Swann, W., Masterton, M. and Potts, P. (eds) *Policies for Diversity in Education*. London: Routledge.

Booth, T. (1994) 'Continua or chimera?' *British Journal of Special Education*, **21 (1)**, 21–24.

Borthwick-Duffy, S. A., Palmer, D. S. and Lane, K. L. (1996) 'One size doesn't fit all: Full inclusion and individual differences', *Journal of Behavioral Education*, **6 (3)**, 311–29.

Carlberg, C. and Kavale, K. (1980) 'The efficacy of special versus regular class placement for exceptional children: A meta-analysis', *Journal of Special Education*, **14 (7)**, 295–309.

Chapman, J. W. (1988) 'Special education in the least restrictive environment: Mainstreaming or maindumping?', *Australia and New Zealand Journal of Developmental Disabilities*, **14 (2)**, 123–34.

Clark, C., Dyson, A. and Millward, A. (1995) *Toward Inclusive Schools?* London: David Fulton.

Cole, T. (1989) *Apart or A Part? Integration and the Growth of British Special Education*. Milton Keynes: Open University Press.

Cruickshank, W. M. (1974) 'The false hope of integration', *The Slow Learning Child*, **21 (2)**, 67–83.

Danby, J. and Cullen, C. (1988) 'Integration and mainstreaming: A review of the efficacy of mainstreaming and integration for mentally handicapped pupils', *Educational Psychology*, **8 (3)**, 177–95.

Davies, J. D. and Davies, P. (1988) 'Developing credibility as a support teacher', *Support for Learning*, **3 (1)**, 12–15.

Dean, J. (1989) *Special Needs in the Secondary School: The Whole School Approach.* London: Routledge.

Dean, J. (1996) *Managing Special Needs in the Primary School.* London: Routledge.

Dearing, R. (1993) *The National Curriculum and its Assessment: Final Report.* London: School Curriculum and Assessment Authority.

Deno, E. (1970) 'Special education as developmental capital', *Exceptional Children*, **37**, 229–37.

DES (1978) *Special Educational Needs (The Warnock Report).* London: HMSO.

DES (1992) *Getting in on the Act. Provision for Pupils with Special Educational Needs: The National Picture (Audit Commission/HMI Report).* London: HMSO.

DfE (1994a) *Code of Practice on the Identification and Assessment of Special Educational Needs.* London: Department for Education.

DfE (1994b) *The Organisation of Special Educational Provision (Circular 6/94).* London: Department for Education.

Dunn, L. M. (1968) 'Special education for the mildly retarded: Is much of it justified?' *Exceptional Children*, **35**, 5–22.

Dyson, A. (1990) 'Effective learning consultancy: A future role for special needs coordinators?' *Support for Learning*, **5 (3)**, 116–27.

Evans, J. and Lunt, I. (1993) 'Special education provision after LMS', *British Journal of Special Education*, **20 (2)**, 59–62.

Fish, J. and Evans, J. (1995) *Managing Special Education: Codes, Charters and Competition.* Buckingham: Open University Press.

Forest, M., Pearpoint, J. and O'Brien, J. (1996) '"MAPS": Educators, parents, young people and their friends planning together.', *Educational Psychology in Practice*, **11 (4)**, 35–40.

Forlin, C., Douglas, G. and Hattie, J. (1996) 'Inclusive practices: How accepting are teachers?' *International Journal of Disability, Development and Education*, **43 (2)**, 119–33.

Fuchs, D. and Fuchs, L. S. (1988) 'Evaluation of the Adaptive Learning Environments Model', *Exceptional Children*, **55**, 115–27.

Gardiner, J. (1996) 'Voice of pragmatism queries inclusion ideal', *Times Educational Supplement*, **1 November**, 2.

Garner, P .(1996) 'Students' views on special educational needs courses in Initial Teacher Education', *British Journal of Special Education*, **23 (4)**, 176–79.

Garnet, J. (1988) 'Support teaching: Taking a closer look', *British Journal of Special Education*, **15 (1)**, 15–18.

Gartner, A. and Lipsky, D. K. (1989) 'New conceptualizations for special education', *European Journal of Special Needs Education*, **4 (1)**, 16–21.

Gottlieb, J. (1981) 'Mainstreaming: Fulfilling the promise?' *American Journal of Mental Deficiency*, **86 (2)**, 115–26.

Hegarty, S. (1993) *Meeting Special Needs in Ordinary Schools: An Overview.* London: Cassell.

Hegarty, S., Pocklington, K. and Lucas, D. (1982) *Integration in Action.* Windsor: NFER-Nelson.

Henderson, D. (1991) 'Swimming in the mainstream', *Times Educational Supplement*, **25 October**, 18.

HMI (1989) *A survey of Pupils with S.E.N. in Ordinary Schools*. London: DES.

Hockley, L. (1988) 'On being a support teacher', *British Journal of Special Education*, **12 (1)**, 27–29.

Hocutt, A., Martin, E. and McKinney, J. D. (1991) 'Historical and legal context of mainstreaming'. In Lloyd, J. W., Singh, N. N. and Repp, A. C. (eds) *The Regular Education Initiative: Alternative Perspectives on Concepts, Issues and Models*. Sycamore, Ill: Sycamore, pp. 17–28.

Hornby, G. (1990) 'A modular approach to training', *British Journal of Special Education*, **17 (4)**, 156–60.

Hornby, G. (1992) 'Integration of children with special educational needs: Is it time for a policy review?' *Support for Learning*, **7 (3)**, 130–34.

Humberside County Council (1988) *Mainstreaming Approaches to Meeting Special Educational Needs: Policy and Guidelines for Schools and Colleges*. Beverley: Humberside County Council.

Hurt, J. S. (1988) *Outside the Mainstream*. London: Batsford.

Johnson, D. W. and Johnson, R. T. (1987) *Learning Together and Alone*, (2nd edn.). Englewood Cliffs, NJ: Prentice-Hall.

Jones, N. (1990) *Special Educational Needs Review* (Vol. 3). Lewes: Falmer Press.

Jordan, A. (1994) *Skills in Collaborative Classroom Consultation*. New York: Routledge.

Katsiyannis, A., Conderman, G. and Franks, D. J. (1995) 'State practices on inclusion', *Remedial and Special Education*, **16 (5)**, 279–87.

Kauffman, J. M. (1991) 'Restructuring the sociopolitical context: Reservations about the effects of current reform proposals on students with disabilities'. In Lloyd, J. W., Singh, N. N. and Repp, A. C. Iu *The Regular Education Initiative: Alternative Perspectives on Concepts, Issues and Models*. Sycamore, Ill: Sycamore, pp. 57–66.

Kauffman, J. M. and Hallahan, D. P. (1995) *The Illusion of Full Inclusion: A Comprehensive Critique of a Current Special Education Bandwagon*. Austin, Texas: PRO-ED.

Kidd, R. and Hornby, G. (1993) 'Transfer from special to mainstream', *British Journal of Special Education*, **20 (1)**, 17–19.

Kirk, S. A. (1964) 'Research in education'. In Stevens, H. A. and Heber, R. (eds) *Mental Retardation*. Chicago: University of Chicago Press.

Kirkaldy, B. (1990) 'Special education: Towards a question of civil rights', *The Psychologist*, **3 (10)**, 466–67.

Lewis, G. and Howell-Jones, M. (1991) 'Perspectives on support teaching', *Education 3–13*, **October**, 44–49.

Lindsey, G. (1989) 'Evaluating integration', *Educational Psychology in Practice*, **5 (1)**, 7–16.

Lingard, T. (1994) 'The acquisition of literacy in secondary education', *British Journal of Special Education*, **21 (4)**, 180–91.

Lingard, T. (1996) 'Why our theoretical models of integration are inhibiting effective innovation', *Emotional and Behavioural Difficulties*, **1 (2)**, 39–45.

Little, S. G. and Witek, J. M. (1996) 'Inclusion: Considerations from social validity and functional outcome analysis', *Journal of Behavioral Education*, **6 (3)**, 283–91.

Lloyd, J. W., Singh, N. N. and Repp, A. C. (1991) *The Regular Education Initiative:*

Alternative Perspectives on Concepts, Issues, and Models. Sycamore, Ill: Sycamore Press.

Lowenbraun, S., Madge, S. and Affleck, J. (1990) 'Parental satisfaction with integrated class placements of special education and general education students', *Remedial and Special Education*, **11** (4), 37–40.

McDonnell, J. (1987) 'The integration of students with severe handicaps into regular public schools: An analysis of parents' perceptions of potential outcomes', *Education and Training in Mental Retardation*, **22** (2), 98–111.

Madden, N. A. and Slavin, R. E. (1983) 'Mainstreaming students with mild handicaps: Academic and social outcomes', *Review of Educational Research*, **53** (4), 519–69.

Marston, D. (1996) 'A comparison of inclusion only, pull-out only and combined service models for students with mild disabilities', *Journal of Special Education*, **30** (2), 121–32.

Meyers, C. E. and Blacher, J. (1987) 'Parents' perceptions of schooling for severely handicapped children: Home and family variables', *Exceptional Children*, **53** (5), 441–49.

Miller, O. and Garner, M. (1996) 'Professional development to meet special educational needs', *British Journal of Special Education*, **23** (2), 70–74.

Mostert, M. P. (1991) 'The Regular Education Initiative: Strategy for denial of handicap and perpetuation of difference', *Disability, Handicap and Society*, **6** (2), 91–101.

NCC (National Curriculum Council) (1989a) *Implementing the National Curriculum: Participation by Pupils with S.E.N. – Circular Number 5.* York: NCC.

NCC (1989b) *A Curriculum for All: S.E.N. in the National Curriculum.* York: NCC.

NCC (1993) *Special Needs and the National Curriculum: Opportunity and Challenge.* York: NCC.

O'Hanlon, C. (1993) *Special Education Integration in Europe.* London: David Fulton.

Oliver, M. (1996) *Understanding Disability: From Theory to Practice.* Basingstoke: Macmillan.

Pijl, S. J. and Meijer, C. J. W. (1991) 'Does integration count for much? An analysis of the practices of integration in eight countries', *European Journal of Special Needs Education*, **6** (2), 100–111.

Pyke, N. (1996) 'Expenditure time bomb fear over special help', *Times Educational Supplement*, **29 November**.

Reynolds, M. C., Wang, C. and Walberg, H. J. (1987) 'The necessary restructuring of special and regular education', *Exceptional Children*, **53**, 391–98.

Russell, P. (1990) 'The Education Reform Act: The implications for special educational needs'. In Flude, M. and Hammer, M. (eds) *The Education Reform Act, 1988: Its Origins and Implications.* Lewes: Falmer Press.

Sayer, J. (1994) *Secondary Schools for All?* (2nd edn.). London: Cassell.

Scruggs, T. E. and Mastropieri, M. A. (1996) 'Teacher perceptions of mainstreaming/inclusion, 1958–1995: A research synthesis', *Exceptional Children*, **63** (1), 59–74.

Self, H., Benning, A., Marston, D. and Magnusson, D. (1991) 'Cooperative teaching project: A model for students at risk', *Exceptional Children*, **58** (1), 26–35.

Shaw, L. (1990) *Each Belongs: Integrated Education in Canada.* London: Centre for Studies on Integration in Education.

Simmons, D. C., Fuchs, L. S., Fuchs, D., Maths, P. and Hodge, J. P. (1995) 'Effects of explicit teaching and peer tutoring on the reading achievement of learning disabled and low performing students in regular classrooms', *Elementary School Journal*, **95** (5), 387–408.

Slavin, R. E. (1996) 'Neverstreaming: Ending learning disabilities before they start', *Support for Learning*, **11** (2), 74–76.

Semmel, M. I., Abernathy, T. V., Butera, G. and Lesar, S. (1991) 'Teacher perceptions of the Regular Education Initiative', *Exceptional Children*, **58** (1), 9–23.

Simpson, R. L. and Myles, B. S. (1989) 'Parents' mainstreaming preferences for children with educable mental handicaps, behavior disorders and learning disabilities', *Psychology in the Schools*, **26** (3), 292–301.

Slee, R. (1995) 'Inclusive education: From policy to school implementation', In Clark, C., Dyson, A., and Millward, A. (eds) *Towards Inclusive Schools?* London: David Fulton. pp. 30–41.

Stainback, W. and Stainback, S. (1984) 'A rationale for the merger of special and regular education', *Exceptional Children*, **51**, 102–11.

Stainback, W. and Stainback, S. (eds) (1990) *Support Networks for Inclusive Schooling: Interdependent Integrated Education*. Baltimore: Paul H. Brookes.

Stakes, R. and Hornby, G. (1996) 'Special educational needs and the national curriculum'. In Andrews, R. (ed.) *Interpreting the New National Curriculum*. London: Middlesex University Press, pp. 208–15.

Swann, W. (1985) 'Is the integration of children with special needs happening? An analysis of recent statistics of pupils in special schools', *Oxford Review of Education*, **11** (1), 3–18.

Swann, W. (1991) *Variations between LEAs in Levels of Segregation in Special Schools, 1982–1990: Preliminary Report*. London: Centre for Studies on Integration in Education.

Thomas, G. (1992) *Effective Classroom Teamwork: Support or Intrusion*. London: Routledge.

Tizard, J. (1978) 'Research in special education', *Special Education: Forward Trends*, **5** (3), 23–26.

Vaughn, S. and Schumm, J. S. (1995) 'Responsible inclusion for students with learning disabilities', *Journal of Learning Disabilities*, **28** (5), 264–70, 290.

Visser, J. (1993) 'A broad, balanced, relevant and differentiated curriculum'. In Visser, J. and Upton, G. (eds) *Special Education in Britain after Warnock*. London: David Fulton, pp. 1–12.

Wang, M. C. and Walberg, H. J. (1983) 'Adaptive instruction and classroom time', *American Educational Research Journal*, **20**, 601–26.

Warnock, M. (1992) 'Special case in need of reform', *The Observer*, Schools Report, **18 October**, 3.

Warnock, M. (1993) Foreword. In Visser, J. and Upton, G. (eds) *Special Education in Britain after Warnock*. London: David Fulton, pp. vii–xi.

Welton, J. (1989) 'Incrementalism to catastrophe theory: Policy for children with special educational needs'. In Roaf, C. and Bines, H. (eds) *Needs, Rights and Opportunities*. Lewes: Falmer Press, pp. 20–27.

Wilton, K. (1994) 'Special education policy for learners with mild intellectual disability in New Zealand: Problems and issues', *International Journal of Disability, Development and Education*, **41** (2), 143–58.

Wisniewski, L. and Alper, S. (1994) 'Including students with severe disabilities in general education settings: Guidelines for change', *Remedial and Special Education*, **15** (1), 4–13.

Zigler, E. and Hodapp, R. M. (1986) *Understanding Mental Retardation*. Cambridge: Cambridge University Press.

6   Exclusions – Whose Needs are Being Met?

The extent of the problem

Evidence indicates that in the 1990s there has been a sharp increase in the number of pupils excluded from schools (DfE, 1992, 1993; ILEA, 1990; Lloyd-Smith, 1993; Merrick and Manuel, 1991; NUT, 1992; Parffrey, 1994; Stirling, 1992). The DfE study of permanent exclusions in state schools showed a rise of approximately 32% between 1991 and 1992 and concluded that the number of children excluded was too great. More recent figures of total permanent exclusions show a rise from 3,833 to 11,181 from 1992 to 1994 (nearly treble) and a figure of 12,458 for 1994–95 (DfE, 1995). Some sources, including the NUT (1992), however, believe that accurate figures are not available so that official figures may be underestimated. The conclusion must be that there is an increasing tendency for schools to use exclusion as a way of resolving the problem of disruptive and difficult pupils. Their expulsion from schools has become a major cause for concern for parents, teachers, local authorities, the government and the public at large (Advisory Centre for Education, 1991; DES, 1989; DfE, 1992; DfE 1994b).

Stirling (1992) highlights evidence of unofficial and informal exclusions which also mask the true figures and which make real exclusion rates difficult to quantify. Pupils may be on the school premises, but excluded by not being allowed to be involved in school activities (Cohen and Hughes, 1994; Secondary Heads Association (SHA), 1992). The view of Booth (1996) is that the issue of exclusion is more complex than purely 'disciplinary' exclusion. He believes that to get a real measure of exclusion rates a whole series of exclusionary events which take place in school needs to be taken into account together. Only in this way can a whole picture be built up and effective strategies for addressing the problem be implemented. Parffrey (1994) concludes that the whole of the education system is becoming increasingly intolerant and exclusive.

The present context

The 1981 Education Act supported the principle of integration and the right for all pupils to have their needs addressed, as far as possible, within mainstream education. This principle was further extended in the 1986 Education Act and the Elton Report (DES, 1989) which focused on discipline in schools. However, the introduction of the 1988 Education Reform Act, with the development of the national curriculum, local management of schools and its emphasis on market forces and league tables has led to a new 'intolerance and impatience towards difference and difficulty' (Parffrey, 1994). Parffrey notes that disaffected pupils are demanding and time-consuming, bad for the image of the school and bad for league tables. Also, that teachers are already pressed for time and already face a multitude of demands.

Under the 1981 Education Act pupils with emotional and behavioural difficulties were defined in relation to learning under the term special educational need. Following the introduction of the *Code of Practice on the Identification and Assessment of Pupils with Special Educational Needs* (DfE, 1994a) this continued to be the case, with these pupils clearly identified within the Code under paragraphs 3.64–3.70 and their difficulties defined in relation to learning in paragraph 2:1(b):

> has a disability which either prevents or hinders the child from making use of educational facilities of a kind provided for children of the same age in schools within the area of the LEA.
>
> (DfE, 1994a: 5).

The *Code*, however, does not make explicit the link between emotional and behavioural difficulties and learning. Pupils with emotional and behavioural difficulties are expected to have their needs met through the staged process and individual education plans in the same way as those with learning difficulties but it is not possible as yet to judge whether the framework of the *Code* is going to help address their complex needs.

The 1993 Education Act introduced legal changes to the exclusion system which were designed to prevent pupils 'drifting' within the system and to reduce the adverse impact of exclusion on pupils. The main changes included limitation of the fixed period exclusion to a maximum of 15 days in any one school term and the abolition of indefinite exclusions. The powers of the LEA to provide 'education otherwise than at school' were replaced by a duty to do so. The DfE also produced six circulars entitled *Pupils with Problems* (DfE, 1994b) in which pupils with emotional and behavioural difficulties are described as being on a continuum with their problems lying between 'occasional bouts of naughtiness, and mental illness'. The document included an explanation of the changes in law governing exclusions together with guidance to schools on the circumstances warranting exclusion and the powers, rights and duties of headteachers, governing bodies, local education authorities, pupils and parents or guardians. It also provides advice for schools on pupil behaviour and discipline, based on the findings of the Elton Report (DES, 1989), and guidance on good practice in the education of children with emotional and behavioural difficulties.

More recently, however the government has announced further measures to address discipline and exclusions (Young, 1996). The new measures, on which the DfEE is to produce further guidance in the future, will include:

1. Provision of a legal basis for detention so that schools can detain pupils without parental permission.
2. Nine weeks' fixed term exclusion per year instead of three weeks per term.
3. Mandatory school discipline policies.
4. Provision for schools to make home–school contracts a condition of admission.
5. The LEA to choose, rather than the parents, the school attended after two exclusions.
6. Improved management of pupil referral units.
7. LEAs to maintain a statement of:
   (a) the arrangements made for pupils with behavioural difficulties including advice and assistance to schools;
   (b) the arrangements made for excluded pupils;
   (c) how they assist children with behavioural difficulties back into schools.

The DfEE will produce guidance on how to achieve this.

However, these changes in policy and procedure, whilst they may be beneficial, do not provide any extra support for teachers in mainstream schools to help address the needs of these pupils and no extra provision for those pupils who will be more likely to be excluded as a result of these measures.

Cooper, Smith and Upton (1994: 2) comment that:

> In the light of the circumstances, there has, perhaps, never been a worse time than the present to be a pupil experiencing emotional and behavioural difficulties in school, or a more challenging time to be a teacher faced with a difficult pupil.

Pupils at risk

The DfE (1992) found that certain groups of children were more at risk of exclusion than others. Over 80% of permanent exclusions are from secondary schools, with the peak rate being at the age of 15 years (DfE, 1992, 1993; Mitchell, 1996; Parsons and Howlett, 1996). However, Parffrey (1994) notes the alarming appearance and increase in the number of primary school exclusions. Recent statistics (DfE, 1995) show that in 1994–95 this figure continues to rise and is giving cause for concern (Hayden, 1996; OFSTED, 1993; Parsons, 1996). Boys are between four and five times more likely to be excluded than girls (DfE, 1992; DfE, 1993; Parsons *et al.*, 1995; SHA, 1992) and African–Caribbean boys are most at risk (Cohen and Hughes, 1994; Commission for Racial Equality (CRE), 1985; DfE, 1993; Grant and Brooks, 1996; Mayet, 1992; NUT, 1992).

Pupils who have been formally assessed for special educational needs account for between 12% and 15% of permanently excluded pupils (DfE, 1993). With regard to pupils with special needs in mainstream schools, Blythe and Milner (1996) believe that, given the length of the assessment process, it is not surprising that researchers have found that schools are increasingly resorting to the speedier exclusion process, sometimes using it to secure additional resources for the child (Cohen and Hughes, 1994; Searle, 1994; Stirling, 1992; Todman *et al.*, 1991). The number of pupils excluded from special schools which are specially designed to cater for their needs is also rising (Parffrey, 1994; Parsons *et al.*, 1995; Parsons and Howlett, 1996).

Other children particularly at risk of exclusion are those in the care of the local authority. Stirling (1992) found that children in care comprised 23% of all those permanently excluded. Galloway *et al.* (1982) found that nearly a quarter of excluded pupils had been in local authority care at some stage in their lives. In a joint review of the education of 'looked after' children the health authority and the education department record their concern about the high percentage of children aged 14–16 who are excluded from school or who do not attend on a regular basis (Social Services Inspectorate (SSI) and OFSTED, 1995).

Reasons for exclusions

Current evidence indicates a wide variety of circumstances result in exclusion from school. Almost the entire population of permanently excluded pupils has, however, been excluded on the grounds of behaviour which may variously be described as aggressive, violent and disruptive, but always as unacceptable (Parsons and Howlett, 1996). Generally exclusion is associated with issues relating to the management and control of pupils (Blythe and Milner, 1996). Disobedience of a variety of forms, i.e. failure to respond to authority, plays a major role (DfE, 1993) including negative, disruptive, insolent and uncooperative behaviours (DfE, 1992,1993; NUT, 1992). The National Union of Teachers lists five main reasons for pupil exclusions. In order of priority these are disruptive/negative attitude to school (including verbal abuse, defiance, bad language, insolence, refusal to obey instructions); assaults/bullying; pilfering; malicious damage; absconding from schools/poor attendance. These reasons broadly equate with those found by Mitchell (1996). Exclusion for violent behaviour remains at a relatively low level (DfE, 1992; Gale and Topping, 1986; Imich, 1994; NUT, 1992) although concern about physical and sexual violence towards teachers must be seen in the context of the current climate of preserving the image of the school, which militates against the reporting of violent incidents (Blythe and Milner, 1996). In many incidences of exclusion it appears that the precipitating factor may be relatively minor, e.g. wearing an earring (Cohen and Hughes, 1994; Garner, 1994). McManus (1995), however, expresses a note of caution as categorisation of reasons is open to individual interpretation or even idiosyncrasy, which he believes is partly responsible for the school differences in exclusion rates.

The Advisory Centre for Education (ACE) blames pressure on resources for pupils with special educational needs leading schools to regard pupils as 'naughty' rather than 'needy' in order to access resources (ACE, 1991). OFSTED (1993) indicated a number of possible hypotheses for the increasing rate of exclusions, including increased family stress, reduced teacher tolerance, a way to bring parents into school, a means of raising the image of schools by being seen to be tough, as a response to pupils who fail to turn up regularly for school, staffing difficulties in inner city schools, loss of informal arrangements for transfer between schools and, in addition, a means of securing special educational needs resources for pupils.

The NUT study places a different emphasis on the causes and blames insufficient resources under local management of schools, league tables, deteriorating home circumstances and lack of parental discipline (NUT, 1992). The pressure on schools to achieve in performance tables and compete for admissions has left heads reluctant to help such pupils as they are bad for the image of the school (Stirling, 1992). It is more beneficial, for example, for a school to exclude a truant rather than record their absence as 'unauthorised' (Blythe and Milner, 1996), although the government has expressed disapproval of the use of exclusion with truants (DfE, 1994b). Educational reforms, such as the introduction of the national curriculum, has led to less flexibility and responsiveness to pupils who are experiencing emotional problems or those who are not orientated to achievement with consequent adverse effects on attendance, achievement and behaviour (Blythe and Milner, 1993, 1994). The introduction of local management of schools with increasing independence from local authority control has also increased the reluctance of schools to admit previously excluded pupils. This has been more evident the more independent the school is (SHA, 1992; Stirling, 1992).

Parsons and Howlett (1996) group reasons for exclusions into four main categories: psychosocial problems, family and social problems, stretched educational resources, and cultural factors. They point to larger classes, a limiting and demanding National Curriculum causing teachers to have to ration time, care and attention to the most demanding pupils, the tension between business ethic and professional ethic and the local management of schools. Factors cited outside the school include the rise in psychiatric disorders of young people (Department of Health, 1994; Smith and Rutter, 1995) and an increase in poverty, family breakdown and lack of parental discipline (Hayden, 1996;

NUT, 1992; Parsons, 1996). McManus (1995) believes that a fifth of a school's level of exclusion can be accounted for by catchment area poverty.

Excluded pupils are seen by many teachers as culprits rather than victims and their behaviour is seldom viewed as evidence of a need (Parsons and Howlett, 1996). This locates the problem firmly within the child and allows schools to abdicate responsibility for them. Many teachers believe that the children's rights movement has taken away their authority and left them feeling that the only option they have left often is exclusion (Dineen, 1993; O'Leary, 1995; Preston, 1993; Stirling, 1992). In a similar way the increase in parents' rights has resulted in pressure being placed on some heads to exclude pupils (Blythe and Milner, 1996).

Different reasons have, therefore, been cited by different people, but, whether caused by stresses on children (such as home break-up or bereavement) or stresses in the school system (such as more children with special needs in mainstream schools and larger classes), the result is a rising number of children receiving home tuition or education in a pupil referral unit.

The variation in exclusion rates between schools

The available evidence suggests that the underlying trend for the increasing number of exclusions lies within a context-related rather than a child-related rationale (Mitchell, 1996). This is also suggested by the difference in exclusion rates between schools which is well documented (DfE, 1992, 1993; Galloway, 1982; Imich, 1994; McManus, 1990; NUT, 1992; SHA, 1992). The DfE (1992) found that there was a large variation in exclusion rates between schools which could not be explained by differences in intake or catchment area, that existing exclusion procedures were not properly adhered to and that provision for excluded pupils showed unacceptable variations in both quality and quantity from one area to another. There is also a large amount of evidence which shows that headteachers' attitudes, school status, policies and practices may exert a greater effect on the likelihood of exclusion than a pupil's behaviour (Galloway *et al.*, 1982; Imich, 1994; McManus, 1995). McManus estimates that differences in school policies could account for about half of the difference between schools which exclude relatively large numbers of pupils and those that exclude relatively few. Mitchell (1996) indicates that a difference in internal practices within schools may be responsible. It has been found that exclusions rates, for example, are higher in schools where behaviour problems are not dealt with in the classroom and are quickly referred up through the system (DES, 1989). Benson (1996) and Mitchell (1996) suggest that exclusion rates may be influenced by philosophical beliefs of the headteacher or senior management team which filters down through the hierarchy of the teaching staff through school policies, teaching styles, support structures and disciplinary processes.

The implications of exclusion

It is well established that when exclusion takes place there is considerable distress to the children themselves, their families and also the school involved (Blythe and Milner, 1993; Cohen and Hughes, 1994). The educational, social and emotional implications for those who are excluded can be considerable and there has been long-standing concern about these adverse effects (Carlen, 1985; DfE, 1992; Hibbett and Fogelman, 1990; Hibbett *et al.*, 1990). Although a relationship between delinquency and school behaviour has been long established, the relationship between delinquency and exclusion has only recently been investigated (Searle, 1994; Stirling, 1996; Cullingford and Morrison, 1996). Parffrey (1994) notes that we are increasing the likelihood of delinquent behaviour by excluding adolescents from the very means by which appropriate behaviour may be learnt, by giving them so little to do with their time that vast amounts of it are spent aimlessly and by emphasising their non-acceptability through intolerance and exclusion. Graham (1988) reviews the research evidence which suggests that delinquency is at least in part dependant on being rejecting of or rejected by school. The DfE itself expresses concern that excluded pupils may be becoming involved in crime (DfE, 1993) and the National Association for the Care and Resettlement of Offenders (1993) emphasises the preventative role that schools can play by holding on to disaffected pupils. Already vulnerable pupils feel rejected and increasingly alienated from society. Cullingford and Morrison (1996), Stirling (1996) and Booth (1996) have also identified a 'psychological' exclusion which significantly affects the child even before physical exclusion occurs. For those in care, for whom stability is a major concern, the school may well be the only constant source of stability in a disrupted and troubled life (Firth and Horrocks, 1996). There is also evidence that excluded pupils may be placed at increased physical and emotional risk and that the impact may be felt by the family through aggravation of financial problems and increased emotional tension (Cohen and Hughes, 1994). Grant and Brooks (1996), concerned about the increasing number of black children excluded from school, suggest strategies to be used by parents for coping if this happens to their child.

The financial costs of exclusion may also be considerable. Parsons (1996) argues that other parts of the educational system and other services, particularly social services, often bare the cost of supporting the excluded child to the extent that the aggregate cost of this support is greater than if the child were maintained in mainstream education. He notes that the child becomes 'debris' outside of the system with services moving more slowly to address the 'ejected' problem and the child is left with no support. The way back for the pupil is difficult and the various means are under-financed and under-resourced. He argues that a significant change in orientation needs to take place if these children are to be given a chance to remain integrated or to be re-integrated in such a way that they become accepted and accepting members of society. Finance aside, the principle should be that we do not permit such damaging rejection experiences to happen to the developing young. There are, therefore, a number of financial, economical, social, psychological and educational implications of exclusion.

The educational future of excluded pupils is clearly also in question. Headteachers appear to be increasingly reluctant to accept children who have been excluded from other schools and relatively few permanently excluded pupils are readmitted to another mainstream school (NUT, 1992; Parsons *et al.*, 1993; SHA, 1992; Stirling, 1992). Recent statistics (Young, 1996) show that only 15% of pupils excluded permanently from secondary schools return to mainstream schooling. There is often considerable delay between the different stages of the exclusion process and delay in providing alternative educational provision for pupils (DfE, 1992; Mitchell, 1996). They may be out of the educational system for several months or even years leading to considerable disruption of their educational careers with little chance of returning successfully to a system which has ignored their needs for so long (Mitchell, 1996). Alternative provision, usually through a pupil referral unit or home tuition, has often been criticised for being inadequate in terms of both quantity and quality (DfE, 1992; Parffrey, 1994; Parsons *et al.*, 1995).

Educational provision for excluded pupils

Young (1996) states that 40% of excluded pupils attend pupil referral units for half time or less and 25% receive home tuition for a few hours per week. Only three LEAs provide more than 10 hours per week tuition for permanently excluded pupils. Parffrey (1994) reviews provision in one LEA and questions whether it is adequate in both quality and quantity. She notes that education in a pupil referral unit or exclusion unit is usually only part-time and places are limited, although there is a good teacher:pupil ratio and teachers usually have experience of working with pupils with challenging behaviour. She expresses concern, however, that greater provision of such units may allow schools to abdicate responsibility for these pupils and stresses that these units need to work in partnership with schools to re-integrate excluded pupils (Parffrey, 1990).

Home tuition is only provided for a few hours per week and usually by teachers who have no training in dealing with difficult pupils. Mitchell (1996), studying one LEA's provision, noted that approximately 50 pupils were receiving home tuition for 2 hours daily and that although this was originally intended for pupils who were out of school for medical reasons almost half were excluded from school or exhibited severe behavioural difficulties.

Some excluded pupils are offered temporary placements in psychiatric units if their emotional difficulties predominate. Staff at such units, however, report that schools are increasingly unwilling to accept these pupils back into school even after a period of treatment. Parffrey (1994) concludes that the provision available for these pupils sums up the system's attitude to them, that they do not matter or 'out of sight out of mind'. It is questionable as to whether they are receiving their entitlement to education.

The relationship between exclusions and special educational needs

The Advisory Centre for Education (1991) found that the highest proportion of excluded pupils were children with special educational needs. Despite this, the relationship between exclusions and special educational needs has largely been left unexplored (Booth, 1996). Whilst pupils with emotional and behavioural difficulties are clearly identified under the *Code of Practice* (DfE, 1994a), Parsons and Howlett (1996) claim that this has not offered much for these pupils thus far. Parsons *et al.* (1995) highlight the variation in LEA practices with regard to implementation of the *Code* and the guidance in *Pupils with Problems* (DfE, 1994b). If the *Code* is being implemented properly for these pupils one would expect pupils at risk from exclusion to have been assessed at stage three of the *Code* for emotional and behavioural difficulties, but only a small proportion of LEAs stated that they expected this to be the case. Similarly, only a small number regarded the behaviour of excluded pupils as evidence of special educational need. On the other hand eight LEAs regarded all pupils out of school to be at stage three and a further 14 made some connection between exclusion and special educational needs.

The connection between behaviour and learning is recognised in official reports, such as the Elton Report (DES, 1989), and within the *Code of Practice* (DfE, 1994a) pupils with emotional and behavioural problems are described as having learning difficulties. Despite this, Booth (1996) notes the separateness of disciplinary exclusions and special needs which he believes is part of a pervasive and unproductive separation of difficulties of behaviour and learning in schools. This is also illustrated by divisions between pastoral and special needs staff. In practice, therefore, it may be a matter of chance whether a pupil is subject to formal disciplinary action, sent to an off-site unit, deemed as having emotional and behavioural difficulties or learning difficulties, or formally assessed for a special school placement. It has been shown, for example, that admission to pupil referral units is rarely determined by clear and consistent LEA policy (DfE, 1994b).

Booth (1996) argues that by avoiding the formal assessment process for pupils who are excluded the school retains a fast disposal route out of mainstream education for pupils who cause them a problem. Schools need to examine their internal procedures especially with regard to the *Code of Practice* and its use with pupils with emotional and behavioural difficulties (Normington, 1996). Normington argues that the needs of those who are disruptive and disaffected are as special as those with more obvious disabilities.

They should be assessed and provided for in the same way and with the same dedication if we are to prevent an increase in the number of alienated adolescents growing up into unfulfilled adults. There needs to be a recognition that the difficult behaviour of some pupils is evidence of a special educational need (Parsons and Howlett, 1996). This is an attitude which, Parsons and Howlett argue, is encouraged through the *Code of Practice*.

Teachers' needs

Parffrey (1994) believes that exclusion of pupils is a response to professionals not knowing how to solve problems, feeling overwhelmed and powerless and fearful and anxious that they do not have the time, resources, support or skills to cope with these children. She describes these pupils as:

> scapegoats of a system that cannot cope, a system which feels increasingly under pressure to meet a variety of conflicting demands in ever decreasing time deadlines, a system overwhelmed and failing in coping with its own change (p. 117).

Mainstream teachers now require expertise in dealing with pupils with emotional and behavioural difficulties as part of their role, but there is evidence to suggest that they feel ill-equipped to do so (Cooper, Smith and Upton, 1990, 1991; DES, 1985, 1989). The Elton Report (DES, 1989) showed that many teachers continue without the professional and emotional support which they could receive from those with special expertise, such as their own pastoral, counselling and special needs staff or outside specialists. Medway (1976) states that teachers often become defensive with disaffected pupils, whose needs then become even less likely to be met. Pik (1986), for example, discusses the strong, uncomfortable feelings which confrontation situations may provoke in teachers and the effects that these may have if not addressed. Sivanandan (1994; quoted in Searle, 1996: 46) states that:

> Exclusion is seldom the measure of a child's capacity to learn; it is an indication instead of the teacher's refusal to be challenged.

Teachers cannot be expected to meet such children's needs if they get no support with their own needs (Hanko, 1993). Hanko states that teachers need support for their work with pupils who are disturbed or disturbing. She comments that the specialist skills, principles and practices required to relieve emotional problems are as yet rarely conveyed to teachers. These pupils tend, therefore, not to receive the early help to which they might be able to respond and they continue to indicate their needs in ways which schools find unacceptable, thereby worsening their difficulties.

For some time there has been official recognition of the need to improve the professional development of teachers to enable them to respond appropriately to the exceptional needs of pupils which they encounter (The Advisory Committee on the Supply and Education of Teachers, 1984). This is supported by Dessent (1987) and Hegarty (1989). The Elton Report (DES, 1989) recommended that whole school policy be developed to deal with discipline problems and recent government initiatives include placing a duty on schools to have a discipline policy. There is, therefore, a need for associated in-service training to foster this. The integration of pupils with emotional and behavioural difficulties into mainstream settings demands the widening of subject teachers' skill base to include the ability to cope effectively with these pupils (Cooper, Smith and Upton, 1994).

Inter-agency response

Trying to help support children with complex difficulties and needs in school is likely to require the expertise and support of several agencies and professions (Hayden, 1996). The literature emphasises that the network of inter-agency support is crucial in addressing pupil's needs (e.g. Beveridge, 1993; Dessent, 1987; Garner, 1994; NUT, 1993; Normington and Kyriacou, 1994). There are a number of outside agencies and support services which provide pupil-centred and teacher-centred support in the field of emotional and behavioural difficulties. These include educational psychologists, teachers from the special needs support service, outreach workers from pupil referral units, education welfare officers and school nurses. Any network of support is only likely to be effective where there is clear understanding and communication about complementary roles and responsibilities of all concerned in meeting pupils' needs (Beveridge, 1993). Evidence suggests that most teachers perceive the experts as inaccessible (Desforges, 1988; Hegarty and Pocklington, 1981) and often only use these services when they are convinced that the child is impossible to cope with rather than at an earlier stage when there is more chance of remediation (Hanko, 1993). Specialists can only hope to meet the increasing need by augmenting the ability of teachers to help these pupils. This has been advocated in a number of official reports (DES, 1968, 1989), circulars (e.g. DES/DHSS, 1974) and by leading experts in this field (Tizard, 1973; Wall, 1973).

Hayden (1996), believing that pupils who are in the greatest need of social and educational support are most at risk of exclusion, illustrates with case studies how a multi-disciplinary approach can be used to mobilise resources for these pupils. This is supported by Normington (1996) who shows how inter-agency collaboration can make flexible use of available resources. Hayden jusifies providing this support before a pupil reaches the stage of exclusion because exclusion creates additional pressure on services and, by allowing the situation to deteriorate to permanent exclusion, adds to the difficulties of already vulnerable children. Failing to support these children at this early stage is likely to present society greater problems later on. *Pupils with Problems* (DfE, 1994b) sets out a framework designed to promote inter-organisational and inter-professional co-operation and partnership in providing services for schoolchildren and identifies critical areas where inter-agency co-operation should occur, for example, joint education and social services strategies to meet the educational needs of children in care.

Concern is now deepening about the prospects of these pupils, who will become increasingly marginalised if teachers do not get adequate support and help in understanding how best to respond to their needs.

Conclusion

Exclusion is used increasingly by schools as a way of resolving the problem of disruptive pupils and this is becoming a major cause for concern. Those pupils identified as being particulary at risk of exclusion are Afro-Caribbean boys, pupils with special educational needs and those looked after in local authority provision. Many factors have been cited as the reason for the increasing use of exclusion, but whether factors within the family, school or the system are responsible the result has been more pupils alienated from mainstream schools and rising numbers of children receiving limited education in pupil referral units or through home tuition. Increasingly schools are reluctant to accept excluded pupils. The implications of exclusion for the child, the family, the school and society are great. These include financial, economical, social, psychological as well as educational implications and their impact cannot be overemphasised. More, therefore, needs to be done to ensure that these pupils receive their entitlement to education and to re-integrate them back into mainstream education where not only their educational but also their social and emotional needs can be met.

The issue of exclusion cannot be separated, however, from the issue of special educational needs. Pupils with emotional and behavioural difficulties are identified within the special needs *Code of Practice* and are entitled to have their needs addressed through the staged process and individual educational plans in the same way as those with learning difficulties. In this way pupils' needs can be identified at an early stage before the exclusion, which only creates additional pressure on services and on an already vulnerable pupil. This requires, however, a recognition by teachers that those who exhibit behavioural difficulties are demonstrating evidence of need and a recognition that there is much that schools can do to alleviate the difficulties of these pupils. They cannot do this, however, without adequate support and training and without their own needs being met. Excluded pupils often have complex and varied needs that cannot be addressed by the school alone and require the expertise and support from several agencies and professions. By working collaboratively with other agencies teachers may feel more able to meet the needs of this challenging group of pupils.

References

Advisory Centre for Education (1991) 'Exclusions', *ACE Bulletin*, **47**, 4–5.

Advisory Committee on the Supply and Education of Teachers (1984) *Teacher Training and Special Educational Needs*. London: ACSET.

Benson, C. (1996) 'Resisting the trend to exclude'. In Blythe, E. and Milner, J. (eds) *Exclusion from School: Inter-professional Issues for Policy and Practice*. London: Routledge, pp. 208–23.

Beveridge, S. (1993) *Special Educational Needs in Schools*. London: Routledge.

Blythe, E. and Milner, J. (1993) 'Exclusion from school: a first step in exclusion from society?' *Children and Society*, **7 (3)**, 20–34.

Blythe, E. and Milner, J. (1994) 'Exclusion from school and victim-blaming', *Oxford Review of Education*, **20 (3)**, 293–306.

Blythe, E. and Milner, J. (1996) 'Exclusions: trends and issues'. In Blythe, E. and Milner, J. (eds) *Exclusion from School: Inter-professional Issues for Policy and Practice*. London: Routledge, pp. 3–20.

Booth, T. (1995) 'Mapping inclusion and exclusion: concepts for all?' In Clark, C., Dyson, D. and Millward, A. (eds) *Towards Inclusive Schools*? London: David Fulton.

Booth, T. (1996) 'Stories of exclusion: natural and unnatural selection'. In Blythe, E. and Milner, J. (eds) *Exclusion from School: Inter-professional Issues for Policy and Practice*. London: Routledge, pp. 21–36.

Carlen, P. (1985) 'Out of care into custody'. In Carlen, P. and Worrall, A. (eds) *Gender, Crime and Justice*. Milton Keynes: Open University Press.

Cohen, R. and Hughes, M. (1994) *School's Out: the Family Perspective on School Exclusion*, London: Family Service Units, Barnados.

Commission for Racial Equality (1985) *Birmingham LEA and Schools: Referral and Suspension of Pupils*. London: CRE.

Cooper, P., Smith, C. and Upton, G. (1990) 'The qualification and training requirements of teachers in schools for pupils with emotional and behavioural difficulties in England and Wales', *British Journal of In-service Education*, **16 (3)**, 188–95.

Cooper, P., Smith, C. and Upton, G. (1991) 'The qualifications and training of workers for pupils with EBD', *Maladjustment and Therapeutic Education*, **9 (2)**, 83–87.

Cooper, P., Smith, C. and Upton, G. (1994) *Emotional and Behavioural Difficulties: Theory to Practice*. London: Routledge.

Cullingford, C. and Morrison, J. (1996) 'Who excludes whom? The personal experience of exclusion'. In Blythe, E. and Milner, J. (eds) *Exclusion from School: Inter-professional Issues for Policy and Practice*. London: Routledge, pp. 130–48.

Department for Education (1992) *Exclusions: A Discussion Paper*. London: HMSO.

Department for Education (1993) *National Exclusions Reporting System*. Press Release. London: DfE.

Department for Education (1994a) *The Code of Practice on the Identification and Assessment of Special Educational Needs*. London: DfE.

Department for Education (1994b) *Pupils with Problems (Circulars 8/94 to 13/94)*. London: DfE.

Department for Education (1995) *National Survey of LEAs' Policies and Procedures for the Identification of and Provision for Children who are out of School by Reason of Exclusion or Otherwise*. Pupils and Parents Branch. London: DfE.

Department of Education and Science (1968) *Psychologists in the Education Service*

(The Summerfield Report). London: HMSO.

Department of Education and Science and the Department of Health and Social Security (1974) *Child Guidance, Circular 3/74*. London: HMSO.

Department of Education and Science (1985) *Education Observed: Good Teachers*. London: HMSO.

Department of Education and Science (1989) *Discipline in Schools: A Report of the Committee of Enquiry chaired by Lord Elton (The Elton Report)*. London: HMSO.

Department of Health (1994) *A Handbook on Child and Adolescent Mental Health*. Manchester: HMSO.

Desforges, C. (1988) 'Psychology and the management of classrooms'. In Jones, N. and Sayer, J. (eds) *Management and the Psychology of Schooling*. Lewes: Falmer, pp. 10–23.

Dessent, T. (1987) *Making the Ordinary School Special*. Lewes: Falmer.

Dineen, B. (1993) 'Teachers pay high price for classroom control', *Yorkshire Post*, **8 March**, 9.

Firth, H. and Horrocks, C. (1996) 'No home, no school, no future: Exclusions and children who are "looked after"'. In Blythe, E. and Milner, J. (eds) *Exclusion from School: Inter-professional Issues for Policy and Practice*. London: Routledge, pp. 76–91.

Gale, I. and Topping, K. (1986) 'Suspension from high school: the practice and its effects'. *Pastoral Care*, **November**, 215–24.

Galloway, D. (1982) 'A study of pupils suspended from school', *British Journal of Educational Psychology*, **52**, 205–12.

Galloway, D., Ball, T., Blomfield, D. and Seyd, R. (1982) *Schools and Disruptive Pupils*. London: Longman.

Garner, P. (1994) 'Exclusions from school: towards a new agenda'. *Pastoral Care in Education*, **12**, 3–9.

Graham, J. (1988) *Schools, Disruptive behaviour and Delinquency: A Review of Research*. Home Office Research Study No. 96, London: HMSO.

Grant, D. and Brooks, K. (1996) 'Exclusions from school: responses from the black community'. *Pastoral Care in Education*, **14 (3)**, 20–27.

Hanko, G. (1993) *Special Needs in Ordinary Classrooms*. Hemel Hempstead: Simon & Schuster.

Hayden, C. (1996) 'Primary school exclusions: the need for integrated solutions'. In Blythe, E. and Milner, J. (eds) *Exclusion from School: Inter-professional Issues for Policy and Practice*. London: Routledge, pp. 224–36.

Hegarty, S. (1989) *Special Needs in Ordinary Schools*. London: Cassell.

Hegarty, S. and Pocklington, K. (1981) *Educating Pupils with Special Needs in the Ordinary School*. Windsor: NFER-Nelson.

Hibbett, A. and Fogelman, K. (1990) 'Future lives of truants: family formation and health related behaviour', *British Journal of Educational Psychology*, **60**, 171–79.

Hibbett, A., Fogelman, K. and Manor, O. (1990) 'Occupation and outcomes of truancy', *British Journal of Educational Psychology*, **60**, 23–36.

Imich, I. (1994) Exclusions from school: current trends and issues. *Educational Research*, **36 (1)**, 3–11.

Inner London Education Authority (1990) *Expulsions and Exclusions from Schools*. London: ILEA.

Lloyd-Smith, M. (1993) 'Problem behaviour, Exclusions and the Policy Vacuum', *Pastoral Care in Education*, **11 (4)**, 19–24.

McManus, M. (1990) *Troublesome Behaviour in the Classroom*. London: Routledge.

McManus, M. (1995) *Troublesome Behaviour in the Classroom: Meeting Individual Needs*. (2nd edn.) London: Routledge.

Mayet, G. (1992) 'What hope is there for children with learning and behavioural difficulties?' *Concern*, **81 (Summer)**, 3.

Medway, P. (1976) 'Back with Nellie', *British Journal of Teacher Education*, **2 (2)**, 161–66.

Merrick, N. and Manuel, G. (1991) 'Authorities want an end to exclusion loophole', *Times Educational Supplement*, **25 October**, 1.

Mitchell, L. (1996) 'The effects of waiting time on excluded children'. In Blythe, E. and Milner, J. (eds) *Exclusion from School: Inter-professional Issues for Policy and Practice*. London: Routledge, pp. 116–29.

National Association for the Care and Resettlement of Offenders (1993) *Exclusions: A Response to the DfE Discussion Paper*. London: NACRO.

National Union of Teachers (1992) *Survey on Pupils' Exclusions: Information from LEAs. May*. London: NUT.

National Union of Teachers (1993) *Pupil Behaviour in Schools*. London: NUT.

Normington, J. (1996) 'Exclusion from school: the role of outside agencies'. In Blythe, E. and Milner, J. (eds) *Exclusion from School: Inter-professional Issues for Policy and Practice*. London: Routledge, pp. 237–49.

Normington, J. and Kyriacou, C. (1994) 'Exclusions from High Schools and the work of outside agencies involved', *Pastoral Care in Education*, **12**, 12–15.

Office for Standards in Education (1993) *Exclusions: A Response to the DfE Discussion Paper*. London: OFSTED.

O'Leary, J. (1995) 'Parents failing in duty to discipline, say headteachers', *The Times*, **31 May**, 6.

Parffrey, V. (1990) 'Tor Hill: an alternative to exclusion?' *Journal of the Association of Educational Psychologists*, **5**, 216–21.

Parffrey, V. (1994) 'Exclusion: failed children or systems failure?' *School Organisation*, **14 (2)**, 107–20.

Parsons, C. (1996) 'The cost of primary school exclusions'. In Blythe, E. and Milner, J. (eds) *Exclusion from School: Inter-professional Issues for Policy and Practice*. London: Routledge, pp. 107–115.

Parsons, C. and Howlett, K. (1996) 'Permanent exclusions from school: a case where society is failing its children', *Support for Learning*, **11 (3)**, 109–112.

Parsons, C., Benns, L, Hailes, J. and Howlett, K. (1994) *Excluding Primary School Children*. London: Family Policy Studies Centre.

Parsons, C., Hailes, J., Howlett, K., Davies, A. and Driscoll, P. (1995) *National Survey of Local Education Authorities' Policies and Procedures for the Identification of, and Provision for, Children who are Out of School by Reason of Exclusion or Otherwise*. Final Report to the Department for Education. Canterbury: Christ Church College.

Pik, R. (1986) 'Confrontation situations and teacher support'. In Cohen, A. and Cohen, L. (eds) *Special Educational Needs in the Ordinary School*. London: Harper and Row, pp. 199–218.

Preston, B. (1993) 'Teachers must learn to play safe', *The Times*, **27 February**, 15.

Searle, C. (1996) 'The signal of failure: school exclusions and the market system of education'. In Blythe, E., and Milner, J. (eds) *Exclusion from School: Inter-professional Issues for Policy and Practice*. London: Routledge, pp. 37–52.

Secondary Heads Association (1992) *Excluded from School: A Survey of Secondary School Suspensions*. Bristol: SHA.

Smith, D. and Rutter, M. (1995) 'Time trends in psycho-social disorders of youth'. In Rutter, M and Smith, D. (eds) *Psycho-social Disorders in Young People*. London: Wiley.

Social Services Inspectorate and OFSTED (1995) *The Education of Children who are Looked After by Local Authorities: A Joint Report Issued by the Social Services Inspectorate and the Office for Standards in Education*. London: Department of Health and OFSTED.

Stirling, M. (1992) 'How many pupils are being excluded?' *British Journal of Special Education*, **19** (4), 128–30.

Stirling, M. (1996) 'Government policy and disadvantaged children'. In Blythe, E. and Milner, J. (eds) *Exclusion from School: Inter-professional Issues for Policy and Practice*. London: Routledge, pp. 53–61.

Tizard, J. (1973) 'Maladjusted children and the child guidance service', *London Educational Review*, **2** (2), 22–37.

Todman, J., Justice, S. and Swanson, I. (1991) 'Disruptiveness and referral to the Educational Psychology service', *Educational Psychology in Practice*, **6** (4), 199–202.

Wall, W. (1973) 'The problem child in schools', *London Educational Review*, **2** (2), 3–21.

Young, S. (1996) 'LEAs return to exclusion zone', *Times Educational Supplement*, **15 November**, 23.

III Controversial Group Interventions

7 Conductive Education – Is it Effective?

What is conductive education (CE)?

CE is a system of education for children and adults with motor disorders, that is, those with problems controlling their body movements due to damage to the brain or spine, such as in cerebral palsy and spina bifida. CE is a comprehensive educational programme for children with motor disorders which originated from the work of Andras Peto at the Peto Institute in Hungary in the 1940s (Cottam and Sutton,1986). Its leading proponent today is Dr Maria Hari.

Context

Prior to 1985 CE was virtually unknown outside of Hungary, except for the work of Cotton (1965) who, following her observations at the Peto Institute, introduced the approach into a few schools in England in the 1970s. However, disappointing results of research on its effectiveness led to little importance being attached to this initiative. At the end of 1985 information on the work being undertaken in Budapest started to appear in the UK and some parents, learning of the success claimed for CE, went there to see for themselves (Sutton, 1986). Accounts were presented in the media of individual children apparently benefiting greatly from periods at the Peto Institute. An example of this was the television documentary *Standing up for Joe* (BBC1, 1 April, 1986) which evoked an enormous national response (Sutton,1989) and the setting up of the national pressure group Rapid Action for Conductive Education. Its aim was to ensure that CE was made available to motor disordered children in the UK.

Intense interest was also shown in other countries, including the USA. Subsequently, children from outside Hungary arrived in increasing numbers at the Peto Institute but because of the increased pressure for places they were only able to obtain short-term placements. The Foundation for Conductive Education, a national charity, was formed to meet the demand in the UK. The Foundation negotiated an agreement with the Peto Institute to transfer CE, initially on a small scale, to the Birmingham Institute for Conductive Education, which opened in September, 1987.

Other countries such as Australia, Hong Kong, Germany, New Zealand and the USA, influenced by anecdotal evidence and reports of success emanating from Hungary (Hari and Akos, 1971) have attempted to replicate CE (Coleman and King, 1990; Cotton, 1987; Hedges, 1988; Sigafoos *et al.*, 1993; Weber and Rochel, 1992, cited in Stukat, 1995; Yen, 1990). However, transplantation of CE to other countries has generally proved difficult and little success has been reported (Kozma,1995).

Theory and principles of CE

CE is based on the view that despite damage, the nervous system remains flexible and has a residual capacity which can be brought into use by teaching children to overcome the limitations imposed by their disabilities. The belief is that under the right conditions the central nervous system will restructure itself, although Oliver (1989) states that there is no evidence that this actually happens. The motor problems are regarded as learning difficulties to be overcome rather than medical conditions to be treated and therefore education, rather than therapy or training, is used to develop new skills (Presland, 1990; Sutton, 1989). The aim is for individuals to learn new ways to control their movements and thus to become independent.

CE is often described as a 'unified' or 'holistic' system of education (Hari and Akos, 1971; Sigafoos *et al.*, 1993). Proponents believe that children with cerebral palsy, for example, require an approach which confronts all of their problems in a unified way and that their problems consist not only of the initial presenting difficulties but also of a variety of other problems which interact with one another. Treatment and education is, therefore, aimed at the whole personality rather than directed to the disability in isolation (Swann, 1992). Peto's theory of education is 'conductive' in that the underlying belief is that children and adults learn and develop best when they have determined their own goals and set out determinedly to achieve them. This requires the conscious and motivated participation of the learner. The teacher facilitates the learning process by helping the learners to solve their own problems and structure their own methods (Sutton, 1989).

Aims and objectives

The aim of CE is that of 'orthofunction', which Swann (1992) believes is to teach individuals to master their disordered movements to the degree that they are able to function in the world despite their underlying physical disorders. The primary goal is to stimulate a developmental process which would not occur spontaneously and which will continue even after the child leaves the Institute (Hari and Tillemans, 1984). Orthofunction is both a process and a product, involving the re-establishment of a normal cycle of active learning and success in solving the problems of everyday living and attainment of a level that ensures functional independence (Sutton, 1989). CE aims to give individuals the ability to function as members of society without special apparatus such as wheelchairs, ramps or other artificial aids, adaptations, special measures or auxiliary helpers. This includes going to school and following the curriculum appropriate to the child's age and mental ability. CE aims also, therefore, to return children to mainstream schools, or to special schools if their learning difficulties necessitate this. More specific objectives such as sitting and walking are derived from these general aims (Presland, 1990) and the key objective is that children should eventually learn to do these tasks through their own efforts. Bairstow and Cochrane (1993) state, however, that there is no clear and coherent account in English of the aims, methods and principles of CE. Bairstow et al. (1993) also claim that there is no clear, specific definition of orthofunction.

Who is it for?

The Peto Institute provides education for those who suffer from motor disorder, which refers to an inability of the central nervous system to control movement in any part of the body. Of those children attending the Institute approximately 95% have cerebromotor dysfunction, 4% spinomotor dysfunction and 1% have peripheral motor dysfunction (Hari and Akos, 1971). The majority of individuals attending the Peto Institute suffer from cerebral palsy (Cottam and Sutton, 1986; Hari and Akos,1971). Children with muscular dystrophy or other degenerative conditions, or with defective limbs as a result of congenital conditions and not brain damage are deemed unsuitable.

Cerebral palsy is a neuromuscular dysfunction caused by non-progressive injury to the immature brain and results in various impairments of the ability to co-ordinate muscle action to maintain normal posture and movement (Hur and Cochrane, 1995). Two to three children in every 1,000 live births have cerebral palsy (British Medical Association, 1990). Cerebral palsy, however, presents a very wide range of manifestations including some children who are profoundly mentally handicapped and for whom their mental impairment must be regarded as the primary problem defining their special educational needs (Sutton, 1989).

British special schools set up to provide education for children with physical disabilities serve a more varied population than those in Hungary which provide CE. The British schools include children with severe learning difficulties, multiple handicaps and rare or degenerative conditions such as muscular dystrophy. In their evaluation of CE in the UK, Bairstow et al. (1993) state that the wide range of clinical conditions and functional characteristics of children have led to a high proportion of potential British clients for CE being judged unsuitable by senior Hungarian conductors. Only about 35% of British children with cerebral palsy have been deemed suitable. This is one factor which makes it very difficult to make comparisons between the reported effectiveness of CE in Hungary with that of the education provided for children with physical disabilities in the UK.

Characteristics of CE

The conductor

All teaching is done by conductors who train at the Peto Institute for 4 years before qualifying. The conductor's role is central to the implementation of CE and has developed out of the integrated system of CE (Hari and Akos, 1971; Kozma, 1995). In traditional methods of treatment the different needs of disabled individuals are dealt with by different professionals such as doctors, physiotherapists and teachers, but this is seen by the proponents of CE as the greatest obstacle to progression. The Peto Institute is strongly against dividing the work into specialist areas and sees this as a fragmented approach which is unhelpful for the child. In CE the conductor implements the entire programme and is responsible for all teaching and therapy. Conductors, therefore, combine several roles (Hur and Cochrane, 1995). The conductor's role is to facilitate learning by establishing goals which are attainable and desirable, and generate the motivation to persist and to succeed. The conductor regulates the activities of the group and occasionally works individually with children ascertaining the conditions necessary for them to complete tasks so that everyone in the group is able to achieve the group goal in their own way. Much emphasis is placed on the inter-personal relationship between the child and the conductor, as the aim is to educate the whole child (Hari and Akos, 1971; Sutton, 1988).

The group

Every activity in the daily schedule is conducted in a group, which is viewed as a 'therapeutic force' or a 'pedagogic tool' (Cottam and Sutton, 1986). A typical group consists of about 20–30 children, often with a wide age range and having various disabilities (Swann, 1992). The group, however, is considered to be united by the common educational aim and the daily work schedule, despite differences between its members (Hari and Akos,1971). The entire atmosphere is shaped by sharing common goals and tasks. Close interpersonal relationships between the individual members of the group are important for facilitating social and personal development, which are considered to be a vital part of achieving orthofunction. Children are arranged in the group so that those who are less able can observe and learn from the more able. Emphasis is placed on the function of the child in the group situation and the effect of the group on the child (Hur and Cochrane, 1995). However, the precise nature of the group organisation remains unreported and uninvestigated by those outside of Hungary (Sutton, 1989).

Rhythmical intention

Singing and rhythmic activities are incorporated into the programme of physical exercises with the words sung being used to describe the movements being performed (Hur and Cochrane,1995). In this way the goal is made conscious and explicit. Also, the rhythm aids concentration and provides impetus for the execution of the movement and accomplishment of the goal. Rhythmical intention also involves members of the group working together, however different their level of task accomplishment may be.

Daily schedule

The programme is very intensive and the daily timetable determines every aspect of the children's lives from 6.30 am in the morning to 9 pm at night (Hari and Akos, 1971). For the conductor every single item in the daily schedule is part of the educational programme (Hari and Akos,1971). Teaching, therefore, is not restricted to particular activities but covers the entire day and all its demands. CE involves a complex mix of training in specific motor skills and in all-round general development. Particular attention is paid to mastery of movement, but motor development is viewed as part of the wider process of education aimed at the development of the person as a whole. Motor, social and academic activities over the course of the day are closely integrated. Although a large part of the day is taken up with the task series (explained below), school-age children also follow a normal school curriculum in the afternoons (Swann, 1992). Although rest breaks of 15–20 minutes occur throughout the day, the children work extremely hard and this involves a great deal of mental concentration and physical effort (Cottam and Sutton, 1986).

Task series

Specific motor practice occurs in 'task series' which are allotted about 6 hours per day with each lasting between 20 and 90 minutes (Hari and Akos, 1971). Task series teach the performance of tasks learned spontaneously by healthy children and are seen as the main pathway leading to orthofunction. Every task series is constructed out of 20–30 separate tasks. Construction of a task series is begun with an activity consisting of goals already achieved and is built up from actions which each indidvidual can carry out successfully (Hari and Akos, 1971). Tasks are always practised as part of the desired action and never in isolation (Jernqvist, 1985). Great emphasis is placed on ensuring children's commitment and attention to learning (Swann, 1992). Tasks are therefore varied frequently to ensure success and learning is made enjoyable through songs and games. If the children are losing interest this is viewed as a signal for the conductor to rethink the programme.

Evaluation of conductive education

Until relatively recently most of the available information on CE consisted of statistical data from the Peto Institute and anecdotal accounts provided by those who have visited it (e.g. Cotton and Parnwell, 1967; Presland, 1990; Sutton, 1989). Presland (1990), for example, concluded that although there is little research evidence to substantiate the effectiveness of the approach as a whole, it is hard to see it in practice and not to believe that, at least for many children, it is highly effective. In contrast to this view, and the statistics provided by the Peto Institute, the findings of research conducted to evaluate the effectiveness of CE in several countries have been disappointing. The available evidence on the effectiveness of CE is presented below.

Hungary

The success rate of the Peto Institute is often quoted as 70% (e.g. Cottam and Sutton, 1986, back cover), that is, 70% of its pupils achieving orthofunction. Hari and Akos (1971) provide figures of those discharged from the Institute in the year 1968. Thirteen per cent were considered as having 'achieved nothing', 39% were deemed 'improved' and 48% were considered 'restored to health' or orthofunctional. This suggests a success rate of 48% rather than 70%.

Statistics for the year 1983 taken from the Hungarian National Register (Cottam and Sutton, 1986) using the total number of closed cases, show that only 65% of motor-disordered children received CE, as the other 35% were deemed unsuitable for treatment. The latter probably include cases of late identification and those with profound mental handicap. Of those who received CE 71% achieved orthofunction. This, therefore, suggests a 46% success rate for the total number of motor disordered who originally registered. Although this figure is nearer to that of the 48% calculated above than the one of 70% cited by the Peto Institute, it still appears impressive.

However, it must be remembered that the motor disordered in Hungary do not equate with the physically disabled in the UK, who exhibit a much wider range of disabilities, as discussed earlier. Also, since the Peto sample is limited to those patients for whom CE is deemed appropriate or more likely to respond, this obviously biases the results in favour of a high success rate (Beach,1988). In fact, the Peto Institute has been criticised for being highly selective in its intake, admitting only those children who would perhaps succeed in becoming independent anyway and who are quite different from the overwhelming majority of children in British special schools for the physically disabled (Sutton, 1989).

Australia

Short-term intensive programmes of CE have been used to compensate for the lack of trained conductors in countries other than Hungary and the lack of success in transporting CE in a 'pure' form to other countries. Sigafoos *et al.* (1993) note, however, that despite the proliferation of such courses in a variety of countries there are no published studies evaluating the effectiveness of this provision. They, therefore, conducted an evaluation of a short-term programme of CE in Australia. A group of conductors from the Peto Institute was employed as consultants to implement a 6-week intensive CE programme with ten children. Parental views were sought through questionnaires and observations of the children were videotaped. Although conclusions about programme effectiveness could clearly not be reached following only a 6-week period the results suggested that parents were positive about its impact and valued the CE training which they received. Trevarthen and Burford (1995) support the view that these parents play a central role in their child's progress and that they benefit from training.

Great Britain

Attempts were made during the 1970s to introduce CE into schools in the UK largely on the basis of Esther Cotton's account of the approach (Cotton, 1965). Whole-school attempts to implement her approach were introduced at Claremont School and at Ingfield Manor Residential School. The Claremont CE programme was never formally evaluated but several studies were carried out at Ingfield Manor (Clark,1973; Conochie, 1979; Jernqvist, 1978, 1980; McCormack, 1974; Morley, 1979; all cited in Cottam and Sutton, 1986).

Clark (1973) used a control group of children from another school who were matched for age, sex, length of time at the school and severity of initial handicap. The average age was 12 years. The assessment concentrated on eight areas: basic motor skills, fine finger control, gross motor control, eating skills, dressing skills, helping skills, grooming skills, and social responsiveness. Following the CE programme analysis of the results indicated that the only significant difference in scores between the experimental and control groups was in the area of gross motor control, and this favoured the control group. Clark concluded that he had been unable to find any of the dramatic gains which had been expected and that there were no advantages of CE over conventional approaches (Cottam and Sutton, 1986). McCormack's (1974) results on the same children a year later supported this view, with the control group scoring significantly higher in basic motor skills and gross motor control than the CE group.

Jernqvist (1978, 1980) assessed 12 children, of average age 4 years on admission, after 1 and 2 years of CE. The same checklist was used as previously but no comparison group was involved. The children exhibited improvement in all areas but all of them went on to residential special schools rather than mainstream schools.

Titchener (1986) carried out a study on eleven children aged 5–14 years who, at the start of the programme took little or no active part in looking after themselves. A variety of skills or short-term goals were assessed, the criteria for success being maintenance of the activity for more than 10 seconds. The children were assessed at the start of the programme and again after 20 months and 28 months. Results showed that a certain amount of success was achieved although this was not so striking as to suggest that CE was a considerably better approach than conventional methods. This, however, was not a comparative study.

The most rigorous evaluation of CE to date was conducted in association with the Foundation for Conductive Education (FCE) which established an Institute in Birmingham in 1987 to provide CE in the UK. Close links with the Peto Institute were formed and two conductors from Hungary were used to help train ten British conductors. The aim of the Institute was to replicate as far as possible the work undertaken in Hungary. Independent researchers were assigned to evaluate the effectiveness of the programme and determine whether CE could be successfully replicated in this country.

The group of children involved in the evaluation consisted of some of the first intake, the second intake and some replacement children added subsequently. A sample of children with cerebral palsy – matched for age, severity of disability, intelligence, communication skills, self-help skills and academic ability, and who were deemed suitable for CE – were used as the control group. The CE and control groups were assessed annually. The assessments were specifically designed to cover a range of domains important in the development of children regardless of the particular programme they were following.

Initial results (Cochrane et al., 1991) only reported progress made by children on the CE programme. They had advanced in many of the domains tested but they had not advanced in relation to their age norms. In cognitive abilities, for example, they were slightly further behind their age norms at the second assessment and in interpersonal and independence skills they had fallen a long way behind the development of their non-disabled peer group. However, without the data from the comparison group none of these changes could be attributed to CE.

More recently, Bairstow, Cochrane and Hur (1993) published a report of the comparative findings of the CE and control groups. They found that children receiving CE made progress on a wide range of variables. However, the control group children, who had been following a more traditional special school programme, made equivalent or better progress on most of the variables measured. In none of the domains assessed were CE group children found to have made greater progress than those in the control group. The overall findings of this research therefore suggest that the CE provided at the Birmingham Institute was less effective than traditional approaches used in British special schools.

In another study, Hur and Cochrane (1995) compared the differences in academic performance of children at the Birmingham Institute with children undertaking special education programmes in the Greater Manchester area. The children ranged from 5 to 6½ years and the two groups were similar in age, IQ, severity of disability, conductors' diagnosis, parental social class and initial levels of independence. The Comprehensive Reading Test (CRT) and the Basic Mathematics Test (BMT) specifically designed for use with children with cerebral palsy aged 5–8 years were used. The results showed that there were no significant differences between the two groups in reading and mathematics, although both groups performed significantly better in their second year.

The problems in transferring CE to Britain

In addition to attempting to evaluate the effectiveness of CE for children with cerebral palsy compared with the effectiveness of traditional British programmes one of the aims of the research at the Birmingham Institute was to determine the extent to which the form of CE developed in Birmingham is an accurate replica of that established at the Peto Institute (Cochrane *et al.*, 1991). Bairstow and Cochrane (1993) have outlined the difficulties of transplanting CE to Britain in a follow-up report. They point out that CE was developed in Hungary in a particular historical, social and political climate and in response to a particular need. At the time there was no system of education in place for the disabled. The expectation was that disabled people adapt to the environment rather than the environment be adapted to suit their needs. Children who were unable to get about independently were not accepted in Hungarian mainstream or special schools. In Britain, however, a system of special education for children with disabilities has been in place for many years.

Since the introduction of the 1981 Education Act more physically disabled children are being educated in mainstream schools. Anderson and Cope (1977), for example, conclude that there is no reason why physically disabled children of normal intelligence should not attend mainstream schools. Hegarty (1987) suggests that integration from an early age encourages greater independence, self-confidence, tolerance and acceptance of disability. Whilst Kozma (1995) argues that CE serves integration by aiming to return children to mainstream schools and by using group education at all ages, Bairstow and Cochrane (1993) indicate that the introduction of CE in Britain against this background was bound to be difficult. They suggest that a direct transfer of the Hungarian programme of CE into the British education system may not be meaningful or desirable and that instead CE should be adapted to the requirements and current thinking of the country's own system of special education. This is a view also put forward by Weber in his review of developments in CE in Germany (Weber, 1995).

Bairstow and Cochrane (1993) suggest that if the major principles of CE could be identified and evaluated it may be possible to incorporate essential aspects into existing British practices. This possibility is also suggested by Sutton (1989) and by Sigafoos *et al.* (1993). Stukat (1995) advocates that the distinct components of CE should be the object of further study. However, Bairstow and Cochrane (1993) point out that many of the principles of CE already appear to be incorporated into British programmes. This is supported by Presland (1990) who states that it is not easy to identify the characteristics which distinguish CE from other approaches. He notes that learning in groups, breakdown of tasks into easily mastered steps and a variety of ways of guiding children very specifically in activities are all characteristics of approaches already used in British special schools.

Provision for the motor disordered in the UK

Therapy for motor disordered children in Britain is extremely varied and practices differ from school to school and from therapist to therapist. There are many different approaches, each with their own philosophy, aims and methods, for cerebral palsy alone. This makes comparison of the British and Hungarian provision extremely difficult. It is impossible here to go into detail about all the different approaches, but they include the Bobath or Neurodevelopmental approach (Bobath and Bobath, 1984), the Doman–Delacato approach (Haskell *et al.*,1977; see also Chapter 1), the Phelps approach (Slominski, 1984) and Aim Orientated Management (Scrutton, 1984).

The relative effectiveness of these different approaches is difficult to assess. Comparative research methodology in this field is fraught with difficulties (Scrutton, 1984; Scrutton and Gilbertson, 1975). Aims vary depending on the underlying philosophy and criteria for success are hard to define. Also, children with similar disabilities are difficult to find to establish matched control or comparison groups. Despite all these difficulties, however, a small number of comparative studies on the effectiveness of physiotherapy have been attempted. In response to the outcry for CE to be introduced into Britain practitioners pointed out the success of traditional methods of treating and educating children with motor disorders and at the same time stressed the difference in selection procedures between the Peto Institute and physiotherapy referrals. They highlighted one study carried out in East Anglia which gave a mobility rate, aided or unaided, of over 80% for a group of children taught with a traditional approach (Tonkin, 1988). Thirty-one children aged 3–5 were assessed following treatment at the centre. Nineteen (61%) were able to walk, seven (23%) were able to stand or walk with support, three were able to sit and two were not ambulant apparently due to severe global delay (Chartered Society of Physiotherapy (CSP), 1988). The CSP believes that 'there is much excellent and successful treatment in Britain' (CSP, 1988) and that 'it is not necessary to have conductive education to get children with cerebral palsy on their feet and walking' (p. 6).

In America, however, where similar approaches are implemented, Palmer *et al.* (1988) reviewed several studies and went on to report their own research from which they concluded that physical therapy produced no measurable benefits. They argue that there is a need to examine traditional interventions and widely accepted theories within physiotherapy critically as they have not been supported by research evidence.

Conclusion

The success rate claimed for conductive education in Hungary has been estimated from statistics supplied by the Peto Institue, supported by anecdotal evidence, rather than being backed by research evidence. These statistics have been criticised as being biased in favour of success by the substantial proportion of motor disordered children deemed unsuitable for treatment. Evaluation has been hampered by the lack of a clear account of the aims, principles and practices of conductive education in English. Attempts to transport conductive education to countries outside of Hungary has proved difficult because of differences between countries in social, political and educational climates.

The results of several well-controlled comparative studies have shown CE to be less effective than the traditional methods of teaching and therapy used in special schools in the UK. However, there is clearly little agreement regarding the most effective therapy for motor disordered children, since it has been shown that traditional physiotherapy methods are not supported by research evidence. Despite this finding there is at present not enough evidence of the potential or achieved success of CE to justify abandoning traditional approaches in favour of this highly specialised system.

References

Anderson, E. and Cope, C. (1977) *Special Units in Ordinary Schools*. London: University of London Institute of Education.

Bairstow, P. and Cochrane, R. (1993) 'Is conductive education transplantable?' *British Journal of Special Education*, **20** (3), 84–88.

Bairstow, P., Cochrane, R. and Hur, J. (1993) *Evaluation of Conductive Education for Children with Cerebral Palsy*. London: HMSO.

Beach, R. (1988) 'Conductive education for motor disorders: new hope or false hope?' *Archives of Disease in Childhood*, **63**, 211–213.

Bobath, B. and Bobath, K. (1984) 'The neurodevelopmental treatment'. In Scrutton, D. (ed.) *Management of Motor Disorders of Children with Cerebral Palsy*. London: Spastics International Medical Publications.

British Medical Association (1990) *Complete Family Health Encyclopaedia*. London: Darling Kindersley.

Chartered Society of Physiotherapists (CSP) (1988) *Conductive Education: A Statement by the Chartered Society of Physiotherapy*. London: CSP Publications.

Cochrane, R., Bairstow, P. and Hur, J. (1991) 'The evaluation of conductive education', *International Journal of Special Education*, **6** (2), 223–30.

Coleman, G. and King, J. (1990) *A Pilot Evaluation of Conductive Education in Victoria*. Bundoora, VA: La Trobe University.

Cottam, E. and Sutton, A. (eds) (1986) *Conductive Education: A System for Overcoming Motor Disorder*. London: Croom Helm.

Cotton, E. (1965) 'The institute for movement therapy and school for "conductors", Budapest, Hungary', *Developmental Medicine and Child Neurology*, **7**, 437–46.

Cotton, E. (1987) 'Conductive education and the profoundly, multiply-handicapped, cerebral palsied child', *Conductive Education Association Journal*, **2**, 3–6.

Cotton, E. and Parnwell, M. (1967) 'From Hungary: The Peto Method', *Special Education*, **56**, 7–11.

Hari, M. and Akos, K. (1971) *Conductive Education*. English Translation by Horton-Smith, N. and Stevens, J. (1988) London: Routledge.

Hari, M. and Tillemans, T. (1984) 'Conductive education'. In Scrutton, D. (ed.) *Management of the Motor Disorders of Children with Cerebral Palsy*. London: Spastics International Medical Publications, pp. 19–35.

Haskell, S., Barrett, E. and Taylor, H. (1977) *The Education of Motor and Neurologically Handicapped Children*. London: Croom Helm.

Hedges, K. (1988) 'The Bobath and Conductive Education approaches to cerebral palsy: Treatment-management and education models', *New Zealand Journal of Physiotherapy*, **16**, 6–12.

Hegarty, S. (1987) *Meeting Special Needs in Ordinary Schools: An Overview*. London: Cassell.

Hur, J. and Cochrane, R. (1995) 'Academic performance of children with cerebral palsy: a comparative study of conductive education and British special education programmes', *British Journal of Developmental Disabilities*, **80**, 33–41.

Jernqvist, L. (1985) *Speech Regulation of Motor Acts as Used by Cerebral Palsied Children*. Gotenberg, Sweden: Acta Universitatis Gothoburgensis.

Kozma, I. (1995) 'The basic principles and present practice of conductive education', *European Journal of Special Needs Education*, **10** (2), 111–23.

Oliver, M. (1989) 'Conductive education: if it wasn't so sad it would be funny',

Disability, Handicap and Society, **4** (2), 197–200.

Palmer, F., Shapiro, B. and Watchtel, R. (1988) 'The effects of physical therapy on cerebral palsy', *New England Journal of Medicine*, **318**, 803–08.

Presland, J. (1990) 'Understanding conductive education: Reflections on a visit to Kiskunhalas', *Positive Teaching*, **1** (2), 63–70.

Scrutton, D. (ed.) (1984) *Management of the Motor Disorders of Children with Cerebral Palsy*. London: Spastics International Medical Publications.

Scrutton, D. and Gilbertson, M. (1975) *Physiotherapy in Paediatric Practice*. London: Butterworths.

Sigafoos, J., Elkins, J. and Kerr, M. (1993) 'Short-term conductive education: an evaluation study', *British Journal of Special Education*, **20** (4), 148–51.

Slominski, A. (1984) 'Winthrop Phelps and the Children's Rehabilitation Institute'. In Scrutton, D. (ed.) *Management of the Motor Disorders of Children with Cerebral Palsy*. London: Spastics International Medical Publications.

Stukat, K. (1995) 'Conductive education evaluated', *European Journal of Special Needs Education*, **10** (2), 154–61.

Sutton, A. (1986) 'The challenge of conductive education'. In Booth, T. and Swann, W. (eds) *Curricula for All*. Milton Keynes: Open University Press.

Sutton, A. (1988) 'Conductive Education', *Archives of Disease in Childhood*, **63**, 214–17.

Sutton, A. (1989) 'The Impact of conductive education'. In Jones, N. (ed.) *Special Educational Needs Review* (Vol. 2). Lewes: Falmer Press, pp. 161–87.

Swann, W. (1992) 'Introduction'. In Booth, T. *et al.* (eds) *Curricula for Diversity in Education*. London: Routledge, pp. 182–92.

Titchener, J. (1986) 'An approach for the physically handicapped?' In Cottam, P. and Sutton, A. (eds) *Conductive Education: A System for Overcoming Motor Disorders*. London: Croom Helm.

Tonkin, B. (1988) 'Storm and discord round the conductors', *Community Care*, **728**, 13–18.

Trevarthen, C. and Burford, B (1995) 'The central role of parents: how they can give power to a motor impaired child's acting, experiencing and sharing', *European Journal of Special Needs Education*, **10** (2), 138–48.

Weber, K. (1995) 'Developments in conductive education in Germany', *European Journal of Special Needs Education*, **10** (2), 149–53.

Yen, N. (1990) 'Conducting hope for handicapped children', *Conductive Education in Hong Kong*, **4**, 34–37.

8 Instrumental Enrichment – Is This the Answer to Raising Standards of Achievement in Our Schools?

Raising educational standards

Concern with academic standards has been growing over the last few decades. The introduction of comprehensive education for all meant that students who had previously been paid little attention in the education system were faced with curricula designed for the most able and there was a consequent fall in academic performance. With this came the realisation of the wide range of intellectual ability which is now found in secondary schools. This led to the introduction of many courses which involved practical activity, such as the Nuffield courses, but made little use of thinking skills. The orientation towards business and competition in the 1980s led to increasing criticism of standards within the education system (judged mainly by public examination results) by both politicians and the public. The National Curriculum was introduced on the assumption that the publishing of desired standards of achievement would automatically lead to a raising of standards by improving instruction. However, the first Key Stage 3 tests in science, for example, resulted in only 14% of pupils achieving level 6 in the National Curriculum rather than the expected 50%. Recent results released by the Government (Young, 1996) show that 27% of 14 year olds are reaching level 6. Adey and Shayer (1994) believe, therefore, that the National Curriculum was introduced on a false assumption and that it was short-sighted to assume that standards of achievement would be raised.

A survey conducted by Shayer from 1974 to 1980 called the Concepts in Secondary Mathematics and Science (CSMS) survey applied Piagetian tests to a representative sample of 14,000 children between the ages of 10 and 16. It showed that even by the age of 16 only 30% of pupils achieve even the early formal operations stage outlined by Piaget's theory of child development. Learning outcomes described in science (and probably other subjects) at level 6 in the National Curriculum require formal operational thinking so there is, therefore, a limit to the extent to which standards can be raised simply by improving instruction (Adey and Shayer, 1994). In 1993 less than 30% of students achieved a grade C or above in GCSE science subjects. Psychological development appears to set an upper limit to the raising of educational standards and this cannot be achieved by improving instructional teaching or increasing the motivation of pupils alone. Adey and Shayer (1994) believe that standards can only be raised by the introduction of cognitive development programmes which actually alter the intellectual development of individuals and by a corresponding increase in the professional skills of teachers so that they can provide such programmes. The distinction has to be made, therefore, between 'instruction' aimed at content objectives (content dependent) and 'intervention' in cognitive processes aimed at raising levels of thinking (content independent) and so greatly improving children's potential to gain from instruction.

Instrumental Enrichment (IE)

IE is a cognitive intervention method developed by Feuerstein and his colleagues (Feuerstein *et al.*, 1980) which is essentially geared towards helping slow learners and low-achieving adolescents become effective learners and problem solvers (Burden, 1987). It was initially developed to remediate the socially disadvantaged orphaned immigrants arriving in Israel after the Holocaust in the 1950s. It has more recently, however, received considerable interest from educators and is described by Steinberg as 'an exemplary programme for improving intellectual ability'. Emphasis is placed on the process of learning rather than the content of learning. The IE programme involves the learning of basic thinking processes which are applicable across all curriculum areas.

The beliefs underlying IE

Three basic beliefs are fundamental to IE (Feuerstein *et al.*, 1980):

1. *That humans can be intellectually changed.* Anyone can be helped to become a more effective learner at any age no matter what the cause or degree of their handicap (Burden, 1987). Burden believes that there is also a built-in assumption that few people ever actually reach their full potential.
2. *That learning occurs through interaction.* IE proponents believe that low attainment is mainly due to the lack of a mediating agent and that handicaps do not necessarily lead to impaired cognitive functioning. Most learning experiences are not normally available to the learner through interaction with their environment and must be mediated by a mediating agent, usually parent, sibling or other care-giver, who selects and organises the world of stimuli for the child and in this way affects their cognitive structure (Adey and Shayer, 1994). The role of the teacher, therefore, is to provide a mediated learning experience (MLE) which the child can relate

to meaningfully. Feuerstein and colleagues outline the conditions under which mediated learning occurs and highlight the fact that inadequate mediated learning experience can lead to deficient cognitive functions.

3. *That deficiencies in thinking skills are responsible for poor intellectual performance.* By addressing these deficiencies directly fundamental improvements in learning can be brought about.

Assessment

Feuerstein *et al.* (1979) used the Learning Potential Assessment Device (LPAD) for assessing the learning potential of pupils rather than what they had previously learnt. The LPAD was developed as a clinical instrument for obtaining qualitative data. It involves recording cognitive deficiencies through a cognitive map, which is a hypothetical model consisting of seven parameters by which any mental act can be analysed, categorised and ordered. This model is the basis of the dynamic and interactive assessment of retarded learners and of the IE programme itself. Feuerstein argues that static forms of psychometric assessment lead to an underestimate of the abilities of the retarded. A detailed and critical review of Learning Potential Assessment can be found in Shayer and Beasley (1987).

The IE programme

The IE programme is a set of tools to facilitate the role of the teacher in improving students' ability to process data (Adey and Shayer, 1994). It aims to directly address the deficiencies in thinking skills found to be characteristic of adolescent low attainers (Thinkpenny and Howie, 1990). Feuerstein *et al.* (1980) outline one major goal and six sub-goals of the programme. The major goal is to increase the capacity of the learner to become modified by stimuli and experiences provided by life events, that is formal and informal learning opportunities. The six sub-goals are summarised by Burden (1987) as follows:

1. To correct weaknesses and deficiencies in cognitive functions.
2. To teach the basic concepts which are the prerequisites for operational thinking.
3. To develop the motivation to learn through the formation of appropriate habits.
4. To produce reflective and insightful thought processes.
5. To provide tasks that provide both enjoyment and a feeling of success in their completion.
6. To transform poor learners from passive recipients into active generators.

The design of the IE programme is based on a psychometric model of mental abilities, involving cognitive functions such as spatial operations, verbal reasoning and numerical abilities, in conjunction with Piaget's staged model of mental operations (Adey and Shayer, 1994).

The programme consists of 15 'instruments' containing a series of pencil and paper exercises each of which provides the basis of a 1-hour teaching session. The term 'instrument' is used to emphasise that the process of the activity and the problem-solving way in which it is used is more important than the content. Each 'instrument' addresses a particular cognitive function and there is a progression from simple to higher level thinking skills (Burden, 1987). These different cognitive functions are each divided into three phases: gathering all the information required (the input phase), using the information which has been gathered (the elaboration phase) and expressing the solution to a problem (the output phase). This model becomes part of the everyday discussion between the teacher and the student as well as among students and provides students with strategies which assist them to conduct their own problem solving for each task. Instrumental Enrichment, therefore, aims to provide the necessary mental tools for students to construct for themselves the higher level thinking required and in this way they construct their own learning strategies (Adey and Shayer, 1994).

The variety of studies

Since Feuerstein's original study the IE programme has been adapted in a variety of ways and been used with a variety of populations. Sample populations have included pupils in Years 7 and 8 (Adey and Shayer, 1994), selected low-attaining pupils in Years 10 and 11 (Blagg, 1991), mildly handicapped adolescents (Howie *et al.*, 1985) and profoundly deaf adolescents (Thickpenny and Howie, 1990). Within some studies the IE programme has been adapted to include a smaller number of 'instruments' than the original programme (Thickpenny and Howie, 1990) and in others the principles only of IE have been used to assist students' learning (Mehl, 1985; Strang and Shayer, 1993). Whilst IE originally was specifically designed to be implemented in a context-independent manner (Feuerstein *et al.*, 1980; Arbitman-Smith and Haywood, 1980; Arbitman-Smith *et al.*, 1982; Haywood and Arbitman-Smith, 1981) many researchers have adapted this approach to particular subject areas (e.g. Mehl, 1985) or implemented a combination of context-independent and context-dependent programmes (e.g. Adey and Shayer, 1994). Studies have been criticised for not providing the optimum conditions for IE to work (e.g. Blagg, 1991; Weller and Craft, 1993) and for this reason the required conditions will be discussed in the following paragraphs.

Conditions required for the programme to be effective

Staff support

The teaching skills involved in administering the IE programme are new skills which are not part of the normal repertoire of teachers (Adey and Shayer, 1994) and there is, therefore, a need for intensive training. The programme must be delivered by specially trained teachers with a thorough grounding in the underlying theory (Burden, 1987). Shayer and Beasley (1987) stress that there is not only a need for substantial in-service support for teachers, but also for substantial on-site support, involving the trainer's availability for discussion following lessons. They criticise government funded studies in the UK, the Schools Council Instrumental Enrichment (SCIE) project (Weller and Craft, 1983) and the Lower Attaining Pupil Programme (LAPP) project (Blagg, 1991) for lack of the support which they consider vital to the effectiveness of the programme. Teachers directly involved received generous in-service provision but received no assistance with the methodology at the time of administering the programme. In addition, staff in the school, especially the headteacher, needed to support the project (Shayer and Beasley, 1987). Adey and Shayer (1994) criticise Blagg's study (1991) which was hastily organised by the chief education officer only a term before it was due to start, leaving the headteacher and senior management team relatively uninformed about the programme. Also, staff and pupils were reported to be generally hostile to its introduction. Research by Joyce and Showers (1980, 1988) confirms the view that support of internal school policy and on-site training are crucial.

Time

The IE programme is intended to be taught at a rate of 3–5 sessions per week over a period of 2–3 years. It was initially meant to be used with pupils of 12 years of age i.e. Years 7 and 8 (Feuerstein et al., 1980). In contrast, the LAPP project (Blagg, 1991) administered the programme to pupils in Years 10 and 11 when they were already disaffected and without motivation as they were soon to leave school (Adey and Shayer, 1994). Pupils in the Shayer and Beasley study (1987) received IE teaching 3 hours a week over a period of six terms compared with 1½ hours a week over five terms for the LAPP project; that is, there was over twice as much input. However, there was found to be no difference between classes receiving more IE teaching in Blagg's study. Therefore, Adey and Shayer (1994) place less weight on the amount of time pupils are exposed to the programme than to the way in which the programme is supported through training and awareness of teachers.

Integration of elements

Adey and Shayer (1994) list the essential features of any programme designed to promote higher order thinking:

1. Concrete preparation to introduce the necessary vocabulary and clarify the terms in which a problem is to be set.
2. Cognitive conflict at a level to set the students' minds a puzzle which is interesting and attainable.
3. Construction zone activity in which the conflict is at least partially resolved as students' minds go beyond their previous thinking capability.
4. Metacognition in the sense of conscious reflection on the problem solving process and naming of reasoning patterns developed for future use.
5. The bridging of these reasoning patterns to new contexts in order to generalise them and consolidate their use.

They believe that IE goes a long way to integrating these elements and having well-defined time lines for specific phases. The use of the appropriate language for the processes is essential for students to be able to discuss them and to recall the procedure in a new, possibly relevant situation.

Bridging

Feuerstein and colleagues' original programme was deliberately delivered in special thinking skills lessons which were not related to the context of ordinary schooling because the children involved had already failed in this respect (Feuerstein *et al.*, 1980). The problem of relating this learning to other subject areas was addressed by a process called 'bridging'. Bridging is the conscious transfer of a reasoning pattern from a context in which it is first encountered to a new context (Adey and Shayer, 1994). Transfer will only occur if bridging is specifically built into the teaching programme and bridging opportunities are utilised to maximum effect. The more the variety of contexts, the more concrete generalisation is promoted. Context independent learning, however, raises the problem for the teacher and the student of how to use the skills that they have learnt in the context of their ordinary schooling. Adey and Shayer state that their experience and feedback from schools indicate that there is a major problem with using special thinking lessons. If teachers from all subject areas do not take an active part in the programme a communication barrier between teachers and students can be created.

Peer collaboration

Adey and Shayer (1994) state that mediation can just as validly be achieved through another child as through the teacher. Children internalise what they have approved, contributed to and observed in their peers' practice. Feuerstein *et al.* (1980) saw peer collaboration as a general aim of IE procedures and highlighted its value in the learning process. In practice, therefore, the mediating role of the teacher lies in developing the skill of framing the tasks for the pupils in such a way as to direct their attention to the problem which they should discuss with each other. Then the whole class is encouraged to share different insights and difficulties which the working groups have encountered. In this way all pupils benefit.

Evaluation studies

The first evaluative study of a 2-year IE programme was carried out by Feuerstein *et al.* (1980) and involved comparison of General Enrichment and IE programmes. Comparatively modest effects were found in favour of the IE group for crystallised intelligence, participative collaboration and fluid intelligence, although little effect on school achievement was noted. Criticisms are made, however, of the statistical analysis, the data collection and the use of achievement tests in this study (Burden, 1987; Shayer and Beasley, 1987). A follow-up study after 2 years (Rand *et al.*, 1981) showed a large increase in general intelligence, suggesting that immediate post-tests underestimated the effects of the cognitive intervention.

Since this study was conducted other studies have been carried out on a variety of students and using a variety of tests to measure the effectiveness of programmes. Detailed reviews are to be found in Burden (1987) and Adey and Shayer (1994) and only an overview will be provided here.

Large-scale studies by Haywood and colleagues (Arbitman-Smith and Haywood, 1980; Arbitman-Smith *et al.*, 1982; Haywood and Arbitman-Smith, 1981; Haywood *et al.*, 1982) indicate conflicting results with some showing a gain in IQ whilst others do not, but with no significant improvement in achievement measures, except in one study. Other smaller scale studies showing generally positive effects include Bainin (1982) and Beasley (1984) (both cited in Burden, 1987) and Howie *et al.* (1985). Bainin found significant improvements on criterion referenced tests and in reading achievement. In addition, teacher comments were very positive in their estimation of its value for student learning and their own professional growth. Beasley's study with retarded students showed improvements on Piagetian tests but not on crystallised intelligence or achievement. Howie *et al.* (1985), in their study with mildly handicapped adolescents, found a gain in WISC-R results and positive teacher ratings on classroom participation. In addition, they found that, following a period of individualised reading instruction, seven out of eight of their subjects made notable reading gains. This is important as it suggests that generalisation to academic achievement may have taken place.

Thickpenny and Howie (1990) implemented an IE programme with two classes of profoundly deaf adolescents. The control group received 57 hours of remedial teaching followed by 110 hours of IE whilst the experimental group received 167 hours of IE only. At the end of the control phase (57 hours) the experimental group showed significant gains on Picture Completion and Picture Arrangement sub-tests of the WISC-R and on Matching Familiar Figures compared with the control group. At the end of both programmes both groups had made significant gains on high-sensitivity generalisation measures, thus demonstrating generalised use of IE training. However, only the experimental group showed significant gains on low-sensitivity measures. In addition three subjects made significant gains on the Gates Reading Test despite the fact that profoundly deaf subjects normally make minimal gains in reading ages between the ages of 10 and 16 years. Thickpenny and Howie suggest that longer term follow-up studies in the future may provide information on achievement skills which may have been influenced by cognitive changes.

In contrast, studies in the UK by Weller and Craft (1983) and Blagg (1991) have showed little effect of Instrumental Enrichment programmes. However, these two programmes have been criticised by Adey and Shayer (1994) for the lack of support for the teachers involved, a factor which they consider crucial to the effectiveness of the programme.

Shayer and Beasley (1987) provide the most positive results with an IE programme carried out under optimal conditions including the length and time of implementation of the programme and the necessary support for the teachers involved. They found that effects on underlying thinking ability of the order of 2 extra years of development in mental age terms were achieved as a result of 2 years' use of IE. Also, a gain of nearly thirty percentile points on cognitive development was achieved.

Studies by Mehl (1985; cited in Shayer and Beasley, 1987) and Strang and Shayer (1993) show that large effects can be obtained by applying some of the principles of IE to analysing students' learning difficulties and modifying teaching strategies even in context dependent learning. Mehl used Feuerstein's methodology to describe deficits in students' learning and then used this knowledge to change his teaching to address these needs. He obtained a strikingly large positive effect, which did not, however, generalise to the rest of the course. Strang and Shayer (1993) used similar information to write structured worksheets and create lesson plans to direct students' attention selectively. At the end of the module the students were given the usual test to compare their achievement. This group did significantly better than the control group which was taught in the usual way. The principles of IE can, therefore, be used to gain insight into how to assist students to learn and how teaching strategies can be modified in the light of this information. Very large effects on the results of instruction have been obtained in this way but once again evidence for generalisation has been lacking.

Burden (1987) concludes that there is a lack of published evidence for the effectiveness of IE. He highlights the inadequacies of studies to date including the lack of consideration of staff input required, little consideration of formative aspects of evaluation and the appropriateness of criteria used to measure outcome. He suggests other outcome measures which are more directly related to the aims of the programme and provides important suggestions for researchers involved in developing and evaluating cognitive interventions.

More recently, Adey and Shayer (1994) cite two case studies in which a combination of context-independent and context-dependent learning are used. In one school context-independent IE was begun on entry to Year 7 and replaced by a context-dependent IE programme in Years 8 and 9 using a programme called 'Thinking Science'. Another example is given of a school where whole school policy was developed with regard to IE and 20–25% of each subject time was spent in this type of learning with the remainder being available for content work. Adey and Shayer believed that the effect of these programmes would be to give all these pupils greater access to the content. Their enhanced processing skills would increasingly enable them to handle the higher levels of concepts required by levels 5 and above of the National Curriculum. Adey and Shayer (1994) conclude, at this time, that IE has been shown to deliver some large effects on psychological tests, thinking ability, Piagetian tests, cognitive function and various tests of fluid intelligence. However, little evidence exists of accompanying increases in school achievement. They cast doubt on the psychological models used in context-independent programmes and suggest that the use of immediate post-tests (as used in most of these studies) may not be appropriate. They advocate more research using new learning as the measure of school achievement because it may well be 2 years before enough general experience has been re-processed for students' new higher powers to show up on tests. This delay, however, would not apply to school achievement, provided that the knowledge and skills they test are specific to the learning which has taken place after the intervention. Their most recent study, discussed below, appears to support this view.

The CASE project

In this project the theoretical conclusions made by Adey and Shayer (1994) are translated into a working curriculum called Cognitive Acceleration through Science Education (CASE) which was trialed in nine secondary schools between 1984 and 1987. The general aim of the project was to increase the proportion of children with access to formal operational thinking by the beginning of Year 9 to increase the probability of the next 3 years leading to high achievement. CASE materials contain science activities which represent all aspects of formal operational reasoning. Twenty five per cent of the regular science curricular time was replaced by these activities, i.e. a fortnightly double lesson throughout Years 7 and 8. 'Thinking lessons' were, in this way embedded in an existing subject and within a familiar context before generalising to other contexts. Teachers involved received both inservice and on-site training. Experimental and control groups were set up in the same schools.

The children were tested before and directly after the intervention. They were also tested 1 year after the intervention and 2 years after the intervention in the form of their GCSE examinations in Science, Mathematics and English.

It was found that the proportion of those entering Year 9 with early formal operations capacity doubled and subsequently the proportion of those pupils achieving grade C and above in science at GCSE was doubled. In addition, achievement was enhanced in both mathematics and English at GCSE level.

Further CASE studies where 'Thinking Science' is used by the whole school support these findings. More recent research by Adey and Shayer referred to by Susan Young in the *TES*, 22 November 1996 showed that the thinking skills course improved exam performance in mathematics and English as well as science and also improved results in the Key Stage 3 tests. Sixty eight per cent of pupils using the thinking skills course reached level 6 compared with 27% of other 14 year olds. Although the results vary between schools there is evidence of potential for improvement across the ability range. These results are consistent across all classes and subjects, strongly suggesting that there is a fundamental effect within each child.

Conclusion

IE was originally introduced as an innovative cognitive development programme for raising the achievement of low functioning adolescents. As research has developed a number of factors have become clear. To be effective the programme must be implemented over the first two years of secondary schooling and must be allocated sufficient time within the curriculum. Adequate training must be provided for teachers both before and during the intervention so that they understand the theory behind the programme, are able to put it into practice effectively and have on going support.

Studies showing positive effects of the programme gave positive results on many psychological tests, but not for general school achievement. However, many of the initial studies showing little or no effect of the programme have been criticised for not providing the optimum conditions for IE to work.

The work of Adey and Shayer has shown that, by providing the optimum conditions for IE to work, by undertaking long-term evaluation and measuring school achievement on new learning, improvements in long-term achievement can be shown to be made. In addition, the problem of context-independent learning highlighted by research led them to introduce more courses in which the learning of thinking skills is embedded in an existing subject and then generalised to other areas. Although more research is needed, the results shown by the CASE project are impressive and it is difficult not to agree with its advocates that it needs to be more widely introduced into schools and should continue to be monitored. This evidence suggests that it could provide a relatively cost effective way of substantially raising educational standards, illustrated by higher grades in nationally recognised and publicly set examinations, not only for the least able pupils but for pupils right across the ability range.

However, apart from Adey and Shayer's studies, there is little research evidence in favour of IE having any impact on general school achievement. This may be due to ineffective implementation of IE programmes and the use of short-term measures of evaluation. Adey and Shayer's research, therefore, provides room for optimism and emphasises the need for more research and continual development of IE programmes and evaluation of their effectiveness.

References

Adey, P. and Shayer, M. (1994) *Really Raising Standards: Cognitive Intervention and Academic Achievement*. London: Routledge.

Arbitman-Smith, R. and Haywood, H. (1980) 'Cognitive education for learning disabled adolescents', *Journal of Abnormal Child Psychology*, 8, 51–64.

Arbitman-Smith, R., Haywood, H. and Bransford, J. (1982) 'Assessing cognitive change'. In McCauley, C., Sperber, R. and Brooks, P. (eds) *Learning and Cognition in the Mentally Retarded*. Baltimore: University Park Press.

Blagg, N. (1991) *Can We Teach Intelligence?* London: Lawrence Erlbaum.

Burden, R. (1987) 'Feuerstein's Instrumental Enrichment programme: important issues in research and evaluation', *European Journal of Psychology of Education*, II (1), 3–16.

Feuerstein, R., Rand, Y. and Hoffman, M. (1979) *The Dynamic Assessment of Retarded Performers: The Learning Potential Asessment Device, Theory, Instruments and Techniques*. Baltimore: University Park Press.

Feuerstein, R., Rand, Y., Hoffman, M. and Miller, M. (1980) *Instrumental Enrichment: An Intervention Programme for Cognitive Modifiability*. Baltimore: University Park Press.

Feuerstein, R., Miller, M., Hoffman, M., Rand, Y., Mintzker, Y. and Jensen, M. (1981) 'Cognitive modifiability in adolescence: cognitive structure and the effects of intervention'. *Journal of Special Education*, 15, 269–387.

Haywood, H. and Arbitman-Smith, R. (1981) 'Modification of cognitive functions in slow-learning adolescents'. In Mittler, P. (ed.) *Frontiers of Knowledge: Mental Retardation* (Vol. 1). Baltimore: University Park Press.

Howie, R., Thickpenny, J., Leaf, C. and Absolum, M. (1985) 'The piloting of

Instrumental Enrichment in New Zealand with eight mildly retarded children', *Australia and New Zealand Journal of Developmental Disabilities*, **11**, 3–16.

Joyce, B. and Showers, B. (1980) 'Improving inservice training: the messages of research', *Educational Leadership*, **37 (5)**, 379–85.

Joyce, B. and Showers, B. (1988) *Student Achievement Through Staff Development*. New York: Longman.

Rand, Y., Mintzker, R., Hoffman, M. and Friedlender, Y. (1981) 'The instrumental enrichment programme: immediate and long-term effects'. In Mittler, P (ed.) *Frontiers of Knowledge: Mental Retardation*. (Vol. 1). Baltimore: University Park Press, pp. 141–52.

Shayer, M. and Beasley, F. (1987) 'Does Instrumental Enrichment work?' *British Educational Research Journal*, **13 (2)**, 101–19.

Strang, J. and Shayer, M. (1993) 'Enhancing high school students' achievement in chemistry through a thinking skills approach', *International Journal of Science Education*, **15 (3)**, 319–37.

Thickpenny, J. and Howie, D. (1990) 'Teaching thinking skills to deaf adolescents: The implementation and evaluation of Instrumental Enrichment', *International Journal of Cognitive Education and Mediated Learning*, **1 (3)**, 193–209.

Weller, K. and Craft, A. (1983) *Making up our Minds: an Exploratory Study of Instrumental Enrichment*. London: Schools Council.

Young, S. (1996) 'Cognitive course boosts exam results', *Times Educational Supplement*, **22 November**, 3.

9 Peer/Parent Tutoring – is it Effective?

A brief history

The old saying that there is nothing new under the sun is most surely true of peer tutoring. As far back as ancient Greece, teachers made use of peer tutoring. Aristotle is said to have used student leaders, known as *archons*, to help him; and the Romans, adapting many of the educational practices of the Greeks, used older pupils to teach and test younger students (Wagner, 1982).

In the 1500s, Sturm and Trotzendorf used peer tutors. Sturm did not record why he used them but Trotzendorf wrote that he taught the older pupils who then taught the younger ones because it was too expensive to employ more teachers. Towards the end of the eighteenth century, Andrew Bell made systematic use of peer tutors and saw the psychological benefits of involving pupils more deeply in their learning. In 1801, Joseph Lancaster taught 350 boys in streamed classes using monitors to supervise the peer tutoring of these classes, discovering that both pupils and teacher benefited from this approach (Alder, 1989). Again, this was necessary because it was not possible to employ enough teachers (Allen, 1976).

In all the above-mentioned situations, peer tutoring was a financial and practical expedient rather than an educationally based strategy. Its value as an educational tool became apparent through its use. Peer tutoring was primarily a way of teaching large numbers on a very small budget and its revival in the USA in the early 1960s was, in part, due to an impending shortage of teachers. The emphasis of that time upon individualised instruction also fuelled interest in peer tutoring. With the recognition of under-achievement and the value placed upon compensatory education and anti-poverty drives in the 1970s, research into the use of peer tutoring became intense (Topping, 1988).

Interest in peer tutoring was to emerge later in Britain than in America and only really developed pace in the 1980s with the development of various projects on parental involvement in children's reading (Topping and Wolfendale, 1985). In today's climate of value for money and ever-decreasing funds for education, it is worth considering the ways in which peer tutoring may be effectively employed.

Definitions

The term 'peer tutoring' has been used to describe a wide range of systems down the years but generally refers to situations where children teach other children. As any parent knows, the second and subsequent children in a family often progress through many developmental stages more quickly than the first child due, in part, to the assistance and role models of their elder siblings. Older students teaching younger children is sometimes labelled cross-age tutoring. However, in much of the literature, the term 'peer tutoring' is used to describe the use of any non-professional in the role of teacher. Accordingly, peer tutoring has been defined as:

> ... someone belonging to the same group in society where membership is defined by status. In this case, the status is that of being a fellow-learner and not a professional teacher.
>
> (Goodlad and Hirst, 1990: 1).

There are many forms of peer tutoring. They can be:

- one-to-one, same age tutor and tutee
- older tutor to younger child
- more able to less able child of the same age or younger
- less able child or student as tutor to younger child
- college or university student to individual or group of children
- behaviourally disturbed child or student as tutor to younger less able child
- untrained adults or parents as tutors.

All these, and more, have been studied under the umbrella of peer tutoring.

The subjects and groups with which peer tutoring has been used are as varied as the reasons for its implementation. It has been used in individual classes by specific teachers or as a whole school or community approach. For example, a large, national project, the Perach Tutorial Project in Israel, operates a one-to-one tutoring system for socially disadvantaged children tutored by university and college students who are compensated for their efforts by a rebate in their own tuition fees of approximately 40%. Tutoring takes place outside school and the tutors and tutees are paired on religious grounds and with regard to the distance between their homes. At one time, as many as 12,000 tutor–tutee pairs were involved in the programme (Goodlad and Hirst, 1990: 75).

Peer tutoring has been used to support and increase learning in every subject of the curriculum, including social and personal development, in both schools and colleges, as well as for counselling, drama therapy, language development, bilingual and ethnic group support and behaviour modification. The majority of research, however, has been in academic areas such as mathematics, science, spelling and most especially in reading.

The rationale for peer tutoring

The reasons for using peer tutoring are almost as many as the areas of the curriculum in which it is employed. Its original use was a financial expedient to cater for large numbers of pupils on a limited budget which allowed a minimum of teachers. As class sizes continue to grow, especially in the primary sector where the acquisition of reading skills is so essential, peer tutoring may be a way of giving children practice in reading which the increased demands of the National Curriculum have made so difficult for class teachers to maintain at the level they consider is necessary.

The benefits of peer tutoring are wide ranging and will be considered in more detail below. In some instances, tutors gain more academically than the tutees, in others, the greatest benefits are for the tutees. Behaviourally disturbed tutors may show improvements in self-esteem as a result of the responsibility of tutoring:

> By being given the role of teacher, it is anticipated that they will adopt behaviours consistent with that role.
>
> (Goodlad and Hirst, 1990: 8)

It has been suggested that the positive changes, which many teachers involved in peer tutoring projects claim take place in the behaviours and attitudes of the pupils involved are not detected by tests of self-confidence or self-esteem. In the writer's own experience of a peer tutoring project carried out in a primary school class, acknowledged by the whole staff to be the 'worst class in the school', the improvements in the behaviour and attitudes of the class as a whole during the period of the experiment were so marked that the class teacher chose to continue the peer tutoring after the project time ended. Similarly, staff in a secondary school, learning of the benefits of a peer tutoring project in chemistry, chose to adopt a similar system for themselves (Bland and Harris, 1989).

So, in a variety of ways, peer tutoring has been used to free the teacher to help those most in need; to increase academic learning in both tutee and tutor; to enhance self-confidence and self-esteem; and to reduce disruptive or unacceptable behaviour. As will be seen, different systems of peer tutoring have been found to benefit tutors and tutees to differing degrees. Teachers considering using peer tutoring must therefore decide which system will best meet the needs of the pupils as a whole, as well as those of the teacher. A range of different systems is described below.

Some approaches to peer tutoring

Same-age peer tutoring

Interactive, pairs, or same-age peer tutoring, is a system used commonly in most schools, especially at primary level. This form of tutoring takes limited teacher time and can be used to help pupils who need support to keep up with the task of the group by having text read with or by a more able child (Goodlad and Hirst, 1989). Co-operative work situations such as drafting and editing written work or testing and rehearsing facts, can all be done reciprocally by same-age tutors.

The value of this form of tutoring is in freeing the class teacher to assist those who most need help. Where a more able child tutors a less able child, both tutor and tutee have been found to benefit. Co-operative learning has been found to 'promote higher self-esteem and greater empathy' so that, in the absence of competition, the success of one pupil can mean success for another (Topping, 1988: 2). It has been the writer's experience that primary school children, on the whole, enjoy supporting one another and benefit in many ways from this. The less able children are helped to succeed where they would have failed and the more able children can develop in understanding and caring as well as reinforcing their own skills.

Unstructured peer tutoring

This approach generally uses older students or pupils to tutor younger ones and is sometimes referred to as cross-age tutoring. It offers no guidance to the tutors as to how to present the lessons which are to be taught. This demands a great deal of organisation and planning of sessions from the tutors and therefore benefits the tutors far more than the tutees in most instances.

An after-school tutorial programme for low achievers in the Lower East Side of Manhattan (Mobilisation for Youth Inc.) was set up in 1963 to deal with reading problems in the Puerto Rican and black pupil population. Older pupils from the same background were used to tutor younger children. Local high school students were hired and trained to help children with homework. Training was for the purpose of helping tutors to relate to their tutees, not with regard to the content of lessons. Over a 5-month period, tutees gained an average of 6 months in reading ability whilst tutors made remarkable gains of 3.4 years on average (Allen, 1976). The need to plan, organise and rethink the content of lesson information to help their tutee perhaps gave tutors a re-learning situation themselves and a new attitude to learning which brought about improvements in many areas of the curriculum, not simply those in which they were tutoring (Gartner, Kohler and Riessman, 1971).

Science and law undergraduates from the University of Auckland in New Zealand acted as tutors in secondary school classrooms producing positive outcomes for themselves, the tutees and the school. Students said the project helped them to communicate better and to develop deeper understanding of their subject. Tutees also gained in confidence and academically and the school benefited from the additional support to staff. The unstructured nature of the tutoring meant that the students had to plan and develop teaching strategies as well as seeing their subject from another perspective (Jones, 1990).

Another cross-age tutoring project, in a British comprehensive school, used poor readers to tutor younger pupils. The project involved eleven 20 minute sessions during a period of just less than 4 weeks. Tutors increased their reading scores significantly more than the control group. By tutoring others, low attaining 14–16 year olds had improved their own reading comprehension skills (Kennedy, 1990).

The difference in age between tutor and tutee appears to be critical in this form of peer tutoring and determines who reaps the greater benefit from the scheme. It has been found that the greater the difference in age and ability, the more gains accrue to the tutees, whereas the closer in age and ability the pairs are, the greater are the improvements for the tutors (Goodlad and Hirst, 1989).

Semi-structured peer tutoring

Here, the tutors have a given worksheet or programme to complete, but are able to adjust what they say to help the tutee as they feel appropriate and to add additional examples or practice when they feel this is necessary.

An example of this method can be seen in 'the Pimlico Connection', a scheme carried out by college students in local schools, focusing on mathematics, science and craft design technology. Although this project could not be said to fulfil strict research criteria, it was suggestive of positive results in relation to improvements in learning, behaviour and attitudes of the pupils. Also the tutors developed teaching skills which were to become the basis from which many would decide that teaching was the career for them (Goodlad and Hirst, 1989).

More recently, Bland and Harris (1989) carried out a peer tutoring project in chemistry using semi-structured methods. Again, this was not organised on formal research lines but brought such positive results that other members of staff in the same school adopted the approach for themselves in other curriculum areas. The pupils were paired by putting the most able pupils with the least able and so on. The lesson began with information and instruction from the teacher, then the most able of the pairs carried out the instructions while the partner observed and commented or checked from the worksheet that the pupil's responses were correct. Then the instructions were carried out by the less able peer with support and guidance from the more able student. In this way, the less able pupils had three opportunities to cover the lesson material.

This approach had structured materials and work sheets with clear guidance from the teacher at the start of each lesson but the dialogue and support which each pair employed were wholly individual and unstructured. The gains which were noted by the teachers were in the increased motivation of the students, better concentration, less talk other than work-related conversation, greater repetition for the less able and instant prompting and praise. All these improvements were additional to the academic improvements which the teachers believed resulted from the project (Bland and Harris, 1989).

Structured peer tutoring

This system uses highly structured materials or rigidly set procedures. Tutors have no ownership of the lesson format and must adhere faithfully to the pre-planned programme which is designed to take the tutee step by small step towards each clearly defined goal before moving on to the next lesson. This method benefits the tutee with very little academic benefit to the tutor. Early studies of peer tutoring carried out by Harris (1967) and Ellson *et al.* (1968) found that structured tutoring was more effective than unstructured systems from the point of view of tutee gains. This form of tutoring requires careful instruction of the tutors before the project can commence and may make the teacher feel more in control than with less rigid peer tutoring structures. However, this need for initial training of tutors may reduce a teacher's willingness to implement a system which could be seen to demand considerable additional work.

Parent tutoring

The need for teachers to give time to training tutors is also an element to be found in many forms of parent tutoring. Although some parents, as far back as biblical times, have spent many hours tutoring their offspring in a wide range of skills, in recent times various attempts to orchestrate this form of tutoring have been tried and researched. Parents may not be 'peers' in exact terms but as a non-professional method of support, parent tutoring can be compared with the various forms of peer tutoring and has been researched under the peer tutoring umbrella.

Some trials of parent tutoring have not brought about significant academic improvements in children's reading (e.g. the Belfield Reading Project referred to below) but the value of parental interest and involvement in children's progress and motivation has been recognised by several studies. Douglas (1968) found that a child's capacity to do well at school was to some extent dependent upon the amount of encouragement from home and Hewison (1979), investigating reading attainment, found that the strongest influence upon a child's reading level was whether he or she was heard read regularly at home.

The Dagenham Project, albeit a small study in which not all groups provided complete data, did find that, out of four factors (high IQ, a favourable language environment at home, help with reading at home, and parents who were keen readers) that the one most strongly associated with reading success was help from parents at home (Hewison, 1979).

Regular practice at home may be seen to affect not only academic progress in the area of reading but also to influence a child's attitudes and enthusiasm for reading and so bring about improvements. Parents have been usefully employed as tutors in many areas of the curriculum and as supporters of behaviour modification programmes but chiefly they have been used in the vital area of reading development. It is in this area of support for reading that three principal approaches have been used to increase the amount of practice children receive in reading. They are: listening to children read; paired reading; and the pause, prompt and praise technique. These three forms of parent tutoring will be considered below.

Parental listening to children read

Listening to children read involves no training, merely a regular supply of reading matter and a willingness on the part of the parents to make time each day to sit with their child and listen to what is read. There is no set technique or pre-set programme in this form of parent tutoring and thus listening to children read can be equated with unstructured peer tutoring.

There have been comparatively few studies on this form of parent tutoring. Perhaps projects which used this approach and failed to bring about significant reading gains such as the Belfield Reading Project (1978) may have influenced teachers unfavourably with regard to its usefulness. A similar project carried out in 32 ILEA infant schools (Hannon and Tizard, 1987) showed little difference between those children who have parental help and those who did not. However, in all such studies it is difficult to obtain control groups since many parents hear their children read, therefore the control group children may also have had help at home.

Not all parent listening projects have been unsuccessful. The PACT projects (PACT being an acronym for Parents and Children and Teachers) begun in ILEA schools in Hackney, encouraged children to take books home and read to parents or siblings and produced positive results in the changed attitudes of the parents and children as well as gains in reading ability (Griffiths and King, 1985).

The Haringey Project (Hewison and Tizard, 1980) compared three groups: parents listening to children read; additional teacher support in reading; and no added support. After 2 years, the first group was well ahead in that over half the children were reading at or above their chronological age compared with only one third of the pupils in the other two groups. The success of the Haringey project in the face of less than successful replications may in part be due to the element of home visits which were made by teachers two or three times a term to parents who were difficult to contact in other ways.

Although this project did not claim to train parents, guidance was given to parents and perhaps home visits developed that element further.

The training factor would seem to be as influential in increasing reading gains as is the selection of those to be tutored. Without parental training sessions or the selection of pupils with the greatest reading difficulties, many projects have shown no significant gains in reading using standardised tests. In contrast, low competence readers, supported by parents who were carefully trained to use set procedures have shown 'repeated and substantial gains' (Toomey, 1993: 229). How much training is necessary to achieve success is not yet clear from present research but training appears to be a crucial element in successful parental tutoring programmes.

Paired reading

This is another method which has been employed by both parents and peers to accelerate children's reading. It was developed by Roger Morgan (1976) and uses behaviour modification principles from psychological learning theory. This method does demand training. Parents are trained to read simultaneously with their tutee at the child's own pace until the child chooses to read alone. Mistakes are corrected and the parent models the correct word or phrase. As confidence increases, the child reads more and more independently.

The great body of research projects in this area show gains up to four times the normal rate for reading accuracy and five times the normal rate for comprehension. This approach thus 'frees the struggling reader from the preoccupation with laborious decoding and enables other strategies to come into play' (Topping and Wolfendale, 1985: 112). Because reading is uninterrupted, a child's interest in the text and comprehension of what is read is improved (Elliott and Hewison, 1994).

In a review of nine studies of paired reading, the experimental group gains for both reading accuracy and comprehension were significantly greater than those for the control groups. On average, where the project period was an average of 2.7 months, the control group gains were 4.4 months for comprehension and 2.9 months for reading accuracy, whereas the experimental group gains were 9.8 months for comprehension and 6.5 for reading accuracy (Toomey, 1993).

As has been noted in several peer tutoring projects, the more structured the tutoring, the greater are the benefits to the tutees. Thus paired reading projects might be expected, as a semi-structured approach, to be more likely to achieve significant reading and comprehension gains than unstructured parental listening. In a review of the few comparison studies of parental involvement in children's reading which used control groups Toomey (1993) found no significant differences in effectiveness between parental tutoring approaches. This conflicts with the findings of Leach and Siddall (1990), who compared four types of parent tutoring: direct instruction;

pause, prompt and praise; paired reading; and traditional 'hearing'. Of these four approaches, the most structured direct instruction method proved the most effective. Reviews by Topping and Wolfendale (1985) and Topping and Lindsay (1992) also found that most of the comparative studies suggested that paired reading is more effective than just listening to children read.

From a class teacher's point of view, perhaps the ten projects (reported by Topping, 1987) which were carried out by mainstream class teachers using peer tutored paired reading may carry more weight despite the fact that they were not truly experimental and used a variety of training, monitoring and evaluation procedures. Nevertheless, they were carried out by teachers in 'the real world of teaching and learning' (Topping, 1987: 135). Most of these projects used same-age tutors and tutees who both gained at approximately four times the normal rate in reading skill. Such results may influence teachers to use paired reading techniques in both peer and parent tutoring situations.

Pause, prompt and praise

This method of facilitating children's reading was first researched in New Zealand. It grew out of the research of professor Marie Clay and was used in her 'Reading Recovery Project' (1979) which established that self-correction was not only natural and desirable but was also more frequently seen in better readers. Further development of this approach by McNaughton *et al.* (1981) found that both self-correction and reading accuracy were improved by a delay in attention to errors.

The emphasis of this method is upon training the tutors, focusing upon the meaning of the text and the need to give time for the tutee to self-correct errors. Parents are trained to pause before correcting an error. If the tutee fails to self-correct, a prompt or clue will be given related either to the graphic or contextual nature of the error. Only after two such prompts is the correct word modelled. Whenever a sentence is read, self-corrected or completed, the tutor praises the tutee in such a way as to make it clear exactly what is being praised. This is done to help the tutees develop more varied strategies to support their own reading (Merrett, 1988).

The level of difficulty of the reading matter is considered important and should be between 80% and 95% accuracy level. Above that level of accuracy the text would prove too easy; below this level, too difficult (Wheldall and Mettem, 1985). The need for training is also considered important. Although there are booklets and videos available to support parent training sessions, the overburdened teacher may feel disinclined to use what little leisure time she or he has to conduct parental training meetings. However, since no pause, prompt and praise '... studies were identified as showing non-significant effects on children's reading competence and parents' training behaviour' (Toomey, 1993: 226) perhaps the effort required would be a valuable investment.

Research begun in 1986 by the School Curriculum Development Committee found that by using this approach, pupils were gaining on average at almost three times the normal rate (Merrett, 1988). In this semi-structured pause, prompt and praise tutoring project, tutees in the experimental group made reading accuracy gains of 6.0 months over the 24 tutorial sessions involved but the control group, who were tutored by untrained tutors, made an average gain of only 2.4 months. The whole programme took 8 weeks and although half the children in the experimental group gained more than 6 months, none of the control groups made such improvements. The gains appeared not to be due solely to the additional time spent each week in reading but to the structured approach of the trained tutors (Merrett, 1988).

A peer tutoring project using this method with secondary remedial readers found that 16-year-old pupils with reading difficulties were successfully trained to use the pause, prompt and praise technique with 12-year-old remedial readers, to the benefit of the tutees. Tutees with reading deficits made greater improvements when tutored by trained as opposed to untrained tutors (Wheldall and Mettem, 1985). The authors suggested that the training was valuable and manageable:

> ... the technique offers a clearly specified and relatively easily trainable set of key tutoring behaviours which are shown to be effective and which can be readily monitored.
>
> (Wheldall and Mettem, 1985: 43)

One study which compared the training and use of paired reading with the pause, prompt and praise approach (Winter, 1986) found no significant differences between the improvements made by pupils tutored in either method. This study also showed that peer tutors could be used effectively to back up the support given by parents:

> ... it appears that both parents and peers can be trained to use 'pause, prompt and praise' procedures relatively quickly and easily and that their application is successful in bringing about important changes for the better in low-progress readers.
>
> (Merrett, 1988: 22)

Despite the difficulties of research into parent tutoring, there appear to be benefits worth working towards. When parents are enabled to feel that they are in partnership with the school their attitudes towards school may improve, especially as they come to believe the school is doing the best for their child. Parents who thus become more supportive of the school may increase their child's eagerness to learn through their own changed attitudes (Bloom, 1987).

There appear to be definite advantages of using parents as tutors especially employing the two methods, in which training is involved. Teachers who find it difficult to hear children read themselves might profitably consider organising parent tutoring of some sort. It may not be possible in the light of the present review to be sure why parental involvement in reading benefits children (i.e. is it simply extra practice; one-to-one tuition; more immediate feedback; more valuable reinforcement) but it seems from this review that parent and peer tutoring are resources which should be used as fully as possible. Peer tutoring has been shown to bring a variety of benefits to teachers, tutors and tutees. These advantages will be considered below.

Advantages of peer tutoring – to the teacher

Having someone to listen to pupils read and practise academic skills with other than the class teacher, may be helpful both in terms of the gains to the children and the additional time it gives to the teacher to do other things. Twenty years ago, it was noted that:

> Every child should spend part of each day in reading or pre-reading activities. The teacher should give each child individual attention several times a week, helping him with his reading and keeping meticulous check on progress.
>
> (DES, 1975: 523)

Most primary teachers would say that individual attention 'several times a week' is desirable but unattainable. This is probably the most advantageous aspect of peer tutoring from a teacher's point of view. Whilst the teacher may be unable to provide such a high level of individual attention, a level clearly essential to the learning development of some pupils with learning difficulties, peer and parent tutoring can be a way of meeting this need, if it is used properly.

It is sad that some teachers fear peer tutoring seeing it as a threat to their own role. It would be far better to see it as an opportunity to deal with the complex tasks of curriculum planning, monitoring, assessment, evaluation and the development of the learning environment. It requires a high degree of professional organisation to implement a successful peer tutoring project and this can only enhance a teacher's status. Peer tutoring should be viewed as one of many educational techniques from which teachers choose in order to meet the needs of their pupils (Topping and Wolfendale, 1985).

As the class is reduced from one large community to several smaller units or even pairs, the problems of indiscipline may also be reduced. Research has shown that peer tutoring pairs not only improve academically but that improvements in social behaviour and attitudes to each other can also take place (Sharpley and Sharpley, 1981). In many classrooms today, an improvement in behaviour and attitudes would make peer tutoring valuable even if its value academically was nil! There is considerable research which suggests that 'peer tutoring helps to improve the social climate of the classroom and this is considered to be just as important as any academic gains which might accrue' (Atherley, 1989: 146). This same article refers to the development of new friendships within the tutoring pairs, to an acceptance of differences in ability and personality, a readiness to praise someone else's efforts and an increase in motivation towards reading. Such changes benefit not only the pupils but the teacher, too.

Advantages of peer tutoring – to the tutors

The improvements in behaviour mentioned earlier have been found to extend to children with learning and behaviour problems, especially when they are given the role of tutor (Topping, 1990). Tutoring can give pupils of any age or ability level a responsibility for someone else which can greatly alter the behaviour of the tutor.

When fourth, fifth and sixth grade students were asked to apply for 'jobs' in a Peer Education Programme to support students with intensive need, the tutors developed patience and a deep understanding of their partners' difficulties. Students also 'demonstrated significant growth in positive attitudes toward individuals with disabilities'. Although these developments helped to achieve academic gains for the tutees, the gains in social maturity for the tutors were considered to be important, too (Fulton *et al.*, 1994: 8).

Taking on the role of tutor/teacher has been seen as a way of developing a person's ability to put themselves in someone else's place; to develop an empathy with others. Having played the role of the teacher, a pupil will be better able to see things from the teacher's view and a more responsible attitude to learning can begin (Allen, 1976).

The role of tutor is not restricted to academically superior pupils. When mentally handicapped pupils tutored able-bodied peers in sign language, both tutors and tutees gained in skills, with additional gains to the tutees of understanding and acceptance of the pupils (Topping, 1988).

By assuming the teacher's role, pupils with learning difficulties and behaviour problems can change the tutor's perception of themselves and so bring about changes not only in their behaviour but in the learning of those they tutor. Tutoring younger children can bring a sense of self-worth and success to children who have previously experienced little but failure. With proper training, even pupils with special educational needs can benefit as tutors whilst accruing gains for their tutees (Osguthorpe and Scruggs, 1986).

The need to rehearse known facts and organise them, is believed to benefit tutors, especially when the age and ability of the tutors is close. It can also be a less embarrassing way for older students to go over subject matter for a younger pupil which they themselves can benefit from practising. For some pupils, tutoring can give the curriculum purpose and relevance. A substantial amount of research has shown that tutors make significant gains in their own reading when tutoring others, even when they themselves are of low ability:

> Helping somebody improve their reading skill leads to improvements in the reading performance of the tutor at the same time.
>
> (Merrett, 1988: 18)

The staggering gains made by the tutors on the New York project, Mobilisation for Youth, referred to earlier, led researchers to suggest that pupils may learn how to learn by teaching others:

> ... children learn more from teaching other children ... every child must be given the opportunity to play the teaching role ... through playing this role ... he may really learn how to learn.
>
> (Gartner, Kohler and Riessman, 1971: 1)

Advantages of peer tutoring – to the tutees

As has been documented above, peer tutoring does benefit the tutees academically to varying degrees depending upon the type of tutoring employed and the pair combinations involved. Tutees have been shown to benefit most from being tutored by older and more able students rather than by same-age tutors. In same-age tutoring, tutors themselves tend to benefit the most.

Structured peer tutoring has been found to bring the greatest gains to the tutees. When carefully planned and executed programmes are followed by tutors or parents who have been given sufficient instruction in carrying out the necessary procedures, recordable academic improvements accrue to the tutees.

Teachers who feel that the time spent in training the tutors is counterproductive should not be put off, since research findings show that the benefits far outweigh the additional time spent in training the tutors or parents and planning the structured programmes. In such structured situations the tutee is provided with far more positive feedback and repetition of correct responses than the teacher can possibly give. The advantages to the tutee are great, not only in academic terms but in terms of the self-esteem which can grow out of regular successful situations. If tutors give positive responses each time the tutee is correct, learning will be reinforced and peer tutoring offers the chance of more individual instruction than can be given by a class teacher.

Children, especially those who experience difficulties with their work, are often happier being helped by their peers than by the teacher. This proved to be the case in a project carried out by the writer. In a same-age tutoring project carried out in a mainstream Year 2 primary class, the researcher and the class teacher found that children who had previously been reluctant to read to the teacher because of lack of ability and a consequent dislike of reading, were happy to read to their partner and less embarrassed about admitting that a book was proving too difficult for them. In this situation their partner changed the book for them which meant they themselves did not need to speak to the teacher about their difficulty:

> Tutees often feel more comfortable being helped by other children than by teachers and parents.
>
> (Winter, 1986: 103)

Conclusions

If peer tutoring is to be effective, which research would seem to indicate that it can be, it must be planned to meet the needs of the pupils. Teachers must decide whether the tutors or the tutees are their main priority since the approaches to peer tutoring are varied and bring benefits to tutors and tutees in differing degrees depending upon the strategies employed.

The most extensive research into peer tutoring which took place in the 1960s and 1970s in the USA shows that in many situations it is the tutors who make the most significant gains academically. Also, that it is possible to train tutors to employ complex and highly structured approaches to tutoring to improve benefits to the tutees. When the pause, prompt and praise strategies are taught to tutors, the tutees make significant improvements in their reading skills (Topping, 1988). Despite the time taken to teach, for example, the constant time delay method, it has been shown that tutors can employ the strategy with 97% accuracy (Wolery *et al.*, 1994). Some writers have been led to comment:

> The student is an educational tool with great potential as an instructional agent.
>
> (Ehley and Larsen, 1980: 20)

Not everyone is convinced of the effectiveness of peer tutoring. Because the majority of research into peer tutoring takes place in the 'real' educational world of school and college, there may be a desire, on the part of those involved in the projects, to report success, which leads to the publication of only those projects which have had positive results. It has been noted by Cohen *et al.* (1982) that the effects of such projects are smaller in unpublished dissertations than those that appear in books and journals.

Nevertheless, the effectiveness of peer tutoring has been demonstrated in many classrooms to the satisfaction of the teacher and to the benefit of the pupils. It offers the child with learning difficulties individual attention on a level beyond the capacity of a class teacher, in a non-threatening environment. Children receive frequent and immediate feedback and positive reinforcement of their efforts from a role model with whom they feel comfortable.

It must be stated that there are possibly many unpublished peer tutoring studies which have not produced significant academic gains for either the tutees or the tutors. Although many of the studies into peer tutoring would not satisfy the demands of rigorous experimental research, much of the American research of the 1960s and 1970s was meticulous. This research generally demonstrates the effectiveness of peer tutoring, especially for the tutors. From this grew the belief that every child should have the opportunity to play the role of tutor. This role apparently improves the pupil's self-esteem, attitudes to work and interest in his or her own learning processes (Gartner, Kohler and Riessman, 1971).

Finally, the fact that millions of teachers around the world employ these strategies and believe sincerely in their effectiveness probably carries more weight with classroom-based educationalists than any number of research studies could. Further support for peer tutoring comes from recalling that centuries ago, Comenius recognised its value when he wrote: 'He who teaches, learns'.

Peer tutoring has much to recommend it as an effective educational tool:

- all those involved in it benefit;
- teachers have more time to organise and support where the need is greatest;
- tutors develop their own skills in order to better support their partner;
- tutees improve in confidence and academic learning through intensive one-to-one support and praise.

In addition, benefits of improved behaviour, attitudes and motivation enhance the effectiveness of peer tutoring in the eyes of those who use it.

References

Alder, P. (1989) 'Report from the London Conference on peer tutoring', *Times Educational Supplement Scotland*, **13 January**, 20.

Allen, V. L., (1976) *Children as Teachers – Theory and Research on Tutoring*. New York: Academic Press.

Atherley, C. A. (1989) 'Shared Reading: an experiment in peer tutoring in the primary classroom', *Educational Studies*, **15** (2), 145–53.

Bland, M. and Harris, G. (1989) 'Peer tutoring as part of collaborative teaching in chemistry'. In M. Hinson (ed.) *Teachers and Special Educational Needs – Coping with Change*. Harlow: Longman.

Bloom, W. (1987). *Partnership with Parents in Reading*. Sevenoaks: Hodder and Stoughton.

Clay, M., (1979) *Reading: The Patterning of Complex Behaviour*. (2nd edn.) Auckland: Heinemann.

Cohen, P. A., Kulik, J. A. and Kulik, C. L. C. (1982) 'Educational outcomes of tutoring: a meta-analysis of findings', *American Educational Research Journal*, **18** (2), 237–48.

Department of Education and Science (1975) *A Language for Life. (The Bullock Report.)* London, HMSO.

Douglas, J. P. (1968) *All our Future*. London: MacGibbon and Kee.

Ehly, S. W. and Larson, S. C., (1980) *Peer Tutoring for Individualised Instruction*. Boston: Allyn and Bacon.

Elliott, J. A. and Hewison, J. (1994) 'Comprehension and interest in home reading', *British Journal of Educational Psychology*, **64**, 203–20.

Ellson, D. G., Harris, P. L. and Barber, L. (1968) 'A field test of programmed and directed tutoring', *Reading Research Quarterly*, **3** (3), 307–67.

Fulton, I., LeRoy, C., Pinkney, M. and Weekley, T. (1994) 'Peer education partners', *Teaching Exceptional Children*, **Summer**, 6–11.

Gartner, A., Kohler, M. and Riessman, F. (1971) *Children Teach Children – Learning by Teaching*, New York: Harper and Row.

Goodlad, S. and Hirst, B. (1989) *Peer Tutoring – A Guide to Learning by Teaching*. London: Kogan Page.

Goodlad, S. and Hirst, B. (1990) *Explorations in Peer Tutoring*. Oxford: Blackwell.

Griffiths, A. and King, A. (1985) '"PACT": development of home-reading schemes in the ILEA'. In Topping, K., and Wolfendale, S., (eds) *Parental Involvement in Children's Reading*. London: Croom Helm.

Hannon, P. and Tizard, B. (1987) 'Parent involvement: a no-score draw?' *Times Educational Supplement*, **3 April**, 23.

Harris, P. L. (1968) 'Experimental comparison of two methods of tutoring – programmed versus directed', *Dessertation Abstracts International*, **28 (8-A)**, 3072.

Hewison, J. (1979) *'Home Environment and Reading Attainment – A study of Children in a Working-class Community*. Unpublished PhD thesis. University of London.

Hewison, J. and Tizard, J. (1980) 'Parental involvement and reading attainment', *British Journal of Educational Psychology*, **50**, 209–15.

Jackson, A. and Hannon, P. (1978) *The Belfield Reading Project*. Rochdale: Belfield Community Council.

Jones, J. (1990) 'Tutoring as field-based learning: some New Zealand developments'. In Goodlad, S. and Hirst, B. (eds) *Explorations in Peer Tutoring*. Oxford: Blackwell.

Kennedy, M. (1990) 'Controlled evaluation of the effects of peer tutoring on the tutors: Are the "learning by teaching" theories viable?' In Goodlad, S. and Hirst, B. (eds) *Explorations in Peer Tutoring*. Oxford: Blackwell.

Leach, D. J. and Siddall, S. W. (1990) 'Parental involvement in the teaching of reading: A comparison of hearing reading, paired reading, pause prompt and praise and direct instruction methods', *British Journal of Educational Psychology*, **60**, 349–55.

McNaughton, S., Glynn, T. and Robinson, V. (1981) *Parents as Remedial Tutors: Issues for home and school*. Wellington: NZCER. Now published as McNaughton, S., Glynn, T., and Robinson, V. (1987) *Pause, Prompt and Praise: Effective Tutoring for Remedial Reading*. Birmingham: Positive Products.

Merrett, F. (1988) 'Peer tutoring of reading using the pause, prompt and praise techniques', *Education and Child Psychology*, **5 (4)**, 15–23.

Miller, L. J., Kohler, H. E., Hoel, K. and Strain, P. S. (1993) 'Winning with peer tutoring – a teacher's guide', *Preventing School Failure*, **37 (3)**, 14–18.

Morgan, R. T. T. (1976) '"Paired reading" tuition: a preliminary report on a technique for cases of reading deficit', *Child Care, Health and Development*, **2**, 13–28.

Osguthoorpe, R. T. and Scruggs, T. E. (1986) 'Special education students as tutors: a review and analysis', *Remedial and Special Education*, **7 (4)**, 15–25.

Sharpley, A. M. and Sharpley, C. F. (1981) 'Peer tutoring: a review of the literature', CORE *Collected Original Resources in Education*, **5 (3)**, 7–C11.

Toomey, D. (1993) 'Parents hearing their children read: a review. Rethinking the lessons of the Haringey Project', *Educational Research*, **35 (3)**, 223–33.

Topping, K. (1987) 'Peer tutored paired reading: outcome data from ten projects', *Educational Psychology*, **7 (2)**, 133–44.

Topping, K. (1988a) *The Peer Tutoring Handbook – Promoting Co-operative Learning*. London: Croom Helm.

Topping, K., (1988b) 'An introduction to peer tutoring', *Education and Child*

Psychology, **5** (4), 6–16.

Topping, K., (1988c) 'Peer tutoring of reading using paired reading', *Education and Child Psychology*, **5** (4), 24–28.

Topping, K. (1990) 'Listening to children read', *Child Education*, **August**, 34–35.

Topping, K. (1991) 'Achieving more with less: Raising reading standards via parental involvement and peer tutoring', *Support for Learning*, **6** (3), 112–115.

Topping K. and Wolfendale, S. (1985) *Parental Involvement in Children's Reading*. London: Croom Helm.

Topping, K. and Lindsay, G. A. (1992) 'Paired reading: a review of the literature', *Research Papers in Education*, **7** (3), 199–246.

Wagner, L. (1982) *Peer Teaching – Historical Perspectives*. Westport: Greenwood.

Wheldall, K. and Mettem, P. (1985) 'Behavioural Peer Tutoring: training 16 year old tutors to employ the 'pause, prompt and praise' method with 12 year old remedial readers', *Educational Psychology*, **5** (1), 27–44.

Winter, S. (1986) 'Peers as paired reading tutors', *British Journal of Special Education*, **13** (3), 103–106.

Wolery, M., Werts, M.G., Snyder, E. D. and Caldwell, N. K. (1994) 'Efficacy of constant time delay implemented by peer tutors in general education classrooms', *Journal of Behavioral Education*, **4** (4), 415–536.

IV Controversial Individual Interventions

10 Coloured Lenses and Overlays – Do They Really Work?

Just as dyslexia itself is a highly emotive subject, so some of the remediation techniques advocated for dyslexics are equally controversial. One such treatment, the use of coloured lenses, is considered by some to make reading easier by counteracting the light-sensitive conditions which are believed to affect some children. There is growing interest in the use of coloured filters and lenses and the perceptual dysfunction referred to as scotopic sensitivity syndrome (SSS), which they are claimed to alleviate.

History

In 1980, a New Zealand teacher, Olive Meares, published an article on the use of dirty, opaque perspex sheets for pupils who found the background to the printed page strongly intrusive. Despite the anecdotal nature of much of this work, Meares recorded that the use of filters proved to be helpful. Some pupils used the overlays less as their reading developed whilst others continued to use them even when reading had improved. However, there is no suggestion in Meares' work that her pupils had sensitivity to any specific part of the light spectrum.

It is on this point that the research of Helen Irlen, an American educational psychologist, differs. In a paper presented to the American Psychological Association's 91st annual convention (1983), she put forward her findings on the visual difficulties encountered by some of her adult clients. The difficulties which these people had described were that letters and words seemed to flicker, flash, move or even disappear, thus making reading an unpleasant experience. As a result of a series of questions from the Irlen Differential Perceptual Schedule (IDPS) clients were asked about various visual difficulties they encounter when reading. Lenses were prescribed to relieve these problems. The sufferers were retested immediately using the lenses and questioned further a month later to see if improvements had occurred in their reading performance, concentration, eye strain and writing. Irlen claimed that all her subjects reported improvements in visual resolution and that distortions of clarity and stability had been eliminated due to the use of the lenses supplied (Stone and Harris, 1991). This claim, that some people can read for longer and more comfortably with the use of Irlen lenses, has been extended to include claims about improvements in reading accuracy and comprehension.

The Irlen Institute, California, and centres in the UK, Australia and other states in the USA assess and treat individuals, especially dyslexics, despite the largely anecdotal nature of Irlen's work and the lack of well-designed, rigorous research into the effectiveness of lenses or overlays. The lenses provided are typically expensive compared with the simple overlays found to be effective by Meares, which were extremely cheap. It would seem essential to evaluate carefully the effectiveness of both lenses and overlays to determine if they work, and if so, why they work. It is most important to establish what accounts for the improvements claimed in order to avoid disappointment and distress to pupils who are already experiencing difficulties in learning to read.

There is an important distinction between overlays and tinted lenses or glasses. An overlay absorbs light prior to and following reflection from the printed page. There is a double spectral absorption, whereas with lenses there is only one absorption as reflected light from the page travels to the eyes. The colour of an overlay and an Irlen filter are rarely the same. Irlen considers overlays as an intermediate step towards alleviating symptoms whereas tinted lenses are seen as potentially more effective.

Visual difficulties underlying reading problems are considered by some writers to be widespread. For example, Irlen and Lass (1989) claim that 50% of dyslexics have a visual perceptual dysfunction which may affect their ability to read and write. Some of the symptoms and signs of the syndrome reported by Irlen are listed below from Evans and Drasdo (1991):

1. *Visual resolution* – The inability to keep an image constant. The page becomes distorted with letters moving, getting darker and lighter, blurring, seeing double images, words spreading, flashing and flickering. The whole page can seem to swirl or 'white out' altogether.
2. *Photophobia (called background resolution by Irlen)* – The inability to tolerate bright light and glare. Problems occur with black print on white paper. Shapes become distorted.
3. *Sustained focus* – Sufferers have trouble keeping the words in focus and this is said to be independent of refractive correction. Included in this category are people whose focus is said to be clear but who find that after reading for a short time they are tired, their eyes water, hurt, burn or itch and they have to take a break.
4. *Span of focus* – Irlen refers to the number of letters comprehended during a fixation pause (referred to as the average span of recognition). This is much reduced, punctuation is not used and comprehension is only obtained through re-reading. Irlen describes under this heading an inability to perceive groups of words at the same time and a type of tunnel

vision where a small area or group of letters are clearly defined but everything is out of focus.

5. *Depth of focus* – This is poor, not just when reading.
6. *Eye strain* – This reduces the time spent reading and causes blinking, staring, squinting and poor concentration.

Irlen's contention is that these perceptual dysfunctions are components of SSS which adversely affect a person's ability to read as a result of sensitivity to certain light sources, luminance, intensity, wavelengths and colour contrasts. The Irlen Institute treats such conditions with coloured lenses.

Research

The existence of SSS seems to be substantiated by several researchers. Seventy-four per cent of adults with reading difficulties and 15% of the adult population with adequate or above reading abilities have been found to have such symptoms (Miller, 1984). Other studies report that between 46% and 50% of low-ability readers have symptoms of SSS (Adler and Atwood, 1987; Irlen, 1983; Robinson and Miles, 1987; Whiting, 1988).

However, questions have been raised about the theory that coloured lenses work by filtering out a specific band of light. The suggestion that some individuals respond dysfunctionally to specific wavelengths of light and that for those with SSS, full spectral light produces over-stimulation of the retinal receptors, which in turn can cause problems of seeing, is disputed by ophthalmologists. Evans and Drasdo (1991) believe it is not possible that retinal receptors in a non-diseased eye with normal colour perception would respond abnormally. Also, since Fitzgerald (1989) has revealed that only some of the light at a particular wavelength is filtered out by tinted lenses, Irlen's claim that it is by filtering *out* a band of light that the lenses produce their beneficial effect is difficult to support. In addition, the word scotopic refers to a physiological characteristic related to the levels of illumination at which the eye is dark adapted (Cline, Hofstetter, and Griffin 1989). Over a period of 30–40 minutes when a person is removed from normal illumination to a dark environment, dark adaptation gradually occurs:

> The retinal receptors required for reading are the cones, which provide distinct central vision in normal lighting. The cones are deactivated in the dark. This allows the peripherally located retinal receptors and rods to become activated. The rods provide visual processing under low illumination or night vision conditions. Reading does not occur under conditions of dark adaptation. Hence, the semantic basis for 'scotopic sensitivity syndrome' is questionable.
>
> (Cardinal, Griffin and Christenson, 1993: 277)

The difficulties presented by the theory and definition of SSS aside, several studies have reported the beneficial effects of using Irlen lenses and coloured overlays. A decrease in background distortions, increase in reading time, decrease in fatigue and strain as well as improvements in reading accuracy and comprehension and self-concept are recorded by Irlen (1983), Adler and Atwood (1987), Robinson and Miles (1987), Gregg (1988), Robinson and Conway (1990), O'Connor and Sofo (1988), O'Connor *et al.* (1990) and Whiting (1985, 1988). However, many of these studies are based upon self-reporting data from students who claimed to experience positive improvements and relief from the symptoms of SSS through wearing Irlen lenses. Those interested in the effectiveness and validity of the research are warned that much of the supportive literature appears in publications that do not use a peer-review process (Spafford *et al.*, 1995).

A review of the literature conducted by Rosner and Rosner (1987) warns of the dangers of panaceas and miracle cures which are heavily propounded by developers and marketers only to fade subsequently into obscurity. Concern was expressed in this review over the lack of definition of the criteria for diagnosing SSS and the failure of the Irlen Institute to explain the exact composition of the Irlen Differential Perceptual Schedule. Without such information it is impossible to replicate studies. The criticism that there are few objective reports of changes due to the use of lenses adds to the concerns about the adequacy of the research:

> ... improvement due to the treatment is based only on subjective reports of the clients, rather than on quantitative statistics from objective tests, casts a shadow over the validity of Irlen's findings.
>
> (Cardinal *et al.*, 1993: 276)

Studies on effectiveness

In studies by O'Connor *et al.* (1990) and Robinson and Conway (1990) readers improved significantly in reading comprehension and accuracy when using the prescribed colour overlay. In contrast, the study conducted by Blaskey *et al.* (1990) found Irlen lenses to be ineffective. All three of these studies have been considered methodologically unsound by three experts in the field writing in the same issue of the journal (Hoyt, 1990; Parker, 1990; Solan, 1990).

A study which used coloured overlays, but not specifically prescribed tints, found that 'simply reducing the contrast of text materials, or using colour overlays in books, at practically no expense to the client, produces definite and measurable results' (Williams *et al.*, 1992: 414). In about 80% of the learning disabled children tested, the use of coloured overlays produced measurable gains in reading comprehension. Richardson (1988) used only red filters in a small study involving ten dyslexic boys. The subjects performed better on word reading with the filter, but this perhaps only complicates the situation. It certainly cannot be said to support Irlen's theory that pupils require a specific colour filter to deal with their problem. The use of overlays chosen specifically for each student, over the use of randomly chosen or clear overlays, resulted in significant improvement for word matching, letter recognition and number recognition tasks, but not for word identification (Robinson and Miles, 1987).

Winter (1987) concluded that Irlen lenses did not improve performance in any way when he tested dyslexic pupils using Irlen lenses, untinted lenses, plain grey lenses and no lenses at all. However, some children reported that the untinted or grey lenses actually assisted them with their task. The fact that five of the pupils forgot to bring their lenses with them on the day of the test may suggest that the children themselves had little belief in their efficacy. Other studies have also been unable to demonstrate improvements in reading ability as a result of tinted lenses (e.g. Blaskey *et al.*, 1990; Speld, 1989).

Although there is clearly no firm evidence for the effectiveness of tinted lenses and overlays, there is equally little conclusive evidence to the contrary. The studies of O'Connor *et al.*, (1990) and Robinson and Conway (1990) suggest that some pupils may experience some benefits as a result of wearing coloured lenses. Exactly what they are experiencing and how any improvements are produced remains to be explained. It may be that some children do experience discomfort and difficulties with glare and that any reduction in this may make it easier to concentrate upon the printed text. Those who are susceptible to the 'dazzle' effect can be helped in two ways (Wilkins, 1989): by covering all but the line which is being read and thus reducing the stripe pattern, and by using tinted lenses, especially those which absorb green light, namely red filters, with which improvements have been recorded. However, the overall conclusion regarding the effectiveness of Irlen lenses from the studies conducted to date remains basically that stated by Solan several years ago:

> It appears that when investigations using tinted lenses and overlays are carefully designed and controlled, the results do not lend support to Irlen's hypothesis.
>
> (Solan, 1990: 626)

Implications and conclusions

Research so far into the effectiveness of tinted lenses and overlays is not conclusive. It is also questionable whether lenses should be prescribed to cure a syndrome about which there seems no clear definition from which to determine a diagnosis, especially since such prescriptions remain expensive. Since any sheet of dirty perspex or randomly assigned colour tint appears to be as likely to improve performance as an expensively produced lens, perhaps those pupils and parents who feel that there may be some benefit for them in tinted lenses should be allowed to test out inexpensive sheets to reduce glare or dazzle while researchers investigate more rigorously the Irlen theory.

Although some individuals claim to be more comfortable when using the prescribed lenses, research, as yet, has not demonstrated significant gains in reading. Some researchers believe that tinted lens treatments are subject to the placebo effect. Subjects, believing that the treatment is therapeutic, may experience improvements which are due to factors other than the lenses themselves. By making a previously hidden problem obvious by the wearing of spectacles the subject may receive additional support and understanding which could enhance self-concept. A desire for the lenses to 'work' may also increase motivation and the increased work effort may affect improvement which is not due to the lenses directly (Stanley, 1987). A positive change in pupils' attitude to school as a result of wearing tinted spectacles and the impact of a placebo effect has been reported by several researchers (Fitzgerald, 1989; Hoyt, 1990; Robinson and Conway, 1990).

Much of the research conducted to date on this topic suffers from lack of controls, self-selection of subjects, lack of proper screening for vision defects, confused terminology and a marked lack of scientific data. It is obviously very difficult to produce an effective placebo for use with control groups but this is clearly what is required if research is to begin to unravel the strands of this puzzle. It has been suggested that placebo lenses which look similar to the preferred colour but which are significantly different in light transmission value would be useful (Robinson and Conway, 1994).

Although tinted lenses may seem to be a harmless treatment this writer agrees with Rosner and Rosner (1988) who wrote:

> The 'may as well try this new idea – what harm can it do' attitude is not acceptable. A child's basic resources are time and emotional and physical energy. If these are wasted on useless treatments, that is harmful.
>
> (p.833).

Children who have difficulties in reading and writing require the best we have to offer to alleviate their problems. Any unproven therapy delays the application of more appropriate corrective measures (Spafford *et al.*, 1995). The learning disabled, or dyslexic, child deserves better than that.

References

Adler, L., and Atwood, M. (1987) *Poor Readers – What do they Really See on the Page: A Study of a Major Cause of Dyslexia.* Los Angeles: County Office of Education.

Blaskey, P., Scheiman, M., Parisi, M., Ciner, E. B., Gallaway, M. and Selznick, R. (1990) 'The effectiveness of Irlen filters for improving reading performance: A pilot study', *Journal of Learning disabilities*, **23**, 604–12.

Cardinal, D. N., Griffin, J. R. and Christenson, G. N. (1993) 'Do tinted lenses really help students with reading disabilities?' *Intervention in School and Clinic*, **28 (5)**, 275–79.

Cline, D., Hofstetter, H. W. and Griffin, J. R. (1989) *Dictionary of visual science.* Radnor, PA: Chilton.

Evans, B. J. W. and Drasdo, N. (1991) 'Tinted lenses and related therapies for disabilities – a review', *Ophthalmological and Physiological Optics*, **11**, 206–17.

Fitzgerald, B. A. (1989) *Effect of Tinted Lenses on Contrast Sensitivity in Normal and Dyslexic Children*. Master's thesis, University of Sydney, Australia.

Gregg, P. J. (1988) 'Dyslexia and tinted filters', *Optician*, **29 January**, 17–20.

Hoyt, C. S. (1990) 'Irlen lenses and reading difficulties', *Journal of Learning Disabilities*, **23 (10)**, 624–27.

Irlen, H. L. (1983) *Successful Treatment of Learning Disabilities*. Paper presented at the ninety-first annual convention of the American Psychological Association, Anaheim, Ca.

Irlen, H. and Lass, M. J. (1989) 'Improving reading problems due to symptoms of scotopic sensitivity syndrome using Irlen lenses and overlays', *Education*, **109**, 4.

Meares, O. (1980) 'Figure background, brightness contrast and reading disabilities', *Visible Language*, **14 (1)**, 13–39.

Miller, L. S. (1984) *Scotopic Sensitivity and Reading Disability*. Unpublished Master of Education thesis, California State University, Los Angeles.

O'Connor, P. D. and Sofo, F. (1988) 'Dyslexia and tinted lenses: a response to Gordon Stanley', *Australian Journal of Remedial Education*, **20**, 10–12.

O'Connor, P. D., Sofo, F., Kendall, L. and Olsen, G. (1990) 'Reading disabilities and the effects of coloured filters', *Journal of Learning Disabilities*, **23**, 597–603.

Parker, R. M. (1990) 'Power, control and validity in research', *Journal of Learning Disabilities*, **23 (10)**, 613–20.

Richardson, A. (1988) 'The effects of a specific red filter on dyslexia', *British Psychological Society Abstracts'*, 56.

Robinson, G. L. and Conway, R. N. F. (1990) 'The effects of Irlen coloured lenses on students' specific reading skills and their perception of ability: a 12-month validity study', *Journal of Learning Disabilities*, **23**, 588–96.

Robinson, G. L. and Conway, R. N. (1994) 'Irlen filters and reading strategies: effect of coloured filters on reading achievement, specific reading strategies, and perception of ability', *Perceptual and Motor Skills*, **79**, 467–83.

Robinson, G.L. and Miles, J. (1987) 'The use of coloured overlays to improve visual processing – a preliminary survey', *Exceptional Child*, **34**, 65–70.

Rosner, J. and Rosner, J. (1987) 'The Irlen lens treatment: A review of the literature', *Optician*, **194**, 26–33.

Rosner, J. and Rosner, J. (1988) 'Another cure for dyslexia?' *Journal of the American Optometric Association*, **59**, 832–4.

Solan, H. A. (1990) 'An appraisal of the Irlen technique of correcting reading disorders using tinted overlays and tinted lenses', *Journal of Learning Disabilities*, **23 (10)**, 621–3, 626.

Spafford, C. S., Grosser, G. S., Donatelle, J. R., Squillace, S. R. and Dana J. P. (1995) 'Contrast sensitivity differences between proficient and disabled readers using coloured lenses', *Journal of Learning Disabilities*, **28 (4)**, 240–52.

Speld, S. A. (1989) 'Tinted lenses and dyslexia – a controlled study', *Australian and New Zealand Journal of Ophthalmology*, **17**, 137–41.

Stanley, G. V. (1987) 'Coloured filters and dyslexia', *Australian Journal of Remedial Education*, **19**, 8–9.

Stone, J. and Harris, K. (1991) 'These coloured spectacles: What are they for?' *Support for Learning*, **6 (3)**, 116–18.

Whiting, P. R. (1985) 'How difficult can reading be? New insights into reading problems', *Journal of the English Teachers Association*, **49**, 49–55.

Whiting, P. R. (1988) 'Improvements in Reading and Other skills Using Irlen Coloured Lenses', *Australian Journal of Remedial Education*, **20 (1)**, 13–15.

Wilkins, A. (1989) 'Photosensitive epilepsy and visual discomfort'. In Kennard, C. and Swash, M. (eds) *Hierarchies in Neurology*. London: Springer Verlag.

Williams, M. C., Lecluyse, K. and Rock-Foucheux, A. (1992) 'Effective intervention for reading disability', *Journal of the American Optometric Association*, **63**, 411–17.

Winter, S. (1987) 'Irlen lenses: an appraisal', *Australian Educational and Developmental Psychologist*, **4**, 1–5.

11   Facilitated Communication – Fact or Fantasy?

Facilitated communication has generated considerable controversy as an apparently easy to use method to augment communication among children and adults with autism and other developmental and motor disabilities. It has been the focus of hundreds of training workshops around the world, hailed as a major treatment breakthrough in the media, as well as being the subject of television and newspaper exposés in many countries.

(Bebko, Perry and Bryson, 1996:20)

Facilitated communication (FC) is a method of assisting non-verbal people to communicate through typing using a typewriter, computer, or other keyboard or by pointing to letters on an alphabet board. Manual guidance of the arm, hand or index finger is provided to enable clients to strike keys or point to letters. As the above quotation indicates, FC has been used with children and adults with physical disabilities as well as those with autism and severe learning difficulties. Growth of interest in FC has been rapid in the 1990s and it is currently one the most controversial treatments in the field of special education.

Rosemary Crossley is credited with inventing FC through her work during the 1970s in an Australian hospital with a young woman with cerebral palsy who was also considered to be severely intellectually disabled (Crossley and McDonald, 1980). Crossley showed that, with physical support, the woman was able to point to objects, then to words, then to letters on a keyboard, which eventually led to her developing literacy skills previously thought to be impossible by professionals and family members concerned with her care. This case has become the subject of a book and feature film with the same title, *Annie's Coming Out* (Crossley and McDonald, 1980). Crossley (1992) has recently reported that the young woman has subsequently completed her schooling and several units of a humanities degree course.

In 1986 Crossley established the Dignity through Education and Learning (DEAL) Centre in Melbourne. She claims that 65% of the 430 disabled people referred to the DEAL Centre between 1986 and 1990 demonstrated adequate spelling skills during the first 5-hour assessment session using FC (Crossley and Remington-Gurney, 1992).

Biklen (1990, 1992), a sociologist and professor of special education at Syracuse University in the USA, visited the DEAL Centre in 1989. He subsequently introduced FC to the USA and extended its focus from people with physical disabilities to those with autism and profound learning difficulties. Biklen and his colleagues have conducted several studies of the impact of facilitated communication, mainly in the Syracuse area. In a major study, Biklen *et al.* (1992) reported on the outcome of FC for 43 autistic clients aged from 3 to 26 years. The subjects had been using FC for between 7 and 16 months. Thirty one of the 43 clients were reported to be able to complete academic work at their grade level, with facilitation. Even more startling than this was the finding that most of the clients did not need to be taught how to read or spell since they already possessed these skills! Unfortunately there is insufficient information in the article to determine how the data were obtained.

Components of FC

There are two major components of FC: an attitudinal dimension, and several practical aspects (Biklen, 1990; Crossley and Remington-Gurney, 1992). The attitudinal dimension focused on the ways facilitators relate to clients as well as their views about their clients and FC. Facilitators are instructed not to impose themselves on clients or be patronising to them. They should assume the client's competence and not question the validity of FC.

Practical considerations include:

- *Physical support*: ensuring the client is comfortable, providing physical support under the forearm, wrist or index finger, pulling back the arm after each selection to avoid repetitions and to give the client time to make their next selection;
- *Observation*: watching the client's eyes and the device being pointed to;
- *Being positive*: providing encouragement and helping clients remain on task and avoid errors;
- *Achieving communication*: getting to know the communication style of clients, using structured tasks and ensuring they get plenty of practice;
- *Overcoming problems*: ignoring challenging behaviours and stereotyped utterances;
- *Curriculum*: using interesting materials, allowing clients to choose what they work on and helping them to express feelings naturally.

Several communication devices are used in FC. The simplest is an Alphabet Board which consists of a large piece of cardboard with the letters of the alphabet printed clearly on it. Another commonly used device is the Canon Communicator which consists of a hand-held miniaturised keyboard with a paper tape output. The most frequently used device is a typewriter or word processor with a standard keyboard.

FC is reported to start with clients being given the minimum physical support required to allow them to point to the communication device. They are then given structured activities such as typing the names of their family and friends and pointing to objects. Sentence completion and multiple choice exercises are used to help clients to progress to more complex communication culminating in two-way communications. It is intended that the physical support given to clients be gradually withdrawn, wherever possible, so that clients can eventually access the communication aid of their choice independently (Crossley, 1989).

Research on FC

In addition to the research reports from Biklen and Crossley and their colleagues, which were referred to earlier, there have now been over 50 studies which have investigated the validity of FC. A minority of these have provided support for FC. An example of such research is the recently published work of Sheehan and Matuozzi (1996) who studied FC with three clients aged 8, 10 and 24 years who had diagnoses of autism and mental retardation. Two clients were involved in four, 1–1½ hour sessions, the other participated in six sessions, over a period of 3 months.

The experimental procedure involved presenting each client with a stimulus, such as a video presentation, reading passage or picture, before engaging the client in a discussion about the stimulus with a facilitator by using a Canon Communicator. The client was then asked to discuss the nature of the stimulus with another facilitator who was naive to the subject of the stimulus. The sessions were videotaped so that they could be analysed to check whether clients disclosed any information to the second facilitators about the stimuli which had been presented by the first facilitators. This is a procedure which has been used in many studies of FC and is known as a 'message passing format'.

Results of the analysis revealed that all three subjects disclosed some information previously unknown to their facilitators. For the 24-year-old man, 49 out of the 289 communication interactions included some disclosure of unknown information. For the 8-year-old girl, 25 out of 292 interactions revealed unknown information, while the 10-year-old boy responded with unknown information in 3 out of 139 interactions.

In evaluating the validity of these findings it is important to realise that the clients' parents and the authors of the study acted as facilitators and that the authors had previously used FC with the clients for several months. In this context it is important to consider the authors' statement that:

> The significance of some instances of the participant's disclosure of unknown information may be diminished because we designed the study to allow the naive facilitator to offer feedback, redirection, or at times, yes/no questions or choices in order to elicit a response.
>
> (Sheehan and Matuozzi, 1996: 104)

For example, the authors report that while the 10-year-old boy quickly and correctly typed BUTTERFLI when questioned about the subject of one video he needed '61 instances of redirection, clarification, and eventually, written choices in order to identify a topic seen in another video' (p. 103).

In another recently published article purporting to provide supportive evidence for the validity of FC, Weiss *et al.* (1996) describe a study conducted with a 13-year-old boy with autism, severe mental retardation and a seizure disorder. They report using three independent trials in which short stories were read to him and discussed with the help of FC, followed by a series of questions on the stories to which he responded with the aid of a facilitator who was not present during the reading and discussion of the stories. Results indicated that, in two out of three trials, the boy provided accurate answers to questions on the stories when FC was provided by a facilitator who had not heard the stories. In addition, it is reported that he demonstrated a high level of spelling ability and evidence of abstract thinking in his responses.

However, when considering the likely validity of this finding it needs to be noted that the uninformed facilitator, with whom the boy presented the accurate answers, was the same person who had facilitated him at school on a one-to-one basis for 30 hours per week for 15 months. Little is reported about the actual physical support she uses apart from the statements that she supports below the boy's left wrist and that she offers 'resistance' to his movements. This same person acts as a support teacher in the regular class into which the boy has been integrated. She reports that he is able to complete academic work at his chronological age level and maintain an A to B grade average with the use of FC throughout the school day. All this despite have an assessed IQ of 31 points on the Stanford–Binet Intelligence Scale and a functional oral vocabulary of less than 10 words!

In contrast to the findings of the two studies described above, the majority of studies of FC have found little evidence of valid communication. For example, Cabay (1994) investigated FC with four autistic subjects aged 9–17 years who had used FC at their special school for at least 3 months. The study involved the presentation of 20 cards, 10 blank and 10 with questions, with the facilitator either aware or unaware of which card was presented. An alphabet board was used as the FC device by two facilitators who had been trained by Biklen. Analysis of the results showed that 95% of subjects' responses were correct when the facilitator knew which card was presented while only 19% were correct when the facilitator was unaware. Also, 10 out of the 11 correct responses made when facilitators were unaware involved blank cards which occurred more frequently, which suggests that this was due to chance responding. Cabay (1994) concludes that FC is not authentic communication and that the facilitator is the source of the responses being attributed to clients.

Three important studies of FC were published in a recent issue of the *Journal of Autism and Developmental Disorders*. The first study, by Bomba *et al.* (1996), is particularly interesting because it is an evaluation of a programme of FC which was requested by parents of 14 children attending a special school for autistic students. The parents had seen reports of successful implementation of FC with autistic children and were keen for their children to have the opportunity to experience it. The authors employed a pretest–post-test design to determine whether any of the children could benefit from FC. They found that, at the end of 10 weeks of instruction using FC, none of the children showed any significant gains in their ability to communicate through FC.

The second article, by Simon, Whitehair and Toll (1996), is of particular interest because it describes a follow-up study conducted with a 14-year-old boy with severe learning difficulties who appeared to demonstrate valid facilitated communication in an earlier study conducted by the same authors. In the previous study (Simon et al., 1994) the subject had produced 3 out of 10 correct communications in a double-blind message passing task when using FC. Specifically, he was able to type information regarding a just-completed activity, which was the purchase and consumption of a packet of potato chips. In the follow-up study he was unable to demonstrate any examples of valid FC. Simon et al. (1995) propose that these results suggest that the earlier finding may have been due to the facilitator smelling potato chips on the breath of the subject. They further report that, although the subject could not communicate reliably using FC he could do so using an alternative augmentative communication system, the Picture Exchange Communication System.

The third article, by Bebko et al. (1996), describes perhaps the most thorough analysis of FC training to date. Subjects were 20 autistic students aged 6–21 years. Communication methods used included auditory and visual input, and simple pointing to pictures and words, as well as typing. Data were collected after six weeks of FC and at a seven-month follow-up. Although findings differed across methods, little support for the validity of FC was obtained, whereas significant facilitator influence over responses was found.

In his editorial summary Schopler (1996: 8) comments:

> These three studies not only verified the accumulated evidence showing that 'new communications' in FC originates in the facilitator, they also showed that FC does not contribute to the student's communication competence.

Schopler explains that when FC is used as the only augmentative communication technique it reduces students' motivation to initiate communication and deprives them of the use of other more appropriate augmentative techniques. He concludes that clear support is provided by the results of the three studies for the resolution published by the American Psychological Association (Foxx, 1995) which stated that, not only are FC results refuted by empirical research but that aspects of FC violate the basic human rights of people with autism.

Reviews of research on FC

In a widely cited review, Green (1994) examines 25 well-controlled evaluations of FC, 17 of which have been published in scientific journals. Only 4
out of the 25 studies provided evidence of unexpected skills. These four
studies involved only 7 out of the 203 individuals who participated in the 25
studies. The unexpected skills demonstrated comprised unsophisticated communications such as accurate pointing to five single digits by one subject and
the naming of four objects or pictures by another. Also, it was difficult to
determine whether these responses were really unexpected because of the
lack of information about the subjects' communication abilities without FC.

Felce (1994) reviewed nine studies of FC published in 1993. He reported
that a consistent finding across the studies was that the facilitator, albeit
unknowingly, shapes the message and provides the linguistic and other
knowledge which is attributed to the client by proponents of FC. He considers that FC not only wastes the time and efforts of those involved but also
creates barriers to the adoption of effective augmentative communication
strategies. Finally, Felce (1994: 126) concluded that 'FC must be properly
evaluated if vulnerable people are not to be unwitting and uncomplaining
parties to an illusion'.

Howlin (1994) has reviewed 38 controlled trials of facilitated communication involving a total of 316 subjects which were conducted between 1990
and 1994. She found that in 31 of the studies no evidence of independent
communication was provided. The seven studies in which independent communication was reported included a total of 12 subjects and involved mainly
minimal naming responses, usually single words, as well as partially correct
responses. She considered that, in 99% of cases, the responses which were
attributed to FC were found to come from the facilitators rather than the subjects. Howlin highlights the anomaly evident in FC, that children who are
thought to be able to spell accurately, complete academic assignments and
discuss abstract concepts are unable to indicate their need for food or to use
the toilet. She concludes that there is no case for continued use of FC with
autistic children and further states that, 'There is a real risk that uncritical
acceptance of these methods could impair the quality of life for children with
autism and their families rather than enhancing it' (p.10).

Within their extensive conceptual review of the literature on FC,
Jacobson, Mulick and Schwartz (1995) analysed 15 studies, published
between 1993 and 1995, which they considered representative of scientific
research on FC. The studies included 126 subjects of whom four were
reported to demonstrate valid FC. However, following closer analysis,
Jacobson *et al.* considered that these four individuals did not provide convincing evidence for the validity of FC. They concluded that the findings of
adequately controlled studies have been 'consistently negative, indicating
that FC is neither reliably replicable nor valid when produced' (p. 754).

Explanations

The proponents of FC reject the findings of the research reported in the above reviews on the grounds that qualitative methods are more suitable for studying a phenomenon like FC. Biklen *et al.* (1992) proposes that the following sources of evidence support the assertion that typed responses come from the client and not from the facilitator:

- subjects make typographical errors which are unique to them;
- many subjects produce phonetic or invented spellings unique to them;
- style and speed of fine motor movements to letters or keys is consistent across facilitators;
- some clients type phrases or sentences that are unusual and would not be expected from their facilitators;
- clients sometimes produce content which is not known to the facilitator;
- clients reveal their individual personalities through FC.

Two main explanations are provided by proponents for the failures of experimental validations of FC. The first is concerned with the adversarial nature of tests conducted as part of such studies. Proponents consider that tests are suggested or administered by people who hope that the aid user will fail (Crossley, 1992). They have argued that such testing challenges the confidence of people with severe disabilities to the extent that they are unable to perform. They point out that belief in clients' communication competence is part of the attitudinal qualities required for successful facilitation, as noted earlier.

The second explanation for the failures of experimental validations of FC suggested by its proponents is that people with developmental disabilities, particularly those with autism, have difficulties with word finding. It has been suggested that they have 'developmental dyspraxia' which means that they find it difficult to communicate due to their inability to control motor movements. In fact Biklen (1990) has gone so far as to propose that the cause of autism is 'global apraxia' which presumes a deficit in the ability to express communication rather than to understand it. This then provides a rationale for FC in that the physical support provided by facilitators helps clients to overcome their motor difficulties in order to communicate.

A more plausible explanation for the apparent success of FC in anecdotal reports and its failure in controlled experiments is presented in a recent article by Von Tetzchner (1996). He notes the similarity between the reports of subjects participating in experiments of automatic communication and those of individuals involved in FC. He suggests that messages considered to be the results of FC are actually produced unintentionally by facilitators and are a form of automatic writing, which is a widely researched and well-established phenomenon within psychology. He points out that cognitive processes outside the person's awareness, including automatic writing, are not considered to be examples of extra-sensory perception but are elements of common psychological knowledge. He therefore suggests that the messages produced in FC do not provide information about clients' thoughts but do provide insights into the thoughts and attitudes of facilitators.

Negative effects

The most alarming effect of FC is the high incidence of reporting of cases of sexual abuse which has emerged from individuals exposed to FC. Facilitators working within the Syracuse project have reported that 10 out of the 75 clients involved have made allegations of sexual abuse through FC (Biklen, 1993). In total there are over 60 different cases of allegations of sexual abuse which have been made through FC in the USA alone (Jacobson *et al.*, 1995). These have resulted in legal proceedings charging caregivers, parents, teachers and others with abuse. With only two exceptions, legal proceedings have been terminated before going to trial, but this is not before considerable distress has been caused and possible damage done to parents and others involved. For example, in one case a father was held in prison for 7 months while investigations were conducted (Felce, 1994). As a result of this situation Biklen and others who use FC are being sued for millions of dollars in the US courts by parents claiming damages as a consequence of allegations made against them through the use of FC (Hastings, 1996).

Several other negative effects are associated with FC:

1. FC often creates conflict between parents and professionals. Many parents hear of the success of FC in the media and build up their hopes for the possible gains which their child could make. This makes it hard for professionals to get them to accept the findings of validation studies.
2. The use of FC encourages communication dependence on the part of clients whereas they may be able to achieve greater independence with a more appropriate augmentative communication device.
3. The time and resources spent on FC may deny clients access to proven techniques which are much more likely to facilitate their communication skills.
4. The unrealistically high linguistic and academic output of clients in FC may result in them being wrongly placed in educational settings in which they cannot cope and are likely to gain minimal benefit.
5. FC reinforces a viewpoint in which people are only valued when they have abilities in the 'normal' range thus denying the acceptance of individual differences and of disability itself.

Conclusion

Although the literature on FC reviewed in this chapter contains both favourable and unfavourable reports regarding its validity, it is not difficult to determine the direction in which the vast majority of convincing evidence points. As Jacobson and Mulick (1994) have stated, it is not just the case that there is no reliable support for the validity of FC, but that there is a large amount of evidence indicating that the source of communications produced is facilitators themselves.

As discussed above, several writers have warned that FC is not just a waste of time but has potentially serious effects on clients and their families. It is clear that the balance of current evidence strongly suggests that the use of FC with children or adults with developmental disabilities cannot be justified at this time. Therefore, parents of children with disabilities who wish them to receive FC should be warned of its lack of validity and its potentially damaging effects.

An important concern raised by Jacobson *et al.* (1995) is how FC got to be taken so seriously given its flimsy rationale, extravagant claims and lack of convincing supportive evidence. It raises an important question about the capability of the public, in addition to professionals in the field of special education, of discriminating between interventions that are effective and those which are not. The issue of FC has therefore brought to the fore the need to educate special education professionals so that they can evaluate potential treatments critically to select the most effective ones and advise parents, administrators and policy makers about the ineffectiveness of various 'fad' treatments, including FC.

References

Bebko, J. M., Perry, A. and Bryson, S. (1996) 'Multiple method validation study of Facilitated Communication: II. Individual differences and subgroup results', *Journal of Autism and Developmental Disorders*, **26** (1), 19–42.

Biklen, D. (1990) 'Communication unbound: autism and praxis', *Harvard Educational Review*, **60**, 291–314.

Biklen, D. (1992) 'Typing to talk: Facilitated communication', *American Journal of Speech and Hearing Pathology*, **1** (2), 15–17.

Biklen, D. (1993) *Communication Unbound: How Facilitated Communication is Challenging Traditional Views of Autism and Ability/Disability*. New York: Teachers College Press.

Biklen, D., Morton, W. M., Gold, D., Berrigan, C. and Swaminathan, S. (1992) 'Facilitated communication: Implications for individuals with autism', *Topics in Language Disorders*, **12**, 1–28.

Bomba, C., O'Donnell, L., Markowitz, C. and Holmes, D. L. (1996) 'Evaluating the impact of Facilitated Communication on the communicative competence of fourteen students with autism', *Journal of Autism and Developmental Disorders*, **26** (1), 43–58.

Cabay, M. (1994) 'Brief report: A controlled evaluation of Facilitated Communication using open-ended and fill-in questions', *Journal of Autism and Developmental Disorders*, **24** (4), 517–27.

Crossley, R. (1989) *Communication Training Involving Facilitated Communication.* Caulfield, Va: DEAL Communication Centre.

Crossley, R. (1992) 'Getting the words out: case studies in facilitated communication training', *Topics in Language Disorders*, **12**, 46–59.

Crossley, R. and McDonald, A. (1980) *Annie's Coming Out.* Melbourne: Penguin.

Crossley, R. and Remington-Gurney, J. (1992) 'Getting the words out: Facilitated communication training', *Topics in Language Disorders*, **12**, 29–45.

Felce, D. (1994) 'Facilitated Communication: Results from a number of recently published evaluations', *British Journal of Learning Disabilities*, **4**, 122–26.

Foxx, R. (1995) 'APA passes facilitated communication resolution', *Psychology in Mental Retardation and Developmental Disabilities*, **20**, 18–20.

Green, G. (1994) 'The quality of evidence'. In Shane, H. C. (ed.) *Facilitated Communication: The Clinical and Social Phenomenon.* San Diego, Ca: Singular Press, pp. 157–225.

Hastings, R. (1996) 'Does Facilitated Communication free imprisoned minds?' *Psychologist*, **9** (1), 19–24.

Howlin, P. (1994) 'Facilitated Communication and autism: are the claims for success justified?' *Communication*, **28** (2), 10–12.

Jacobson, J. W. and Mulick, J. A. (1994) 'Facilitated Communication: better education through applied ideology', *Journal of Behavioral Education*, **4** (1), 93–105.

Jacobson, J. W., Mulick, J. A. and Schwartz, A. A. (1995) 'A history of Facilitated Communication: science, pseudoscience and antiscience', *American Psychologist*, **50** (9), 750–65.

Schopler, E. (1996) 'Editorial preface', *Journal of Autism and Developmental Disorders*, **26** (1), 7–8.

Sheehan, C. M. and Matuozzi, R. T. (1996) 'Investigation of the validity of facilitated communication through the disclosure of unknown information', *Mental Retardation*, **34** (2), 94–107.

Simon, E. W., Toll, D. M. and Whitehair, P. M. (1994) 'A naturalistic approach to the validation of facilitated communication', *Journal of Autism and Developmental Disorders*, **24**, 647–57.

Simon, E. W., Whitehair, P. M. and Toll, D. M. (1995) 'Keeping facilitated communication in perspective', *Mental Retardation*, **33** (5), 338–39.

Simon, E. W., Whitehair, P. M. and Toll, D. M. (1996) 'A case study: Follow-up assessment of facilitated communication', *Journal of Autism and Developmental Disorders*, **26** (1), 9–18.

Von Tetzchner, S. (1996) 'Facilitated, automatic and false communication: Current issues in the use of facilitating techniques', *European Journal of Special Needs Education*, **11** (2), 151–66.

Weiss, M. J. S., Wagner, S. H. and Bauman, M. L. (1996) 'A validated case study of facilitated communication', *Mental Retardation*, **34** (4), 220–30.

12 Reading Recovery – Does it Work and is it Cost-effective?

A definition and brief history of Reading Recovery

Reading Recovery (RR) is an early intervention programme aimed at accelerating the reading progress of children who have failed to reach the expected level of achievement by the end of their first year in school. This first year in school allows a child time to settle into the classroom system but not to become totally disillusioned by repeated failures. The programme targets the lowest achieving pupils to help them to function within their own class at an average level. The children receive one-to-one instruction for 30 minutes each day for between 12 and 20 weeks by which time it is hoped the majority of pupils can return to their own classes. If a child is not ready to discontinue the programme after 20 weeks, he or she may be referred for additional support of a more long-term nature. RR aims to teach non-readers to become 'active, independent problem-solvers, who learn because they read and write' (Wright, 1992: 351).

RR was first researched, documented and implemented in New Zealand by Marie Clay during the 1970s. It has since been introduced into parts of Australia, the USA, Canada and the UK. It has been suggested that RR requires changes within both the educational and the political arenas in order to be wholly effective. There needs to be:

(1) Behavioural change on the part of the teachers;
(2) child behaviour change achieved by teaching;
(3) organisational changes in schools achieved by teachers and administrators;
(4) social/political changes in financing by controlling authorities.

(Clay, 1985; cited in Center *et al.* 1992: 264)

RR may thus be seen as 'a systems-based intervention' (Center *et al.*, 1992: 264).

The intensive research which developed the RR programme looked at the sorts of reading materials used in schools and at the ways in which reading was taught. By observing the teaching of reading through one-way mirrors, the various teaching techniques employed were considered and evaluated:

A large number of techniques were piloted, observed, discussed, argued over, related to theory, analysed, written up, modified and tried out in various ways, and most important, many were discarded.

(Clay, 1985: 5)

After 5 years of piloting the programme, it was implemented nationally in New Zealand in 1983. In 1989, more than 10,000 children and 1,000 teachers were involved in the Reading Recovery scheme (Bald, 1992). These teachers attend an intensive course which takes 400 hours of fortnightly in-service training sessions and school based practice of Reading Recovery techniques. As the course progresses, each teacher supports four pupils within their own schools for 10 hours a week during which time they put into practice the new procedures and concepts they have been learning. An important part of the course involves each trainee teacher bringing a child to the training centre on three occasions so that the pupil's lesson may be observed through a one-way mirror by the other teachers. These sessions are later discussed and analysed by the whole group with the RR tutor and thus the specific RR procedures can be learnt and shared, benefiting everyone (Wright and Prance, 1992). The element of in-service training and the discussions related to methods, approaches and pupil and teacher behaviours adds to the intensity of the training of RR teachers. The tutor's role in encouraging the trainees to analyse and reflect upon their own teaching in relation to each pupil they teach must help to develop a deeper understanding of the reading process and their own role within that process. In the year following their training, the teachers remain in contact with their tutor so that the quality of teaching on the RR programme can be maintained.

RR is not a new method or scheme. It was never intended to replace good teaching. It is based upon the 'whole language' approach researched by Clay (1985) in which natural texts offer a wide range of cues to the meaning. Clay argues that some remedial schemes concentrate upon only one or two skills, such as sounding out letters, and do not offer the poorer reader the more effective strategies used by good readers. No one skill or method can be ideal for every learner and an eclectic approach is one of the strengths of RR. The Department of Education and Science and Welsh Office (1990) echo this approach in the statement that every pupil should be taught to:

use the available cues, such as pictures, context, phonic cues, word shapes and meaning of a passage to decipher new words...to make informed guesses, and to correct themselves in the light of additional information, e.g. by reading ahead or by looking back in the text.

(Department of Education and Science and Welsh Office, 1990: 30)

This is what RR is all about. From observing the ways in which children were taught to read, Clay was convinced that competent readers employ many or all of the above strategies but children who struggle with reading generally rely on far fewer ways of deciphering new texts. Such strategies as guessing a word from its initial letter sound can be unsatisfactory because this does not take into account the meaning of the passage. The research which led to the trialing of RR stresses the importance of meaning in the development of successful readers:

> for all children, the larger the chunks of printed language they can work with, the richer the network of information they can use, and the quicker they learn.
>
> (Clay and Cazden, 1990: 207)

If RR can be shown to encourage the development of a wide range of strategies for reading, it would be a most effective way of supporting those pupils who do not employ these cues naturally or automatically.

Rationale of RR

The chief reason for implementing RR has to be to raise the standards of reading for pupils in the lowest scoring range. This is RR's claim and if research into its effectiveness proves conclusively that this is so, then any society which ignores the potential of such a scheme can only be said to be callous and shortsighted. New Zealand's impressive literacy achievements are testament to what can be done if a national commitment is made to raise literacy levels. A report from the office of Her Majesty's Chief Inspector of Schools states that:

> Much of the observed success of the programme is owing to the rigour of the specific training it provides, its comprehensive quality assurance structures, the coherence of its organisation on a national scale and the central provision of its funding.
>
> (OFSTED, 1993: 4)

Failure to learn to read is not only a serious handicap in adult life but a cause of intense misery and despair for many children who spend their entire school careers in one form of remedial programme or another. This is not the intention of RR which is intended to be a short-term boost with permanent changes to the child's reading ability which enables the pupil to join the mainstream again:

> Reading Recovery is not intended to be a long-term or permanent programme.
>
> (Wright and Prance, 1992: 104)

If RR can deliver such long-term change, it will be welcomed by both teachers and pupils, especially those with Special Educational Needs. It may:

> raise esteem, induce curricular change, improve the quality of mainstream provision.
>
> (Wade, 1992: 51)

Indeed, when pupils' reading improves due to the RR programme they are said to make gains in other areas; 'in confidence, school attendance and in other subjects, including mathematics' (OFSTED, 1993).

In the article by Wade (1992), the changes which RR demands of the school organisation are also highlighted as follows:

> reduce the diversity of literacy abilities within a class, thus making mainstream provision simpler; reduce the cost, stress and difficulty of later remediation by its early input, before failure has become ingrained.
>
> (Wade, 1992: 51)

This is one of the foremost aims of RR, to intervene at the age of 6 before pupils have had too much contact with failure and poor self-esteem. This early intervention may not only reduce the pain of individual children but must reduce the need for later funding for remediation:

> If children are helped to recover at an early age, the numbers needing more extensive and more expensive assistance later on can be drastically reduced.
>
> (Pluck, 1989: 347)

This emphasis on early intervention was one of the key components of the research of Clay (1985) and there is considerable evidence to support the notion that failure breeds failure and should therefore be avoided if at all possible:

> The initial specific problem may evolve into a more generalised deficit due to the behavioural/cognitive/motivational spin-offs from failure at such a crucial educational task as reading.
>
> (Stanovich, 1986: 389)

RR, by its very nature, requires changes in many areas, not simply in the narrow confines of the teaching programme itself. It involves intensive retraining, has implications for resourcing and funding and organisational changes within individual schools, all of which require changes in the ways in which schools are financed. This involves political changes if RR is to be implemented in the way envisaged by Clay. If it is implemented nationally, as in New Zealand, on such a scale, RR may influence the practice of many teachers and thus the education of a nation's children if the claims made for the programme can be confirmed:

> Indirect benefits of the programme include the presence of a highly trained early years reading expert in almost every primary school and raised expectations concerning the limits of what is possible in reading progress.
>
> (OFSTED, 1993: 4)

The approaches and application of RR

RR gives additional support of a specific nature to the lowest achievers in a school after their first year. No exceptions are made for behaviour difficulties, IQ, maturity level or disabilities. The ultimate aim of the programme is to help the pupils to develop and employ strategies which make it possible for the child to learn through his own attempts to read (Clay, 1985). Children are encouraged to use meaning and phonics to help decipher passages from natural texts as opposed to the restricted language of many reading scheme books. Great importance is placed upon the need to analyse the strengths and weaknesses of an individual pupil by observing what he or she is able or trying to do and tailor the programme to develop the skills already acquired by the competent readers in the class:

> Writing stories and re-reading them to encourage attention to word details, self-correction and use of cueing strategies are an essential part of teaching and ensure that reading is not taught in isolation from writing and speaking and listening.
>
> (Wade, 1992: 49)

So the RR teacher chooses from the range of procedures within the programme those which will best help an individual pupil to develop the skills he or she is already trying to use and those he or she needs to acquire.

Initially, the class teacher identifies the lowest achievers in her class at 6 years of age and these pupils are then given a battery of tests in both reading and writing to determine the poorest, four of whom will enter the RR programme. Each RR teacher is trained to administer and analyse the six part Diagnostic Survey. The assessment consists of:

1. *Book level* – Children are heard read from a series of graded books which are scored in a range of 0–20.
2. *Letter identification* – Scored in a range of 0–54 this accepts any recognition of the alphabet, both sounds or names, lower and upper case letters.
3. *Concepts of print* – Scored in a range of 0–24 looks at children's concepts of printed language, the direction of reading, the concept of a word or a letter, etc.
4. *Word tests* – A test of a child's ability to read commonly occurring words out of context, scored in a range of 0–15.
5. *Writing vocabulary* – How many words a child can write in ten minutes without help.
6. *Dictation* – Writing a short dictated sentence scored in a range of 0–37.

Once a child has been selected for the programme, he or she will receive half an hour per day of one-to-one tuition. The first two weeks of the programme are used to 'roam around the known' to develop a positive teacher/pupil relationship, and to give the child confidence so that the RR teacher can observe the behaviour and skills used by the young reader.

A typical RR session will include each of the following activities and most likely in this order.

- Re-reading two or more familiar books.
- Re-reading yesterday's new book and taking a running record.
- Letter identification (plastic letters on a magnetic board) and/or word and word-making and breaking.
- Writing a story (including hearing and recording sounds in words).

- Cut-up story to be rearranged.
- New book introduced.
- New book attempted.

As this format reveals, RR is heavily weighted towards reading text. These texts are exclusively real texts since Clay emphasises in all her writings the 'whole language' approach. Re-reading the previous day's books and well-known texts is seen to help the pupil to improve both recognition and comprehension skills. It is important that the books used are well illustrated. To be short, individually bound books which employ much repetition and rhyme in order that the child may experience success and so increase the desire to read more. Reading such a large number of books clearly has implications for resourcing and many reading scheme books would not be suitable for the RR programme. Jean Prance, a former Surrey head teacher who trained in New Zealand as a RR tutor, has assembled an extensive book list graded from 0 to 20. It contains many simple books from Heinemanns' *Sunshine* series and Nelson-Wheaton's *Storychest*. She claims to have no favourite scheme but notes that both the above series had their origins in New Zealand, the home of RR (Moore, 1991: 46).

The importance of practising reading, i.e. reading real messages which are written in sentences and developing a range of strategies for achieving this, is seen by Clay as being the most likely means of accelerating reading progress as opposed to methods which involve learning individual words, letters and phonic rules (Clay, 1979).

There is only a small element of phonic work within the programme but the analysis of words and word patterns is developed through the writing aspect of each session. The child is encouraged to progress as rapidly as possible towards independent writing. Throughout the programme, the running records of the child's progress are used to inform the teacher's future planning and these eventually give a detailed profile of the child's development. Once the pupil reaches the level of the average child in his or her class, the RR programme is discontinued:

> The child is then deemed to be equipped with the requisite skills necessary to increase control over his developing literacy skills.
>
> (Wood, 1994: 6)

Each RR teacher tutors four children daily which takes up half of the working week. Whenever pupils are discontinued, others immediately take their place on the programme. It will be obvious from this that RR is an expensive intervention in terms of teacher training, teaching time, and the relatively small number of children that each RR teacher can support. An additional resource cost of the large number of suitable reading books which are essential to the success of the programme must also be considered by any school, LEA, or government wishing to embark upon RR.

Research into the effectiveness of RR

There is no doubt that reading is central to the educational process and the ability to read affects a child's progress in all areas of the curriculum:

> Children with reading difficulties suffer in our society and are disadvantaged as adults.
>
> (Sylva and Hurry, 1995: 22)

Despite the constant claims in the popular press that reading standards are falling, there remain insufficient data from which to make definite conclusions of that nature. Each LEA has its own policy for testing the reading skills of pupils at 7 years of age. However, only 26 of these supplied data to the National Foundation for Educational Research suitable for investigating reading trends in the 1980s. Some of these LEAs did give evidence of some increase in the number of pupils in the lower-scoring groups (Cato and Whetton, 1991). In contrast, however, the SATs results for 7 year olds in 1991 showed that 21% achieved level 3 (the level of an average 9 year old) and a further 50% reached level 2 which is the expected level for that age group; 28% of pupils did not achieve Level 2, some of whom failed to reach the average level on only one or two of the test items. Dombey (1992: 112) suggests that these figures 'show a normal distribution, skewed slightly towards the lower end.'

Whatever the trend may or may not be in reading attainment nationally and globally, a programme which claims to accelerate the progress of the lowest achievers to the level of their average peers and maintain that position over time, must be considered seriously and its effectiveness thoroughly investigated. Such are the claims of RR.

From figures obtained in 1988:

> Results gained in New Zealand show that for every 100 children in the population at age 6, if 20 participate in the programme, 19 will reach average levels after a maximum of 20 weeks teaching.
>
> (Wright, 1992: 352)

There can be little doubt that on the RR programme, pupils make accelerated progress and greater gains on the Clay battery of tests than do comparison group children, but the fact that the New Zealand research typically excludes 'the 25%–30% of children who failed to benefit and were withdrawn from the Reading Recovery programme' must affect the reported results (Center *et al.*, 1992: 266). In Clay's research, (1985) there is no random assignment of subjects; the lowest scoring children enter the RR programme, while the next lowest scorers become the comparison group with no additional support. It is possible that some children may have made accelerated progress even without RR and that the results may be 'due to error in the initial selection of children for intensive intervention' (Nicholson, 1989: 95).

Research into the effectiveness of Reading Recovery in Australia

(Wheeler, 1986) was carried out along similar lines to those of Clay's original research and produced successfully discontinued pupils who reached the average for their classes. However, as with the New Zealand results, about 25% of the RR subjects were omitted due to their failure to reach satisfactory levels within the 18 weeks of the programme. Such exclusions may bias the evaluation in favour of the intervention pupils. This study did not have a follow-up study so it is not possible to know whether the gains were maintained but a report from the same area of Australia was carried out by Rowe (1989) to look at the impact of RR over the long term. This suggested that the children who had had RR were doing better on reading than non-RR pupils in the lowest 25%. Although this was most marked amongst the 10 year olds which might indicate the positive effects of the early intervention, the number of pupils included who had been part of the original programme was so drastically reduced as to make any real comparisons impossible.

More recent research in New Zealand, although also showing significantly greater gains by the experimental group than the comparison group, showed that 'the net gain which is attributed to Reading Recovery appears to be quite modest by a year or so after discontinuation' (Glynn et al., 1989: 83–84). RR was designed to be implemented in New Zealand, where pupils in the first year of school have a formal reading programme which puts emphasis upon the need to match a child's reading ability to text of an appropriate level. Despite such a programme which links closely with the concepts of RR, the above researchers found that there was a great deal of variability in the level of effective communication between class teachers and RR teachers. One possible reason for the 'wash-out' effect after discontinuation may be related to the unsatisfactory nature of communication between tutors and classroom teachers in that discontinued pupils may still be perceived by the class teacher as poor readers and therefore given texts which are too simple to demand of the child all the new cueing skills he or she has been practising.

It has been suggested that RR lacks the systematic teaching of such skills as phonological awareness, phonological recoding and syntactic awareness, all of which have been associated with competent reading. When RR pupils were also taught explicit code instruction based upon the work of Bryant and Bradley (1985) they attained discontinuation levels more quickly than did pupils who either received RR instruction alone or another standard intervention (Iverson and Tumner, 1993). If this study is replicated with the same results it has been estimated that the saving made by the adoption of the modified RR programme in inner city schools in England would be over £4 million (Bald, 1992).

Research in Ohio State, USA, randomly assigned pupils to the RR programme (Pinnell et al., 1988). The lowest 20% of children from 12 schools were randomly assigned to either the RR programme or to another remedial programme in groups of 10 or 12 with some individual tuition. The tutorial times for the control group were not clearly specified. There were 136 pupils involved in the RR programme and 51 pupils formed the control group. The RR children, both successfully and unsuccessfully discontinued pupils, scored significantly better on all the Clay diagnostic tests than did the control group children. Criticisms arise with regard to the fact that the control group did not receive an equivalent intervention since their support was not individualised as in RR. In addition, the experimental group were largely from classes taught by RR trained teachers and the question arises, did this link between the approaches of their intervention tutors and their normal class teachers affect the success of the RR programme? It is hard to believe that it did not.

This research was followed up a year and two years later at which time the RR children had maintained their gains in terms of book levels:

> However, when the data are converted to effect sizes (Wasik and Slavin, 1990), there is a progressive diminution until, by the end of the second year, the differences between the two groups are almost negligible.
>
> (Center *et al.*, 1992: 268)

Considering how very expensive the RR programme is, suggestions that its gains may be of a temporary nature make it vital that research into the effectiveness of this approach should take into account the need to randomly assign pupils and to provide sufficient funding to offer an equally individualised programme for the control group pupils.

A later study in Ohio (Pinnell *et al.*, 1991) compared four programmes which were:

1. RR with a fully trained RR teacher.
2. A similar programme carried out by teachers trained in a shortened programme.
3. One-to-one skills practice using direct instruction.
4. Groups taught by a RR teacher.

Only the first group was seen to produce lasting effects and the conclusions of the study were that one-to-one instruction was indeed necessary and that it was the intensity of RR which made it so effective (Pinnell *et al.*, 1991). However, the view that RR produces lasting gains is in conflict with the findings of Glynn *et al.*, (1989), mentioned earlier.

A small, short-term project took place in Cumbria in the UK in 1988. Four children received RR tuition and the four children with the next lowest scores were used as a comparison group. The pupils had had two years in school unlike the usual RR children who enter the programme after their first year in school. This project lasted for only 11 weeks but after that time the RR children had made:

> remarkable gains on all measures compared with their initial assessment scores and with the reference group.
>
> (Pluck, 1989: 353)

Results from such a small study which, as with many RR projects, did not randomly assign subjects must be treated cautiously.

The first British LEA to introduce RR was Surrey, which set out to duplicate the programme exactly as developed in New Zealand. Jean Prance, an ex-head teacher, returned to Surrey in 1990 after successfully training in New Zealand as an RR tutor. Training courses were set up, the first beginning in March, 1990. Of the 11 self-selected schools involved in this course and the 10 schools in the second course, there were eventually nine from the first course and 10 from the second which took part in the RR programme. The demands of the training proved to be too much for some of the headteachers and deputy headteachers who began the course.

In addition to the usual diagnostic survey associated with the selection of the lowest achieving pupils for the RR programme, the Burt Graded Word Reading Test was used plus the National Curriculum SATs results. Two rural schools, not matched to the schools involved in the project, were used as a comparison as well as the next lowest achievers in the RR schools who did not receive the intervention. No major difficulties arose in setting up a duplicate of the New Zealand programme and although the Surrey pupils took marginally longer to reach discontinued levels than the New Zealand children they made greater gains in all areas except sight vocabulary. It must be noted that in its homeland of New Zealand, RR may be more easily integrated into the remainder of the school curriculum since:

> the curriculum is fairly narrowly based by English standards and concentrates on giving pupils good literacy and numeracy skills.

> (OFSTED, 1993: 19)

Criticisms of the above study have been made with regard to the progress made by the pupils. At the start of the project, no statistically significant differences in the scores of the various pupils was noted. After three months, the RR children had made more statistically significant gains on book level, concepts about print and writing vocabulary than the comparison groups. However, when the Burt Graded Word Reading Test was administered, the comparison group pupils' scores were statistically significantly above those of the RR children. These conflicting results added to the exclusion from the figures of those children who failed to reach a satisfactory discontinuation level weaken the case for the effectiveness of RR.

A two-year longitudinal evaluation compared RR with a specifically phonological and less intensive programme involving seven LEAs (Bexley, Greenwich, Hammersmith and Fulham, Islington, Surrey, Wandsworth and Westminster) and 120 schools. The report states that within this project, 'inner-city children are over-represented in terms of the national picture' (Sylva and Hurry, 1995). Each LEA randomly assigned two similar schools for each RR school in its area and six of the poorest readers from each school became part of the study. Three or four of the six pupils received RR and the remainder formed a comparison group within the school. Four of the six pupils in the phonological intervention schools were randomly assigned to the training and the other two became the within-school comparison group. In the randomly assigned control schools, all six pupils were the control group. In addition to the RR diagnostic tests, the study used the British Ability Scales Word Reading Test and the Neale Analysis of Reading. The poorest readers were automatically selected for the RR group and the control group had slightly higher scores than the phonological intervention group. An attempt was made to match the children in these groups on the basis of their initial reading ability.

At the end of the first year, the RR children had made significantly more progress on all measures than the control group. Data from the pupils matched for initial scores showed that in 8 or 9 months, the RR children had made 17 months' progress compared with about 9 months' progress for the control group schools. No intervention took place in the second year and although the difference between the RR children's progress and that of the control group pupils had reduced by the end of the second year, the RR children still had a 6-month advantage over the non-RR pupils. This study suggests that RR can be effective in accelerating the progress of the lowest achievers and that this progress can be maintained.

The improvements made by the children on the phonological intervention were not significantly greater than the gains made by the control group. They made gains of 10 months as opposed to 8 months at the first follow-up test. They had made significant gains in three areas of the diagnostic tests; on letter identification, written vocabulary and dictation. By the second follow-up the pupils were still ahead of the control groups but not at statistically significant levels. They had made significantly more progress in reading accuracy and spelling but not in reading comprehension. The conclusion of the authors was that 'the Phonological Intervention is certainly less effective than Reading Recovery and the effects are narrower' (Sylva and Hurry, 1995: 17). This study provides powerful evidence for the effectiveness of RR.

Whatever else research tells us, there can be no doubt that RR can accelerate the reading progress of the lowest achieving pupils and there is some evidence to suggest that these gains may be retained at least in the short term. However, it is not so certain whether these gains can be maintained in the long term nor is it clear exactly what elements of RR are responsible for these improvements. As yet, there have been few studies which have had comparison groups which have been exposed to comparable, individualised programmes as did the Ohio research (Pinnell *et al.* 1991). Also, the very nature of the selection of pupils for RR, i.e. the lowest achieving pupils, makes it difficult to have either matched or randomly assigned subjects. These elements are weaknesses in the present research into the effectiveness of RR.

It is equally difficult to state decisively whether RR is cost-effective. Clearly, it is an extremely expensive programme which in the case of the recent 3-year government funded experiment was costed at £1,030 per child in extra teaching time (Judd, 1995). The cost of the phonological intervention was estimated at £581 per child. It is no simple task to compare these sorts of figures since the sums of money alone mean very little. The cost must be related to the effectiveness of the intervention. The results of the phonological intervention were minimal and the report suggested that perhaps that was due to the short length of time given to the programme which may have been more successful over a 4-year intervention. If the cost remained constant for that length of time, the programme would have been more expensive than RR which is only intended to take between 3 and 6 months. It would seem that although RR is by far the most expensive reading intervention programme, it may also be the most effective, in the short term, at least. Angela Hobsbaum of the RR National Network suggests it may be as expensive to prepare a statement of special educational needs prior to the child receiving any help as it is to offer a child RR (Hofkins, 1995).

Implications for research

The most immediate need regarding research into the effectiveness of RR is clearly stated in almost all the literature; that is the need for more strictly controlled research which involves the random allocation of subjects, the inclusion of all participants in the final results and most difficult of all, a truly comparable, individualised programme of intervention. All the above have proved to be weaknesses of the research to date. Without an equivalent individualised programme for comparison, it is not possible to know whether it is the content of the RR programme which make it effective as opposed to the intensive one-to-one delivery of the programme. Is it:

> the conceptual model/programme content or simply the individualised instruction which is associated with short-term reading gains after exposure to Reading Recovery.
>
> (Center *et al.*, 1992: 273.)

In addition, it is vital that any such research be of a longitudinal nature so that the long-term effectiveness of RR may be assessed. However much RR may be estimated to cost, it is not possible to determine whether it is cost-effective without more carefully controlled, long-term evaluations.

RR may be effective in New Zealand where it is a nationally implemented programme linked closely to the existing approach to the teaching of reading within most schools. But, can it be transferred to a society such as Britain with its different school organisation, curriculum and funding arrangements? It may be that grants to fund new initiatives such as RR which are localised and short term only are not an adequate means of implementing such a programme which is designed to be far more than a local experiment.

The requirements of change on the part of teachers, teaching approaches,

school systems and those in control of the financing of education in relation
to the teaching of reading deemed as essential by Clay (1985) must affect the
successful implementation of RR. Although RR aims to affect the progress
of low achieving readers it also aims to have a positive effect upon the
organisation of individual schools, the practice of teachers and the behaviour
of those who are in charge of funding education. Perhaps a careful look at
what is being done now for the least able readers and at how teachers are
trained to teach this vital subject would be worthwhile. Is there a need for
change in other areas of the educational system in order to achieve long-term
improvements in the literacy levels in the United Kingdom?

> Trainee teachers there [New Zealand] spend twice as long learning how to teach
> reading as do teachers in England and the same national programme is used to
> teach reading in every school. Reading appears to enjoy unrivalled prominence in
> the New Zealand primary school curriculum.
>
> (Hall, 1994: 125)

Many young teachers in the UK feel that they are inadequately trained to
deal with the complexities of teaching reading. This situation is acknowledged by the recent government guidelines for teacher training which set out
precisely how to teach the core subjects of English (including reading),
mathematics and science.

A further implication of the implementation of RR would be the necessity
to provide sufficient suitable books to support the programme. Books are an
expensive, but essential resource in all schools and the financial restraints
now made upon school budgets make it difficult to fund any new venture,
even one with the potential impact of RR.

RR has been criticised for its lack of parental involvement, despite the fact
that there is a wealth of research evidence to support the positive effects of
parental involvement in reading. However, in areas of the country marked by
social and economic decline, high levels of parental involvement are sometimes difficult to achieve. RR requires no parental involvement and so may
be more suited to such areas of deprivation than other reading support initiatives:

> The parents of such children are often educationally disadvantaged themselves
> and consequently less able to participate in such cooperative schemes.
>
> (Wood, 1994: 11)

It may be, however, that some parents may be less willing than others to
become involved in their children's learning due to their own negative
experiences of school, English being their second language or feelings of
inadequacy. These reasons may not always mean that such parents are less
able to give support (Glynn and Glynn, 1986).

For it to be successful, it has been argued that only fully trained RR teachers obtain the best results from the programme (Pinnell *et al.*, 1991) and this
is certainly the view of the programme's designer, Marie Clay (1979). The
British research would seem to support this view, that RR is of particular

benefit to children who come from deprived backgrounds. Because of its lack of reliance upon parental involvement, RR may be worth considering for inner-city areas of deprivation:

> The Reading Recovery intervention was particularly effective for socially disadvantaged children who are over-represented in special needs programmes.
>
> (Sylva and Hurry, 1995: 22)

Conclusions

The effectiveness of RR in accelerating the reading progress of the lowest achieving pupils at age 6 can hardly be in doubt but further research is needed before definitive statements can be made about its long-term effectiveness and overall cost-effectiveness. However, the fact that New Zealand has the lowest illiteracy rate in the world (Wade, 1990) cannot be a coincidence. Any government which faces falling reading levels cannot afford to ignore the effectiveness of RR in its homeland.

With its emphasis upon the essential need for highly qualified teachers and for a more individualised approach to the teaching of reading, RR requires an ethos which pervades not only each whole school and each local authority but one that has a necessary effect upon policy makers at the highest level. In these ways, through its impact upon the provision of resources allocated to this vital area of education, RR certainly provides a potentially useful way forward.

References

Bald, J. (1992) 'Roads to recovery', *Times Educational Supplement*, **18 January**, 42.

Bryant, P. and Bradley, L. (1985) *Children's Reading Problems*. Blackwell: Oxford.

Cato, V. and Whetton, C. (1991) *An Enquiry into LEA Evidence on Standards of Reading of Seven Year Old Children*. National Foundation of Educational Research: Slough.

Center, Y., Wheldall, K. and Freeman, L. (1992) 'Evaluating the effectiveness of Reading Recovery: a critique', *Educational Psychology*, **12**, 263–74.

Clay, M. M. (1979) *Reading: The Patterning of Complex Behaviour*. London: Heinemann.

Clay, M. M., (1985) *The Early Detection Of Reading Difficulties*. (3rd edn.) Auckland: Heinemann.

Clay, M. and Cazden, C. B. (1990) 'A Vygotdkyan Interpretation of Reading Recovery'. In Moll, L. C. (ed.) *Vygotsky and Education*. Cambridge: Cambridge University Press, pp. 206–22.

Department of Education and Science and Welsh Office (1990) *English in the National Curriculum (no. 2)*. London: HMSO.

Dombey, H. (1992) 'Reading Recovery: a solution to all primary school reading problems?' *Support for Learning* **7 (3)**, 111–14.

Glynn, T. and Glynn, V. (1986) 'Shared reading by Cambodian mothers and children learning English as a second language: reciprocal gains', *The Exceptional Child*, **33** (3), 159–72.

Glynn, T., Crooks, T., Bethune, N,. Ballard, K. and Smith, J. (1989) *Reading Recovery in Context*. Report to New Zealand Department of Education, Dunedin, University of Otago.

Hall, K. (1994) 'Conceptual and methodological flaws in the evaluation of the "first" British Reading Recovery programme', *British Educational Research Journal*, **20** (1), 121–28.

Hofkins, D. (1995) 'Study backs cash-starved reading plan', *Times Educational Supplement*, **10 March**.

Iverson, S. and Tunmer, W. (1993) *Phonological Reprocessing Skills and the Reading Recovery Program*. Palmerson North, New Zealand: Massey University.

Judd, J. (1995) 'Top reading scheme axed', *Independent on Sunday*, **5 March**.

Moore, G. (1991) 'The road to reading recovery', *Child Education*, **March**, 45–47.

Nicholson, T. (1989) 'A comment on reading recovery', *New Zealand Journal of Educational Studies*, **24**, 95–97.

Office for Standards in Education (1993) *Reading Recovery in New Zealand*. London: HMSO.

Pinnell, G. S., Deford, D. and Lyons, C. (1988) *Reading Recovery: Early Intervention for At Risk First Graders*. Arlington, Va: Educational Research Service.

Pinnell, G. S., Lyons, C. A., Deford, D., Bryak, A. A. and Seltzer, M. (1991) 'Studying the effectiveness of early intervention approaches for first grade children having difficulty in reading', In *Education Report No. 16*. Columbus, Ohio: Martha King Language and Literacy Centre, Ohio State University.

Pluck, M. (1989) 'Reading Recovery in a British Infant School', *Educational Psychology*, **9** (4), 347–54.

Rowe, K. J. (1989) *100 Schools Project*. Summary Report of Second Stage Results. Melbourne, Australia: School Programs Division, Ministry of Education.

Stanovich, K. E. (1986) 'Mathew effects in reading: some consequences of individual differences in the acquisition of literacy', *Reading Research Quarterly*, **21**, 360–406.

Sylva, K. and Hurry, J. (1995) *Early Intervention in Children with Reading Difficulties: An Evaluation of Reading Recovery and a Phonological Training*. London: SCAA.

Wade, B. (1990) *Reading for Real*. Milton Keynes: Open University.

Wade, B. (1992) 'Reading Recovery: myth and reality', *British Journal of Special Education*, **19** (2), 48–51.

Wasik, B. A. and Slavin, R. E. (1990) *Preventing Early Reading Failure with One-to-one Tutoring: a best-evidence syntheses*. Baltimore, Maryland: Johns Hopkins University, Centre for Research on effective Schooling for Disadvantaged Students.

Wheeler, H. G. (1986) *Reading Recovery: Central Field Trials*, 1984. Bendigo: Bendigo College of Advanced Education.

Wood, K. (1994) 'Reading Recovery: What is it? How effective is it?' *Educational Psychology in Practice*, **10** (1), 3–13.

Wright, A. (1992) 'Evaluation of the first British Reading Recovery programme', *British Educational Research Journal*, **18** (4), 351–68.

Wright, A. and Prance, J., (1992) 'The Reading Recovery programme in Surrey Education Authority', *Support for Learning*, **7 (3)**, 103–10.

V Conclusion

13 Epilogue

The main purpose of this book has been to evaluate the current state of the evidence regarding the major controversial issues in the field of special education. The overall conclusion reached from reading the previous 12 chapters is that some of the controversial diagnoses and treatments appear to be useful while others do not.

Regarding the three controversial diagnoses discussed, autism is well established as a distinct form of disability, whereas the distinctiveness of ADHD and dyslexia remains dubious.

Regarding the two system-wide interventions considered (inclusion and exclusion), widespread implementation of both of these strategies have been shown to be of dubious value to the children involved.

Of the three group interventions discussed, peer and parent tutoring have been shown to be useful in a wide range of settings and formats. The outcomes of Instrumental Enrichment have been mainly disappointing but the results of recent research has provided some hope that, given the right conditions, it could be a useful intervention. Conductive education has been shown to be less effective than existing treatments.

With regard to individual interventions, Reading Recovery has produced some very promising results, although the jury is still out on the topic of its cost-effectiveness. However, Irlen lenses and Facilitated Communication have at present little or no evidence in favour of their effectivenes.

There is also little evidence to support the effectivenes of the three controversial treatments considered briefly in the introductory chapter: Gentle Teaching, the Doman–Delacato programme and cochlea implants. So far sufficient research data are not yet available to evaluate the other controversial issue considered in this chapter, bilingualism in deaf education.

There are several important implications of these findings for professionals in the field of special education:

- Professionals need to be aware of the current state of the evidence regarding these controversial issues so that they can select the most effective interventions.
- Professionals need to be able to communicate these findings to col-

leagues, educational administrators, policy makers, and to parents of children with disabilities, to assist them to make appropriate decisions regarding the education of children with special needs.

- Professionals need to understand the process involved in critically evaluating controversial diagnoses and treatments which emerge in the future so that they can assess their usefulness.

Evaluation of the controversial issues discussed in this book was made possible by the research which has been conducted and published on each of these topics. Without the existing literature base, evaluation of such issues would not be possible. This would leave children with disabilities vulnerable to potentially ineffective or damaging treatments. It is therefore imperative that evaluative research on special education continues and every opportunity is taken to facilitate its dissemination. It is also imperative that professionals involved in the field of special education are committed to keeping up to date with the research relevant to their particular roles. Finally, professional training in special education must continue to emphasise the critical analysis of research in the field. Special educators need to develop the skills for conducting literature reviews on topics of concern to them. They also need the skills required to conduct evaluative studies of their own so that they can contribute to the research literature thereby continuing to extend the scientific data base of the field of special education.

Index